Problem-Solving Therapy

 HARPER TORCHBOOKS

Harper & Row, Publishers, New York
Grand Rapids, Philadelphia, St. Louis, San Francisco
London, Singapore, Sydney, Tokyo, Toronto

To Kathleen, Andrew, and Gregory Haley

PROBLEM-SOLVING THERAPY: NEW STRATEGIES FOR EFFECTIVE FAMILY THERAPY.
Copyright © 1976 by Jossey-Bass, Inc., Publishers, Jossey Bass Limited, and Jay
Haley. All rights reserved. Printed in the United States of America. No part of this
book may be used or reproduced in any manner whatsoever without written
permission except in the case of brief quotations embodied in critical articles and
reviews. For information address Jossey-Bass, Inc., Publishers, 615 Montgomery
Street, San Francisco, California 94111. Published simultaneously in Canada by
Fitzhenry & Whiteside Limited, Toronto.

First HARPER TORCHBOOKS edition published 1985.

ISBN 0-06-131991-0

90 91 92 93 94 95 MPC 20 19 18 17

Contents

Preface

For the ideas presented here about therapy and the teaching of therapists I owe much to colleagues and students at the Philadelphia Child Guidance Center and at the Family Therapy Institute in Washington, D.C. The communication ideas are largely derived from Gregory Bateson. I participated in Bateson's research project for ten years, and from him I not only learned but also learned how to learn. *Strategies of Psychotherapy* (Grune & Stratton, 1963) expressed my version of the communication ideas of that research group.* At that time I was attempting to shift from

---

*See J. Haley, "A History of a Research Project," in C. Sluzki and D. Ransome (Eds.), *The Double Bind* (New York: Grune & Stratton, 1976). A note to clarify a misunderstanding is appropriate here. One often hears references to the "Palo Alto Group" and its communication point of view, but in fact there were two groups in Palo Alto, with quite different ideas. There was the project directed by Gregory Bateson, which developed the double-bind theory. Bateson's project existed in Palo Alto (actually in Menlo Park) from 1952 to 1962. The full-time members of that project were Gregory Bateson, John Weakland, and myself. There were also Don D. Jackson, M.D., and William F. Fry, M.D., part-time a focus on the individual to a more social view, proposing that the unit of research and therapy should be at least a dyad. *Strategies* was an examination of different therapy approaches from a dyadic point of view. The present book differs by offering an approach to therapy that defines the unit as at least a triad.

For the general approach to therapy here, I am indebted to Milton H. Erickson; see *Uncommon Therapy: The Psychiatric Techniques of Milton H. Erickson, M.D.* (New York: Norton, 1973). The directive style of therapy, and, more specifically, the chapter on directives in this work, is derived directly from his teaching. I learned this approach in consultation with Erickson over many years.

For the general orientation to the family expressed here, as well as for many ideas about family interviewing, I am indebted to many colleagues in the field of therapy. The specific approach to families in this work was greatly influenced by my work in Philadelphia. I went there in 1967, commuting daily in a car with Salvador Minuchin, the director of the Philadelphia Child Guidance Clinic, and Braulio Montalvo. Those informal seminars, as well as many other conversations, influenced the views expressed in this work. Equally important was Minuchin's willingness to shelter controversial approaches to therapy and to the training of therapists within his clinic. While Minuchin's recent book, *Families and Family Therapy* (Harvard University Press, 1974) has a different emphasis from this book, it reflects many similar ideas developed during the years we associated with Montalvo and with each other.

---

psychiatric consultants. The group stayed together for a decade and published over seventy articles and books, especially in the fields of schizophrenia, hypnosis, and therapy. The central focus of the group was on paradox in communication.

At the time the Bateson project was ending, Dr. Jackson formed the Mental Research Institute in Palo Alto with a different group of people who had only a social connection with the Bateson double-bind project. Although the two groups have been confused with each other, in actuality Mr. Bateson declined to be a member of the Mental Research Institute and did not like his project to be confused with that group.

I am particularly indebted to Braulio Montalvo for ideas in this work. He shared with me the teaching of therapy as well as the making of training films on therapy. Over the years, we had many hundreds of hours of conversation about the nature of therapeutic change and the ethics of the therapy situation. He also kindly read the manuscript and suggested improvements as the book developed.

I am indebted to Cloé Madanes for her contribution to this work both in ideas and in critical comments on the manuscript. Many of the ideas about training were developed with her, since we shared teaching positions in both Philadelphia and Washington.

I was involved in two training programs that evolved many of the ideas about training therapists presented here. The first, the Institute of Family Counseling, training people from the community to be therapists. The faculty of that project jointly produced many training procedures and included Minuchin and Montalvo as well as Jerome Ford, Mariano Barragan, Lydia Lynan–Gervacio, Cloé Madanes, Carter Umbarger, Rae Wiener, and Marianne Walters. The students also contributed many ideas, particularly those who later became faculty members in the program, including Barbara Bryant, Gerald Hawthorne, Barbara Penn, Edna Smalls, and Peter Urquhart.

The second training program that contributed many ideas was the Institute of Teachers of Family Therapy. In this program, teachers were sent out to various agencies to train staff in family therapy. Along with Minuchin and Montalvo, I was a teacher of teachers in that program. The director of that institute was Kal Flomenhaft and, later, Steve Greenstein. The teachers were Mariano Barragan, Ross Carter, Neal Daniels, David Heard, Gus Kratsa, Gary Lande, Barbara Lewin, Jamshed Morenas, Bernard Raxlen, Samuel Scott, Muriel Shapp, and William Silver.

In recent years I have been directing a program of therapy training at the Family Therapy Institute in Washington, D.C. With my fellow teacher Cloé Madanes and the students there, we have been developing the ideas emphasized in the training section of this work.

Two chapters in this work appeared in somewhat different form in two journals. Chapter Three, "Communication as Bits and as Metaphor," appeared in the *American Journal of Psychotherapy*, *25* (1971), 214–227. Chapter Five, "Examples of Therapy in Stages," was published in different form in the *Journal of the American Academy of Child Psychiatry*, where it was called "Strategic Therapy When a Child Is Presented as the Problem," *12* (1973), 641–659.

Philadelphia, Pennsylvania   Jay Haley
July 1976

Problem-Solving Therapy
New Strategies for Effective Family Therapy

Introduction

~~~~~~~~~~~~~~~~~~~~~~~~~~~~~~~~~~~~~~

Problem-Solving Therapy

~~~~~~~~~~~~~~~~~~~~~~~~~~~~~~~~~~~~~~

This book is for therapists who wish to develop specific techniques for solving human dilemmas and for teachers of therapy who wish to teach specific skills. The therapy approach focuses on solving a client's presenting problems within the framework of the family. The emphasis is not on a method but on approaching each problem with special techniques for the specific situation. The therapist's task is to formulate a presenting symptom clearly and to design an intervention in the client's social situation to change that presenting symptom. Although the book focuses on problems, the approach here differs from other symptom-oriented therapies in that it emphasizes the social context of human problems.

Defining a Problem

In recent years there has been a debate between therapists who prefer to define a symptom in precise behavioral terms, such as a specific avoidance behavior, and those who

1

use a more general category like "anxiety" or a "feeling of helplessness." Some therapists prefer to formulate symptoms in ways that can be counted as acts, while others prefer to formulate a problem as a state of mind or as a character disorder. The approach in this work differs from both such approaches insofar as the emphasis is not on an individual. While this approach assumes that the therapist has failed if he or she* does not solve the presenting problem, and while the symptom is defined in operational terms that are as precise as possible, the therapy focus is on the social situation rather than on the person. It is possible to define a "problem" in different social units. In this book a problem is defined as a type of behavior that is part of a sequence of acts between several people. The repeating sequence of behavior is the focus of therapy. A symptom is a label for, a crystallization of, a sequence in a social organization. Thinking of such symptoms as "depression" or "phobia" as a contract between people and therefore as adaptive to relationships leads to a new way of thinking about therapy.

Shifting one's thinking from the individual unit to a social unit of two or more people has certain consequences for a therapist. Not only must the therapist think in different ways about human dilemmas, but he or she must consider himself or herself as a member of the social unit that contains the problem. The therapist must be considered as part of the social dilemma of the client, and this can be a disturbing idea. Twenty years ago it was a new step to recognize that a family rather than an individual was the therapeutic unit. In time that family unit was expanded to include the extended kin and also the peer group. Now it is becoming uncomfortably evident that a presenting problem includes the professional world in which the problem appears, as well as the larger society.

---

* It is not appropriate only to use the pronoun *he* when referring to a therapist, because therapists come in both sexes. The author uses *he* for reasons of convenience and acknowledges the inequity of the traditional use of the masculine pronoun.

Diagnosis as Part of the Problem. When a therapeutic problem is defined as the social relationships of clients, a therapist must include himself in the issue since he helps define the problem. To label a child as "delinquent" or as suffering from "minimal brain disfunction," or to label an adult as an "alcoholic" or a "schizophrenic," means that one is participating in the creation of a problem in such a way that change may be made more difficult. A therapist who describes a family situation as characterized by "a dominating mother and a passive father" or "a symbiotic relationship between mother and daughter" has created problems, although the therapist might think he is merely identifying the problems put before him. The way one labels a human dilemma can crystallize a problem and make it chronic.

Colleagues as Part of the Problem. The issue of professionally created problems becomes more evident when we examine the ways in which clinicians may become part of the presenting problem. If a therapist accepts in therapy a young adult who is defined as schizophrenic and who is in a mental hospital, how does one define the problem? Therapists have known for years that the social unit in such a case is the young adult and his family. Now it is more evident that the problem includes the psychiatric staff who have authority over custody and medication. The therapist cannot pretend that the therapy problem is only the young person and his family when decision for discharge is in the hands of other people and when the young person may be drugged at any time without the therapist's permission. Similarly, to do therapy with a man or woman on probation requires defining the problem to include the probation officer and court as well as family and friends. When social control is an issue, the professional milieu is part of the presenting problem. In more routine cases, the dissension among professionals involved in a family may be the therapy problem. If different therapists are seeing different family members, they may be in a territorial struggle over who is right and wrong in the family. The social unit for the therapist is thus not merely the family but also the professional colleagues.

A Wider Social Unit

The issues are disturbing if one views fellow clinicians as part of the problems, but there are larger issues as well. When a boy refuses to attend school, his behavior can be defined as a therapeutic problem. His therapist is expected to intervene in family and school and to get the youth to function appropriately. Such a problem is usually routine. Yet suppose the school is in a slum and is such a bad school that the therapist can only sympathize with the young person for avoiding it as a waste of time? The problem is thus not simply a boy's truancy but also a problem school. If one includes the school, the line between therapy and social or political action becomes obscure.

Adopting a social view of the problem makes it difficult for a therapist to limit his thinking to either boy or school without including the economic system and social issues in which such a school is embedded. A boy who will not go to school may be responding to a bad school or to a problem family. But neither issue is separable from the fact that the father may be chronically unemployed because of the nature of the economic system and the mother may be involved in a welfare situation that may distort the organization of the family. Is the therapist's problem not only the individual, family, gang, and school but also the larger society? Although such issues are evident with the poor, they are also present when therapists deal with the upper class. A depressed wife may be defined as the problem or the therapist may include the fact that she is the wife of a harried corporation executive who is driven constantly to move his family from place to place as part of the competitive struggle of his career.

Whither the Therapist?

A therapist can attempt to deal with the social issue by going to extremes. He may define the problem as really a matter of misperception by the client and he may concern himself with the client's fantasies about his social situation. Such a narrow view no longer seems palatable. The therapist can go to the opposite extreme and define all problems as economic and cultural. But then he must become a revolutionary to solve each problem. Such an approach does not seem practical. Not only must the therapist have evidence that a revolution would create a society that would solve the problem, but furthermore, the client must wait in distress while the therapist organizes the revolution.

The issue of radicalism became prominent in the 1960s when therapists were placed in mental health clinics in slums full of poor black people. Such therapists were caught up in arguments of polar extremes. If a therapist helped a poor family deal with a problem, he was accused by radicals of wasting his time since the problem was a racist society and unemployment. Those therapists who shifted to a more radical objective and attempted to do something about racism and the economic system were open to the argument that they were only indulging in rhetoric and not helping even one family in distress.

The task for the therapist has no easy solution. Whatever radical position he takes as a citizen, his obligation as a therapist is to define the social unit that he can change to solve the presenting problem of a client. To war with mental hospitals, courts, and welfare agencies does not usually achieve the goal of the therapy, although sometimes it may be necessary. The effectiveness of the therapist is evaluated in terms of the outcome of his therapy, not in terms of the moral stance he takes or his justifiable indignation at the society that is contributing to the problems he is trying to solve. The most useful point of view for the therapist is the idea that there is sufficient variety in any situation so that some better arrangement can be made. Rather than simply condemn a bad school, a therapist must visit the school and find within it a more suitable place for the youth he is attempting to get back into school.

When one accepts the idea that the problems of a client include the social milieu, including the therapist, the therapist must always consider the coalitions he is involved in when he acts. Not only must he consider whether he is acting as a social control agent of society whose job is to quiet troublemakers, but he must also think of this function in social frameworks smaller than that of society as a whole. Problem solving from this point of view is not as simple as some behavior modifiers would suggest. Behavior therapy has emphasized problems and has brought more precision to the field, as well as a concern with results. Yet there is also a tendency for behavior therapists to define the problem without including the therapist in the social situation. For example, if a child has temper tantrums and the therapist subscribes to a conditioning theory, he will focus on the problem of tantrums and use conditioning procedures to extinguish the problem behavior. Yet whose agent is the therapist in such a case? With whom is he in coalition against whom? A therapist who thinks in terms of the social context will be concerned about the child's temper tantrums as a response to the child's current relationships. He will also consider the hierarchy in the situation and decide if he wants to be employed by parents to shape a child in the ways they wish. In actuality, the therapist might decide to focus on the temper tantrum problem, but if he thinks in terms of sequences in relationships he will also be aware that he is acting as much in relation to mother and father as to child.

A more evident dilemma for the therapist appears when he becomes aware that he is part of the problem in a social control situation. From a narrow view, a therapist on an inpatient unit can be solving behavior problems of patients on the ward when he sets up a "token economy" or uses similar procedures. Yet from an organizational point of view, he is joining the establishment to shape patients into behaving like better patients for the convenience of the staff. Years ago a report described a mental patient who collected towels in her room on a mental hospital ward. A therapist solved the problem by paradoxically imposing towels on the woman until her room was so full she could not get into it. This intervention is typically described without clarifying whether it caused the woman to behave better on the ward or helped her to go out into the community into a normal life. Once a therapist thinks in organizational terms, he must think of himself as a part of the social system that is the client's problem.

Besides dealing with the consequences of thinking about his place in the social system, a therapist who takes a problem point of view has difficulty finding a place in which to be trained to do therapy. A few settings offer training in problem solving through behavioral techniques. Other, quite different settings offer training in family-oriented therapy. It is difficult to find a place where one can learn a problem orientation while also learning to think about problems within a social framework. It is the purpose of this book to provide ways to formulate problems and ways to intervene into human relationships to solve these problems.

This book is designed for therapists and should not be misunderstood as an attempt to map how society and the human family are in actuality or how they should be if all were well. What is offered are simplistic formulations of social situations that can help a therapist recognize typical interchanges and determine what to do.

1

Conducting the First Interview

If successful therapy is defined as solving the problems of a client, the therapist must know how to formulate a problem and how to solve it. And if he or she is to solve a variety of problems, the therapist must not take a rigid and stereotyped approach to therapy. Any standardized method of therapy, no matter how effective with certain problems, cannot deal successfully with the wide range that is typically offered to a therapist. Flexibility and spontaneity are necessary. Yet any therapist must also learn from experience and repeat what was successful before. A combination of familiar procedures and innovative techniques increases the probability of success.

If therapy is to end properly, it must begin properly —by negotiating a solvable problem and discovering the social situation that makes the problem necessary. The act of therapy begins with the way the problem is examined. The act of intervening brings out problems and the relationship patterns that are to be changed.

9

A skillful therapist will approach each new person with the idea that a unique procedure might be necessary for this particular person and social situation. The variables are many but most fall into the categories of time, place, fee, number of people involved, and the special directives necessary to begin. A therapist who had total freedom might find it best for a particular situation to work in the office, in the home, in the place of business, on the street, or, for a school problem, at the school. The first interview could go on for an hour, or half an hour, or several hours. The therapist could immediately move for a change or perhaps be leisurely and not request action at once. In one case a standard fee may be appropriate; in another the client may be asked to pay what he thinks the therapist deserves; and in yet another he should pay if he does not improve. The therapist may interview one person or several on the first visit, and he may include only family members or may include friends and other professionals. For one ethnic group the approach may need to be formal, and for another a casual attitude might be more effective. There are many different ways a master therapist might begin, but what will be offered here is a preferred way for the average therapist to begin a first encounter.

Today it is assumed that to begin therapy by interviewing one person is to begin with a handicap. When it was thought that a therapeutic problem was a one-person phenomenon, then it seemed reasonable to interview only one person. Symptoms, or problems, were considered to be maladaptive and inappropriate. Therefore there was no reason to bring in more than the one person who was being maladaptive. If a wife had anxiety attacks, these were not considered adaptive to her marriage, but were thought to be irrational. Therefore, her husband was not considered to be relevant except as a stress factor for the woman, who was the "real" problem.

It is, of course, possible to change a marriage or a family by seeing only one person, but it can be a slow and difficult procedure and often fails, as therapy outcome studies have shown. It is much more sensible to interview the natural group where the problem is expressed and so to proceed immediately toward the solution.

If it is obvious that one should interview both husband and wife in a marriage, it should be even more obvious that when the problem is an adolescent who must be helped to disengage from his family, then the whole family must be immediately involved. The therapist must bring people together to help them individuate, and it is more sensible to begin that individuation process at once with the first interview.

If one thinks of a problem in its context, the past dichotomy between "individual" and "family" therapy becomes irrelevant. To interview an individual is one way to intervene in a family. If a therapist interviews a man, woman, grandfather, or child and does not see the others in the family, he forms a coalition in the dark without knowing what kind of organization he is entering. Although after therapy has begun the therapist might want to interview family members one at a time for a particular purpose, in the beginning it is better to see everyone who lives in a household so that the therapist can quickly grasp the problem and the social situation that is maintaining it.

Moreover, it is generally accepted that people cannot report properly about their own social situations. Even a trained participant observer gives a biased report, because of his position in his personal social network. A trained anthropologist cannot adequately report the sequences in his own family. In the 1950s, doubt about self-report led to family interviews and also caused therapy supervisors to prefer to watch a therapist at work through a one-way mirror or on videotape. The supervisors learned that a therapist's description of an interview was not adequate when compared with a recording. When patients were seen privately without being recorded, therapists also were seen privately in supervisory sessions, and no one knew what was actually happening in therapy. A wife would report that her husband did something, without mentioning her part in the sequence that led up to the act. For example, she might report that her husband struck her "out of the blue." The therapist would report this reported event to his supervisor without describing how he encouraged the wife to tell him about this incident. The therapist would not mention that he was joining, perhaps outside awareness, with the wife against the husband and encouraging her to condemn him. The supervisor had to guess what might have happened from the reports of a wife as reported by a therapist. Both reports would be biased. It is more sensible to see husband and wife together with a supervisor observing the action when that is possible. With this kind of observation, the therapeutic situation changes from "individual" versus "family" to doing therapy in the dark or in the light.

Part of the difficulty in beginning therapy properly has been the confusion between diagnosis for institutional reasons and diagnosis for therapy purposes. For an institution, it was necessary to see a person alone and to classify him as a diagnostic type. That procedure was irrelevant to therapy and could even handicap the therapist in thinking about how to solve the problem. Now it is known that the best diagnosis *for therapy* is one that allows the social group to respond to attempts to bring about change. A therapist must intervene with a therapeutic act to gather diagnostic information for therapy, so it is best to begin with everyone involved because change will involve everyone.

There are, of course, times when only one person is available to be interviewed and so the initial session must be one-to-one. If the person is in jail or a mental hospital, naturally the therapist would expect the family to be present at a first interview, in order to plan the future outside. If the person is a college student thousands of miles from home who asks for therapy, it may be necessary to see him or her alone for a first interview. Later there can be letters, telephone calls, visits from parents, and other forms of getting together, but in the beginning the single person must be interviewed. This special and unusual situation requires a therapist who can estimate from talking to one person what his situation is and what the consequences of change will be to people who are not there. It is possible to change a person by seeing him alone, but the skill required is often too much to ask of the average therapist.

For the usual first interview, particularly with child problems, the therapist should expect everyone involved to attend. If the problem involves school, it is often best to have the first interview at the school with the teacher, counselor, child, and parents. These persons make up the social group involved and time can be saved if therapy is begun with all members of the group present. (The way of doing a first interview described here applies to such a group.) For most problems, the intimate network should be invited. Everyone who lives in the household is a member of the proper unit, although if the therapist knows about a grandmother who lives around the corner, he should ask that she come too. When the problem is a child, any man seriously involved with the mother should be there.

This emphasis on having everyone at a first interview does not mean that therapy cannot be done if total participation is not arranged. It simply means that bringing everyone in is the easiest way to work. The way to conduct a first interview described here will help a therapist begin properly. The procedure outlined can be used with most problems; of course, there are always unique situations that require special handling.

For example, when a young person is in a mental hospital, this kind of exploratory interview is not appropriate. In such a case, the therapist knows in advance that the problem is the hospitalization. Generally, the problems of severely disturbed young people are not emphasized in this book. Another book, now in preparation, will deal with the therapy of such young people. The strategy in such a case is to be more authoritarian and less exploratory in the beginning since it is a time of family crisis.

There are other times when this type of first interview is not the correct procedure to follow. At times a family is referred in error because of a misunderstanding with the referral source, or the interview is for a "check up" or a consultation and there is no interest in beginning therapy. Some families merely want a child tested and so do not arrive with a purpose of having therapy. (Even if only testing is to be done, the family can be involved. Some clinics now arrange that a child be tested while the parents observe from behind a one-way mirror so they can see their child's responses. Afterwards when tester and parents discuss the results, the parents have a basis for judging the tester's conclusions and do not merely receive a summary report.)

There are also "compulsory" referrals that require special handling in the first encounter. When the family is referred by a court, or at times by a school, the mother or father may be angry and require special courtesy. Whenever a therapist finds a client confusing or apparently behaving in an inappropriate way, he should assume it is the context of the situation that is confusing, and not merely a peculiar person.

Another special situation is a demonstration interview, in which a therapist must interview a family before a group. If the family therapist does this, he must take care that the family does not expose more than it should before a group of strangers. A therapist should never interview a family before a group if one is not going to see that family again. A demonstration interview of a family by a visiting therapist is an exploitation of the family, and the family members do not receive compensation for their exposure (unless they are paid a fee). Such a one-time demonstration also has nothing to do with therapy. It is simply a demonstration of how to use a family to communicate to an audience, and a student therapist should never assume that he should do a therapy interview in that way.

One further comment on getting everyone in for a first interview. Often a young person, either living with parents or not, would prefer not to have the family involved in the therapy. Sometimes, such a young person has had years of individual therapy and prefers that method. A therapist should not let a client decide how therapy should be done, particularly a client who has had previous therapy that was not successful and who wants to continue with the same pattern. Sometimes, too, an adult does not want a spouse brought in. A person may be living alone and the family is in the same area, but the person may not consider family members relevant to his or her problem. Therapy is more effective and more rapid when more people are involved in the interviews. At times one can start with a person alone if he or she insists, but to continue that way makes therapy much more difficult. Often seeing a person alone first makes it even more difficult to get the relevant people involved later. Some therapists, learning from Carl Whitaker, argue that the battle over who will be involved in the therapy can determine the outcome of the therapy.

Stages of a First Interview

An interview begins with the first contact made concerning a problem. Usually someone calls asking for an appointment, and some information is gathered on the telephone. The therapist should ask that everyone living in the household come in for the first interview.

When the family arrives, the following stages occur in the interview: (1) a social stage in which the family is greeted and made comfortable; (2) a problem stage in which the inquiry is about the presenting problem; (3) an interaction stage in which the family members are asked to talk with each other; and (4) a goal-setting stage where the family is asked to specify just what changes they seek. The interview ends by setting an appointment for the next time, with the whole family or with some part of it.

The Social Stage

At every stage of the interview *all* family members should be involved in the action, and particularly during the greeting stage. When the family enters the interview room, they should seat themselves as they wish. After introducing himself, the therapist should speak to each family member and obtain his or her name.* It is important to get a response from each person, in order to define the situation as one in which everyone is involved and important. During this social stage the therapist can also find out who lives in the home and should therefore have been present. If one person starts to talk about the problem, the therapist should stop him until some social response is obtained from each person. The model for this stage is the courtesy behavior one would use with guests in the home. Everyone is greeted and made comfortable.

While the family is being seated the therapist has an opportunity for observation to guide himself in how to begin the next stage.

Most families who come in with a problem feel defensive about it no matter how agreeable the members may seem. It is embarrassing to have to bring a personal problem to someone. Most families have tried all kinds of remedies that have not worked and therefore asking for help can mean to them that they have failed. Often the family members have not been in agreement about the problem or about coming in, and some members have been dragged in when they would rather be elsewhere. They may feel they are going to be blamed.

The therapist should note the mood of the family since he must know their mood in order to get their cooperation in changing. They may be pretending to be more cheerful than they are. They may be unhappy or angry. The family

---

*In this therapy it is expected that the therapist will work alone. The use of a cotherapist is usually for the security of the clinician and not for the value to the client. Outcome studies do not indicate that cotherapy does better, and the cost is twice as much. As for training, cotherapy with a more experienced person teaches the student to sit back and not take the responsibility for the case, which he must ultimately learn how to do. A therapist working alone can develop and carry out ideas without having to delay to consult with a colleague. If the therapist needs assistance, a supervisor (or even a fellow therapist) behind the one-way mirror can provide it.

members may have the attitude that bringing the problem person in is a punishment they are carrying out after threatening him with this action for some time. Or they may be desperate. They may also be coming in as a duty because some authority, like the school or court, told them to come. As the therapist greets the family members, their mood will be communicated to him and he should attempt to match it.

The therapist should note the parent–child relations as the family members organize themselves to come to the room. The parents may be too severe with the children, or they may be too easy, just hoping the children will come with them. The children may spontaneously cooperate in the hallway or they may have to be instructed by the parents. The ways in which parents discipline the children can be observed as parts of the process of getting to the room and getting seated. The therapist should keep in mind that the parents are not merely dealing with the children but *showing* how they deal with the children. For example, they might usually smack a child if he misbehaves but if they are concerned about what they show the therapist they may behave differently. The child will also be demonstrating how he and his parents behave. The therapist is not necessarily getting the facts from them, but, rather, an illustration.

The therapist should note the relationship between the parents or other adults who bring the children (such as mother and grandmother). If there is a child problem in a family, the adults are usually in disagreement about how to deal with the child. Sometimes they show this disagreement immediately and sometimes they present a united front in the beginning. If they seem very much in agreement and too amiable with each other, this situation is different from a situation in which they are showing they have different positions on the child issue. The therapist should also note whether one of the adults is indicating he or she has come reluctantly.

How do the family members deal with the therapist? The behavior of the children will give some indication of what the parents have told them about the place if therapy is being conducted outside the home or school. If the child seems afraid of the therapist, the fear may indicate that he thinks he is there as punishment or that he thinks he will be left there. If the children seem amiable and curious, they may have been told that the place is a pleasant one to visit. In particular, the therapist should note who in the family attempts to engage the therapist on his or her side, even at this greeting stage. If one parent attaches himself or herself too quickly, the therapist can expect a problem in keeping out of a coalition with that person during the session. If a parent is too distant, it may be necessary to work more to get that person involved. If the parents look at the child and then at the therapist with that "sharing exasperation look," they may be bidding to join him against the problem child.

When the family members seat themselves, sometimes the organization of the family is clarified. For example, the mother may be seated among the children and the father at the edge of the group. Or the parents and children may seat themselves in two camps. Or parents and an older child may sit together, isolating the problem child. Perhaps the males seat themselves together and the females together, which gives information about the importance of sex differentiation in the family. Whether or not the problem child is seated between mother and father may suggest his function in their marriage.

It is important to gather information but it is also important to *keep conclusions tentative*. The therapist may be misled and therefore ideas should not be too firm. Observation gives information that can be tested as the session continues. A therapist who gets too set in one idea is not free to consider other ideas.

It is also important that the therapist *should not share his observations with the family*. If the problem child is sitting between mother and father, the therapist may make a tentative hypothesis that the child's problem serves a function in their marriage. But that hypothesis should not be taken too seriously without further data, and the therapist should *never* comment to the family about the child's position. Not only might the therapist be wrong, but if he is right, he is pointing out to the family what the members already know. To point out something like a seating arrangement is asking the family to concede something they might prefer not to concede, and thus that action could arouse defensiveness and cause unnecessary difficulties in the therapy.

The Problem Stage

Up to this point in the interview, there has been a social interchange with the family that may be quite brief or last a few minutes. From this stage it is necessary to shift to the therapy stage where the situation is no longer defined as social but as purposeful. It is an unusual situation when a family comes for help to someone whose job it is to do something for them. There are no standard rules for this kind of situation, and so therapist and family must work out what kind of situation it is.

The most common procedure is for the therapist to inquire why the family is there or what the problem is. This inquiry changes the situation from a social to a therapy situation. It is the "getting-down-to-business" message. There are many ways to make this inquiry and each way has its advantages and disadvantages. The inquiry has two aspects: how the therapist makes it and to whom in the family the therapist speaks.

When the family members arrive, they often do not know why the whole family has been asked to come in. Often what they have sought was help for a particular child or adult, and to be asked to come in as a family may puzzle everyone, even if no one asks about it. Therefore, it is often a good idea for the therapist to begin by clarifying his position in the situation. He can say what he already knows and why he asked everyone to come in. When he has clarified his position, it is easier for the family members to state their positions.

One way for the therapist to begin is to say something like, "I heard what was said on the telephone, so I have some idea what the problem is. But I asked the whole family to come in so I could get everyone's ideas about it." He can then ask more directly about the problem.

Another way to begin is for the therapist to say, "I wanted everyone in the family to come in today so that I could get all your opinions about the situation." Some variation on this phrasing gives at least a partial explanation of why they are all there and creates a readiness on the part of the family members to contribute their opinions.

How the introduction of the therapist's position is phrased depends on the education level of the family since he should state his position in a way that is understandable to everyone. If the therapist has the feeling that it is a secretive family, he should particularly emphasize that he already has some information from the telephone call setting up the appointment. Then it is clear to everyone that someone (usually the mother) has already stated the problem and the therapist has heard that version.

When the therapist asks for more specific opinions about the problem, the way he phrases his inquiry can determine how the interview will develop. Several different ways that are commonly used include:

The therapist can ask, "What is your problem?" This question defines the situation as one in which problems will be talked about. Usually the authority on the problem, typically the mother of the family, has anticipated this question and is ready with a statement about the difficulties with the child. Often a mother is ready to give an historical review of when the problem developed. To ask the question in this way fits with the mother's expectations.

The therapist can make the situation more personal by asking, "What is it you want from me?" This kind of question reduces the possibilities of the family's report. They not only must think about the problem but also must think in terms of what the therapist may be able to do about it. Such an inquiry by the therapist makes the situation less professional and more personal, which may make some therapists uneasy.

Instead of asking what the problem is, the therapist can ask, "What changes do you want?" By putting the question in this way, the framework of the therapy situation is set as one of change. The parent must then state the problem in terms of how the child should change rather than in terms of what is wrong with him. Even if the discussion later shifts to a problem orientation again, this framework allows the therapist to shift back to what the family would like changed.

Another way to phrase the inquiry is to say, "Why are you here?" This phrasing allows the family the opportunity to focus on the problem or on change. Some members of the family will say, "Because of Johnny," and others will say, "To get something done about Johnny."

As a rule, the more general and ambiguous the inquiry of the therapist is, the more room there is for the family members to display their point of view. They may emphasize the problem or the change or even describe it as a family problem rather than as a child problem. The more specific the therapist is, the more the family is focused on one area in the discussion.

Who Should Be Asked about The Problem. When the therapist shifts from the social to the therapy situation, he must speak to the group as a whole or to one person. It is at this point that the personal involvements and biases of the therapist can become an issue. A therapist who considers children to be victims of parents can tend to side with children in the ways he inquires about the problem. Such a therapist may ask the problem child what the problem is, implying that he or she is probably misunderstood. If the therapist sharply divides the world into male and female, the issue of who to ask about the problem becomes a sexist issue. To speak to a male first could imply that the female was inadequate. If a therapist is older and a grandparent, in a family interview with grandparents, he or she may consider the grandparents the ones to speak to about the problem because they are undoubtedly wiser. A family interview, unlike an interview with an individual, forces a selection on the therapist the moment he begins to explore the problem.

There are several relevant dimensions to the issue. First, there is the person who tends to be the one sufficiently concerned about the problem to bring the family in for the interview. Usually there is someone else who disagrees that there is that much of a problem and who comes reluctantly. This is a typical conflict in a family with a problem.

A second dimension is one of hierarchy. In any organization, the members are not equal. The therapist must respect the hierarchy in a family if he is to gain cooperation. Unfortunately, a therapist's bias can cause him or her to be unclear about who has authority. If grandparents are in a room, many therapists would consider them higher in the hierarchy than parents and so would ask them about the problem. Other therapists would not consider the grandparents as authorities, and so they would address the parents about the problem and politely ignore the grandparents. Similarly, some therapists will observe that a father is withdrawn and marginal from the family and will address him first and treat him as if he were the head of the household. This is not necessarily done because the therapist believes that father holds that position but because if he is addressed in this way the father will respond by becoming more involved and assuming more responsibility in the situation. These therapists will make use of the stereotype about fathers being the head of the household, whether they believe it or not, to solve the family's problem. In the same way, if a therapist believes that a mother should be bolstered in her position in order to solve the presenting problem, he will address her first and treat her as if she were the head of the household. But this decision should be made in relation to the presenting problem, not to the therapist's idea about the proper status position of either sex, which is not the issue of therapy.

Yet another dimension is more of an issue in therapy than in other situations. The therapist has a task to get done and he needs to keep the family involved in order to do it.

Often there is one person in the family who can bring the family back, and that person should be treated more respectfully for that reason. For example, one might listen to a grandfather with special respect and find that in actuality he does not think there is a problem worth coming to therapy for, and that even if he did think so the remainder of the family would not come at his request. So a therapist treating him with excessive respect may be dealing with the least powerful person in the family.

As an example of the adroitness necessary by a therapist, there may be a family in which mother has the power to bring the family in and father does not. Yet the therapist must emphasize father's status to increase his involvement when that appears necessary as part of a therapeutic plan. Therefore the therapist must treat father as an authority on the problem of the child, while indicating to mother that this is being done as part of the therapy and not because the therapist does not understand father's usual marginal stance in the family.

If the therapist could merely treat all members of the family as equals and behave as if who was asked about the problem was a random choice, the solution would be simpler. That is how one might behave in an artificial group in group therapy. Yet it is in the nature of natural groups that the therapist must deal with the issue of hierarchy and cannot avoid it.

It is recommended here that the adult who seems less involved with the problem be spoken to first, and the person with the most power to bring the family back be treated with the most concern and respect. Usually the most concerned person is the most burdened with the problem. In a clinic, the most typical arrangement with a child problem in an intact family is a mother quite concerned about the child and a father who is more peripheral. In that situation, it is best to ask father about the problem first because one wishes to define him as involved in the therapy and also to find out how much responsibility he will be willing to take when action is requested.

A certain percentage of families will have a father who is the one excessively concerned about the child while the mother is more peripheral. Sometimes the involvement would seem to be determined by who takes on most of the child caring functions at home and is therefore more aware of the problems. There is another aspect of the situation that is often overlooked by therapists caught up in the issue of sex roles rather than family organization. Quite often, which parent is most involved and concerned about the child is determined by that parent's involvement with parents or in-laws. That is, a mother who is competitive with her mother about child rearing will be excessively concerned about her child's behavior because it is part of an issue in the older generation. Similarly, a father who is proving to his father how a son should be raised may be the one the therapist notices as most involved in the child problem. Any *one* relationship is part of another and it is naive to think of this issue as merely a male or female one. In fact, the same issue of who is overinvolved with the child and who is peripheral is present when the adults involved are of the same sex. A mother and grandmother can express this issue, as can a father and grandfather, or a homosexual pair can be in conflict over whether the child has a problem and who is the authority on it.

In this chapter, a stereotyped view is risked by describing a typical arrangement in which two parents bring in a child with a problem. However, the same interview approach can be taken if it is parent and grandparent or sister and brother or any other relations. The problem may be daughter or son, older or younger child, or it may be one of the parents with symptoms being presented as the problem. The different stages of the initial interview apply whatever the composition of the group.

The issue of who to address about the problem may be thought to be partly determined by the sex of the therapist, but this appears to be a minor issue in a first interview except in some unusual situation. The competence of the therapist is far more important than the sex. If the father seems to behave as if he is feeling left out when mother and female therapist are discussing the problem, the therapist must make special efforts to include him. However, this same coalition issue arises with the male therapist talking with the father about the problem. An awareness of explicit and implicit coalitions on the basis of sex must be assumed by any competent therapist.

Generally, it is not a good idea to start with the problem child and ask him why the family is there. He will feel that he is too much on the spot, and it may look as if the therapist is blaming him for everyone being there. It is better to deal with him later. Every therapist must watch out for a tendency to turn to, or on, the problem person in a benevolent way when he or she (the therapist) is anxious and under stress. It is the function of problem people to get attention when their intimates are nervous and upset, and therapists typically follow the pattern of giving such attention, too. It is usually better for the nervous therapist to deal directly with the parents at nervous moments.

Another consideration is that the problem child is sometimes sullen and quiet because of a misunderstanding about the context and the reason for the interview. As a rule, a therapist should always state his own position and understanding of the situation whenever he sees anyone worried about the situation. A child may be afraid he is going to be locked up in the place, or believe that he is there because people think he is crazy. It is helpful if the therapist states what he knows about why everyone is there at that point and, if he can, to normalize the situation by emphasizing that it is a usual context for problems.

Some therapists sometimes like to start with the least involved child and ask him why the family is there.* By "least involved" is meant the child sitting furthest out of the group and seeming most detached. Often this is quite a young child, and if he is spoken to the therapist is making it clear

---

*Beginning with the least involved child is a procedure I first observed used by Frank Pittman.

that everyone is going to participate in this session. He is pointing out that it is not a situation where adults only talk about children who only listen. Young children may also say perceptive things, since they have not been taught clearly what should be said and what should not be said in public.

By asking a child why he is there, one sometimes finds out that none of the children has been told why the parents have brought them. This discovery provides the therapist with information about secrecy in the family and what sort of splits there may be between adults and children, or among adults and problem child and the remainder of the children.

Sometimes the therapist can look at the floor or the ceiling, not addressing any particular person, and say, "Can someone tell me what the problem is?" This approach will usually draw out the spokesperson for the family. It also provides information about the father's position in the family, since if he responds by stating the problem it is more likely that he is a willing participant in family issues. However, addressing the room generally tends to make the situation more unpredictable and some therapists prefer to address a particular person so that what is said comes out in an orderly manner and in the way he would like it to come out.

Sometimes the therapist may "slide" from the greeting stage to the therapy stage without making an issue of the shift. He may chat with the children during the greeting —ask them about school or some other activity. This conversation can lead to a discussion by the family without any inquiry about why they are there or what the problem is. Sometimes, if he slides into the problem this way, the therapist can bypass a parent's speech and prevent the child being labeled as the problem, because by the time the issue comes up in the middle of the interview it is clear that there are a number of problems or else that all the children are pretty much alike.

There are two basic errors in confusing the greeting and problem stage of a first interview. The first applies to any approach to therapy and the second is relevant to the approach offered in this book. First, the family can begin to be puzzled if the therapist does not focus on the problem because they are not sure whether this is a therapy or social situation. The therapist loses the opportunity of clarifying how this situation is different from a conversation among friends. Sometimes, too, it magnifies the problem by making it seem unmentionable. At some point, the therapist must clarify the situation.

Following the approach of this book, what the therapist wants is a clear focus on a problem so that family relationships can be changed by using that problem as the lever. The therapist does not want the problem child to be minimized as no different from the other children, or the problem to be minimized. Nor does the therapist want a discussion of relationships before having the problem stated. This is not a therapy where relationships are changed by talking about relationships but by requiring new behavior to solve a problem. For example, a 13-year-old girl was brought in by her parents because she was stealing money from a neighbor's house. The mother told the therapist about this on the telephone and said she had recently married so the girl now had a new stepfather. When the family was interviewed, everyone was reluctant to state the problem. The therapist chatted with the family, and father talked about his problem being a stepfather and not knowing how to discipline children in a way that pleased his wife. Finally the therapist was telephoned by the supervisor who required her to ask what the problem was that brought the family to therapy. When the therapist inquired, the girl began to cry and the parents talked about the integration of the stepfather into the family in a quite different way. It was not a conversation about relationships but about why the girl stole and what was to be done.

Listening to the Problem. The family may describe the problem as something unusual or as something routine. As the therapist listens, he or she should do certain things, and not do others.

First, the therapist should not make any interpretation or comment to help the person see the problem differently. He should just accept what is said. If something is not clear, it can be asked about. If the therapist needs to rephrase something to see if he understand it, he should do so—but he should not rephrase anything to help the other person "discover" something.

Second, the therapist should not offer advice at this stage, even if asked for it. He should use a phrase such as: "I need to know more about the situation before I can say what might be done."

Third, he should not ask how someone feels about something, but should only gather facts and opinions.

Fourth, the therapist's attitude should be one of helpful interest. He should not be diverted from what is really outside the question of why the family is there.

While listening, the therapist should encourage the person to talk. Some people talk at great length, and others find it hard to talk. Talking should be made as easy as possible.

If someone interrupts, the therapist should let the interruption happen to observe it briefly, and then should intervene and return to the person first talking. The person interrupting can be told he will get his turn.

Everyone must have a turn. After a statement of the problem from one person, all the others should be asked what they think about it. The therapist should not sound as if he wants a disagreement between two people or to put anyone down. He is only after each person's opinions. When there are disagreements, an issue should not be made of them but the disagreement can be returned to later. Moreover, one person should not talk too long. If the others get restless it is too long. Everyone should be asked to pay attention if he is not doing so.

Making sure that each person takes a turn should happen naturally, if possible. What someone says about someone else may naturally lead the therapist to speak to that other person. However, at this stage the therapist should not return to a previous speaker, but should go on to a third. A dialog between two people is not recommended at this stage.

The therapist wishes to join the universe of the family and so understand them, but at the same time he wishes to make enough changes in their behavior so that the interview can proceed in an orderly fashion. If the family is slow, the therapist should move slowly; if rapid, he should join it at that speed. If a parent keeps interrupting, the therapist must intervene so that everyone can express a view. Not only should everyone speak, but also the therapist should take charge of what is happening. If the family takes charge, it will go on as it has in the past, and there will be no change.

If the therapist only listens to one parent and lets him or her take over each time another person speaks, the therapist is saying by his actions that only that parent's words are important. He must persuade other people to have their say and give them equal respect. By preventing an overtalkative parent from being the only one who talks, the therapist is actually helping him or her, because he must save the family from going on doing what has always failed before.

Sometimes the problem child may be reluctant to talk, particularly after his parents have described his misbehavior. To draw him out, the therapist should be persuasive and may need to move his chair near the child. Usually it is better to talk to the problem child last. After his brothers and sisters have said something, he usually becomes more willing to give his views.

For small children, it is always best to have toys and puppets in the room so that the child is given the opportunity to communicate in a "play" form. The estimate of the child's ability to play may be important, as well as the parents' ability to play with the child when they are asked to by the therapist. Toys and play activities allow action in the room rather than merely conversation about action so the therapist can observe the family members dealing with one another.

Therapist's Observation. When asking about the problem and encouraging people to talk, the therapist should observe how everyone acts as well as what they say. He *should not* share his observations with the family.

As someone talks about the problem, the therapist should notice such things as whether he or she is acting politely but really feels angry; whether the person is talking about a child as if he were a thing instead of a person; whether the person is worried about what the child or others will think about what he or she says; and so on. The therapist should notice particularly whether the person talks about the problem as if he or she has said the same thing many times before or whether he or she is describing it for the first time. (Sometimes the family has had previous treatment and this is important information.) By the way the participants talk, they will also be showing whether they feel the therapist can do something or whether they feel the whole thing is hopeless and they are simply participating as a duty.

The therapist should notice who is given responsibility for the problem. The situation if the mother blames the child is different from a situation in which she blames herself, or in which she blames other people such as relatives who are not present, or the school. Ultimately, the therapist will want to have the whole family take responsibility for solving the problem, and so he will want to note how easily the members accept responsibility for it.

While one person is speaking, the therapist should observe the reactions of the others. They will show with their behavior whether they agree or disagree, have heard all this before and are bored with it, are pleased to see a child getting blamed, and so on. Watching their reactions helps the therapist decide how to talk to them. The therapist should particularly notice how the child who is the problem is responding: if he is upset, or too casual or bored, and so on. The therapist should also notice the father when the mother is talking and the mother when the father is talking, because the therapist will be working with their disagreements.

The more responsive and involved the listeners are, and the more angry and upset at what is said, the more likely it is that the family is in a state of crisis and is therefore unstable. The more calm and detached they are, the more likely it is that the situation is reasonably stable and so may be difficult to change.

When listening to people talk about the problem, the therapist should keep in mind that they are not only telling him facts and opinions but also are saying things indirectly that cannot be said directly. These indirect messages are particularly evident when a mother and father describe a child's problem.

A therapist may listen to the mother's talking about the child in two ways: as statements about the child, but also as statements about her husband and the marriage. For example, if the mother says her son is obstinate, the odds are that she is also telling you that her husband is obstinate. If the father says the child is threatening to run away all the time, it is possible that mother is threatening to leave him.

It is useful to assume that a child problem reflects, or is a performance, of a marital problem. One can get information about that marital problem in advance by listening to the ways the parents talk about the child. The therapist can think about the data tentatively and check it out later, but it is important to keep such information to himself. *The therapist should not verbalize any interpretations to connect the child's problems with the marital situation.* He should just encourage the participants to talk and listen to the different meanings in what they say. Many things cannot be said directly, or there would probably not be a problem.

There are actually three different ways of receiving the problem and all three should be used at different times in the interview. In the first inquiry, the therapist should be general and should allow the problem to be expressed metaphorically. Specificity focuses the problem too much on the child and limits metaphor. Later in the interview, after the interaction stage, one wants a more specific and detailed statement of the problem and the goals so that one can eventually use the statement to check outcome and determine if the therapy has been successful. This statement should have a "how-many-times-a-day" and "for-how-long" sort of specificity, with base rate information. Finally, related to the specific description of the problem is the therapist's request, toward the end of the interview, for a summary defining what changes are wanted. Specifically, what are the goals the family would like to reach? All of these three ways of dealing with the problem are necessary and will provide different information.

At this stage of encouraging a metaphorical discussion of the problem, the therapist should not only avoid being too specific and concrete but should also attempt to communicate at the more general level. If the father is complaining that his daughter is difficult to understand, the therapist can respond that women are often hard for men to understand. Such a statement connects wife and daughter at a more general level without making an issue of it. If the mother says the boy is too aggressive and hits her, or hits girls, the therapist can say that it is too bad when males learn to treat women that way. The mother will recognize that he is hearing her complaint about her husband but is not going to force it out explicitly so that there is more trouble. When the therapist responds at the metaphoric level, he will be given more information, because the family members will know he is not going to be discourteous enough to point out what is "really" being said.

It is particularly important not to comment on indirect information directly. For example, if the mother says her husband is helpful, while covering her mouth with her hand, she could be saying that there are some things about him she would rather not say right now. The therapist should never point out to her that there are some things she is not saying, or explain her movement to her. She already knows and will consider his comment rude. The therapist should just listen and encourage her to talk more. If he does so, communication will become more understandable, partly because she will know it is safe to talk and give hints as well as direct opinions.

The Content of the Problem Presented. When the family members talk about a problem, they will usually describe a person. They will say what is wrong with him or her. This is, however, only one of many ways to think about a problem. For example, the mother may say, "He just never minds." In this way, the son is said to be the problem. However, the mother may say, "I don't know how to make my son mind." By putting it this way, she would still be saying that one person is the problem, but she would be saying it is her and not her son. It would also be possible to think of the problem as not just one person, but as two or more. For example, the mother could say, "My son and I deal with each other in a way that makes us both helpless and we can't get anything done." Then the problem is not one person but two people. Another way to put it would be for the mother to say, "My husband and I can't agree on how to deal with our son, and so my son doesn't mind." If said that way, then three people are defined as the problem.

The important point is that any statement about what is wrong could be put in terms of one person, or two people, or three people, or more. The same behavior by one person looks different in terms of what is wrong and what can be done if one thinks about the problem in terms of different numbers of people. Usually family members say that one person is the problem. The therapist's job is to think of the problem in terms of more than one person. By thinking that way, he is most able to bring about change. Therefore he will be thinking about the problem in a different way from the way the family members think about it, but he does not have to persuade them to think about it his way. He should accept what they say and seem to go along with it, but in his own mind he can be thinking about the problem differently.

In a child clinic, the parent will say the person is a problem and will say what the person does wrong. Usually the family says that the child does not behave himself or mind his parents. Sometimes the family members will say he does not behave or mind his teacher in school. There are at least three ways a child "does not mind": (1) he may be openly rebellious and defiant; (2) he may not do what he is told, but he does not defy anybody, he "just doesn't mind"; or (3) he "doesn't mind," but may show he cannot help himself by being too anxious or afraid, too nervous, getting sick or having pains, or by generally being too clinging and helpless to do what he is asked. In most cases, a parent will say the boy does not mind and the boy will sit there sullenly. Sometimes the parent will say the child is anxious and fearful and only later will the parent say he just does not do anything he is asked and that no one likes to push him because he gets so upset.

When a parent says the problem is at school and the teacher is complaining that the boy will not mind or is not doing well, there are three possibilities. One may be that the problem is at the school; another may be that the boy is responding in school to trouble at home; and yet another may be that there is trouble between the parents and the school and the boy is caught between them and is responding to that situation.

When a parent lists the things the child does wrong, it may be that he never does what he is told to do, lies, cheats, steals, wets the bed, fights with his brothers and sisters, and so on. By giving this list, the parent is also saying that he or she is not competent in dealing with the problem. That is why the parent has come for help. The parent is unable to deal with him, and nobody else in the family can help in such a way that the family can handle the problem by itself. Often parents prefer to say that it is not their fault at all, it is all the child's fault. They like to think that there is something inside the child that is making him misbehave. Thinking about the problem in this way has not been helpful to the parents and if the therapist thinks this way he will not do much better than they have done. It is the situation that needs changing so the child can behave more normally. When listening to the report about the child's misbehavior, the therapist should think about what is happening in the total situation of the child that is causing him to behave as he does.

For example, a mother may say that her nine-year-old son is afraid to go outside the house and clings to her all the time. In the room the therapist may see that he sits beside her and holds on to her. She also may say he lies and will not do anything around the house, but that the problem is mostly that he is afraid and never leaves her side. He even sleeps with her so that the father has to sleep on the living-room couch. The other children do not behave this way, but seem normal.

This information from the mother does not tell the therapist what the problem is or what to do about it. He has only her version that the problem is inside the child and no one else has anything to do with it. To get more information and begin to make a change is the purpose of skillful family interviewing. After the mother has stated that problem the therapist needs to listen to the father and his views. Then he needs to listen to the brothers and sisters and what they say about it. After having spoken to each one, he will see disagreements appearing. For example, he will notice that the father does not quite agree with the mother and thinks she is taking care of the child too much and not letting him be on his own enough. He also does not like to be moved out of his own bed, he may say, although he is willing if it will keep the child from being afraid. Perhaps mother argues that father neglects the child. When mother and father talk about their disagreements, information may appear about how much the child is an issue between them.

During this stage of the interview, it will probably become clearer how to think about this problem in terms of more than the child. The therapist may think of it as a peculiar relationship between mother and son; she has as much difficulty leaving him as he has leaving her. He may also be able to think in terms of three people and consider the possibility that the child is helping mother and father. If they cannot get together without fighting, particularly in bed, then the child is helping them by acting so fearful that they are kept more separate. They can then say it is the child who is the problem, and not bad feelings between them.

When gathering information the therapist should learn whether part of the reason the child stays at home may be a bad neighborhood or real danger on the street. Is his staying at home related to the situation outside the family as well as within the family? All these factors should be considered as the therapist formulates ideas about what to do to bring about change. The interviewing itself, and the way it is done, is a way of bringing about change as a first step. For example, if the therapist asks the child to sit over by his father, the therapist is beginning to move him out of a too close attachment to his mother. The therapist is also learning how movable the child and his mother are as well as how receptive the father is.

Each family is unique, so the therapist must fit what he does to a particular family. Yet what happens in each family is familiar because one sees it in family after family. With experience, a therapist learns to expect certain family patterns of behavior. For example, one parent typically accuses the other of being too hard on the child, while the other says that the first parent is too soft on the child. The therapist's task is to think about what he sees in the family in a way that helps him devise an idea to change the family. He must also think about how to get these particular family members to cooperate in bringing that change about.

The Interaction Stage

There are two steps to asking about the problem. The first step is getting everyone's comments. In this step, the therapist needs to take charge directly. The second step is getting the family members to talk to each other about the problem. At this point the therapist should stop being the center of the conversation. Instead of being the person each family member talks to, he should turn them more and more to speak to each other. This shift tends to occur naturally, since when they have stated their opinions about the problem there will be disagreements. The therapist should continue to be in charge of what is happening, but he must now begin the interaction stage, in which he sits back and encourages the family members to talk to each other about these disagreements. If the family members try to continue to talk to the therapist, he must turn them back on each other. It may be helpful to move them physically next to each other to talk.

Sometimes a therapist will find that he has started the family members talking to each other before he has finished the stage of each family member expressing his opinion. For example, the mother may say how the boy misbehaves and boy may start to argue with her about it. If the therapist encourages them to talk to each other, while neglecting the other family members, he will reach a point where mother and son lock with each other and where it is hard to do anything with them. If this happens, the therapist should stop what is happening and go back and finish the first step. For example, the therapist can say, "Well, before you go further with that, let's get some ideas from the others about this situation." Then he should talk to the father or to a brother or sister, and later go on to the interaction stage in which family members talk with each other.

It cannot be overemphasized how important it is to have the family members interact with each other, rather than with the therapist at this interaction stage. No matter how hard the family members try to involve him, it is necessary to turn them to talk to each other.

When any two people are talking, the therapist should always be ready to introduce a third person into that conversation. Ultimately, everyone should talk to each other. For example, if a mother and son are talking and are getting locked in a struggle, it is appropriate to say to the father something like, "They don't seem able to get this straight; could you help them?" In this way the father is brought in and the therapist can observe how much he can oppose either mother or son and how much he cannot. This approach yields information about how to best intervene later when helping the family solve their problems.

Although the emphasis has so far been on talking, the therapist should prefer action to words as a source of information. There is less consequence, and less result, with talk. Rather than only have a *conversation* about a problem, he should try at this stage to bring the problem *action* into the room. For example, if a child deliberately bangs his head, he can be asked to do so. The family will show how it responds. If a child sets fires, he can set one (in a metal ashtray) so that the knowledge he has of how to handle matches as well as the response of everyone is clarified. With toys in the room, problem situations can be performed. If a wife complains and is depressed, she may be asked to behave that way and then everyone can show how they respond. However, these more active procedures should be attempted only when a therapist has learned to give directives effectively (see Chapter Two).

Family Organization.   The family members cannot tell a therapist about their sequences and patterns of behavior because they do not know what these are. Only observing how they behave with each other can yield this information. Having the family members talk to each other allows the therapist to observe what kind of sequence there is in the family.

A family is a very complex organization and each family is unique. Yet for practical purposes one can think about a family in an oversimplified way. This way of presenting types of family sequences is a guideline and does not deal with all the complex behaviors which the adults typically are employing to "save" the child from each other, as they do in families with problem children. If the interaction stage of the first interview is conducted correctly, the structure of the family will become apparent. When one of the parents is siding with a child against the other parent, this situation will become obvious as they talk. If a grandmother is siding with a child against the mother, the behavior will appear in the interview (if the grandmother is present because she lives in the household; otherwise the behavior must be estimated from what they say about her, and she must be brought to the next interview). If the family organization has a child functioning as a parent to the other children, this situation will become apparent. (For a sequence description, see Chapter Four.)

To describe the organization in another way, one can say that when there is a problem child, one adult in the family has violated a generational boundary by becoming overinvolved and concerned with a child. This adult is the authority on the child's problem and is both benevolently concerned and exasperated with him. When the child talks to another adult, the overinvolved one will intrude and side with the child. For example, in a one-parent family a mother will say that it is a mystery to her why her daughter does not mind and why she lies to her. The therapist can say, "I want you to choose one of the lies and talk to your daughter about it." As mother and daughter start to talk, an overinvolved grandmother will intrude and question the daughter herself or object to the way the mother is talking with the girl. The more difficult it is to keep grandmother from intruding, the more set the family is in that pattern. If the therapist can prevent grandmother from intruding and mother and daughter have a talk, the therapist is simultaneously making a diagnosis and beginning a change, which is what happens when a first interview goes well.

At times, a therapist may want to have a child tested for intelligence or given a special psychological test, but much information about the child can be gathered in a family interview. As part of the interaction stage, the therapist can have a parent ask a child to do something at the blackboard, draw a person on a sheet of paper, or make an arithmetical computation. Both the child's ability to perform and the type of family involvement can become evident in such a procedure. For example, if a father who seems on the periphery of the family is asked to tell his nine-year-old son, who may be retarded, to write his teacher's name, or something more complicated, on the blackboard, a great deal of information can be gathered in the process. How the father asks the boy to do it, whether or not the boy does it, how the mother intrudes to help, and so on, is information that is available from such a simple testing situation.

Defining Desired Changes

After the family members have interacted together, many of the issues in the family will have been clarified. At this point it is important to obtain from the family a reasonably clear statement of what changes everyone, including the problem child, wants from the therapy. This process helps everyone focus on the important issues, and it provides the base line for the goals of the therapy. Essentially, the therapist is making a therapeutic contract. The clearer the contract is, the more organized the therapy will be. If problems and changes desired are left fuzzy and unclear, the family participation and the therapist's chance of success will be more difficult. For example, if the family members say clearly and definitely they want to get a child over the problem of bedwetting, among other problems, then when the therapist gives the members a task later to cure the problem they are more obligated to accomplish the task. If the agreement on the changes wanted is not made clear from the start, the family will respond in a less cooperative way.

It cannot be emphasized enough that the problem the therapist settles on must be a problem that the family wants changed but that is put in a form that makes it solvable. The negotiation that takes place should involve how to make the problem operational. For example, if a family should say the problem is that a person is anxious, that is not a solvable problem. The ways in which this anxiety manifests itself and the responses to it are the problem. No traditional diagnostic category is a solvable problem. To say the problem is "schizophrenia" or "mental retardation" is to say nothing related to therapy. "Identity confusion" or "low self-esteem" or "unhappiness" or most of the terminology of psychodynamic language is not useful when one is formulating a problem. A "school phobia" is not a problem one can resolve, but a child who will not go to school is an operational problem.

Problems, whether one calls them *symptoms* or *complaints,* should be something one can count, observe, measure, or in some way know one is influencing. The kinds of information a therapist needs about a symptom, depending on the type, are such things as: Is it there all the time, or does it come intermittently? Is it unexpected when it arrives, or predictable? Does it go away suddenly or drift away? Is it more intense at some times or at others? Is day or night the most frequent time of occurrence, or the weekday or the weekend? How many times an hour does it occur? If something like bedwetting, does it happen early in the sleep, late, or just before waking up? As with all symptoms, asking what has been tried already clarifies the nature of the problem as well as provides guidance as to what to do.

One of the most important reasons for specifying the problem clearly is so that a therapist can know when he has succeeded. Presumably, when treatment terminates and in a followup interview afterwards, a therapist will want to know definitely whether he has achieved his therapeutic goals. If the contract is cloudy, the outcome evaluation will be unclear.

The problems emphasized here are obviously over-simplified and many unique situations arise that must be dealt with differently. The procedures suggested are for the average case. There are inevitably exceptions, of which one or two can be mentioned here. Ordinarily, one should define a problem as clearly as possible. Yet at times that may not be the best way to proceed.

Sometimes a family or an individual may present a problem so rigidly defined and circumscribed that it is better to seek ambiguity. With an ambiguous situation, the therapist has more room to maneuver. This problem may be a symptom that the patient repetitiously emphasizes again and again, refusing to deal with anything else. Or the family may repetitiously emphasize a person. In some such instances it is best to *un*clarify the problem in order to work with more alternatives.

One unfortunate idea in family therapy was the notion that a person was a scapegoat and that the family should be educated about what the *real* problem is. Sometimes the therapist would "take the pressure" off the problem child by pointing out the problems that all the siblings have. This is an error. Typically, parents feel they have failed when they come in with a problem child, and this feeling is one of the reasons why they attack the child. If they are persuaded that they have also failed with the other children, they may attack the problem child even more because they feel he has forced them to be exposed to such accusations. Generally, the attempt to rescue a problem child activates the family to prove that the therapist does not understand what a dreadful person he is. The family tries to prove this assumption by increasing the attack on him—often at home, after the interview.

In the approach recommended here, it is best to keep the focus on the problem person and to use that focus as leverage to change the situation. Since he is such a problem, therefore more is to be expected from the family to do something about it. Of course, the therapist should bring out the assets of the problem person as well as the defects, but not as a way of proving to the family that it is wrong.

Therapy is more effective if the focus is kept on the symptom and on the problem person. At times, of course, one meets unusual situations and is tempted away from that focus. For example, a crisis situation may require a different approach until the crisis is resolved. Certain presenting situations may seem more important to the therapist than the problem presented. However, if possible, one should always tie the shift in emphasis to the problem focus. For example, a family once came in with a problem with a retarded daughter. The parents had devoted their lives to her. In the interview it was learned that father was dying of cancer and had only a few months to live. This issue was upsetting everyone. A therapist might have been tempted to shift and deal with the issue of death to help the family past this painful period in a direct way. Instead, the therapist took the approach recommended here. She found that the father was concerned because the retarded daughter gave his wife more trouble than the daughter gave him. He was worried about his wife handling the daughter alone. He also regularly had to drive the daughter to a sheltered workshop because mother did not drive. The therapist focused on the father helping mother learn to drive. She also had the father work with the mother on more effective ways of responding to the daughter. This way, the father could leave the world feeling that his wife was competent to drive the girl where she needed to go and to deal with her more effectively. The issue of mother and father dealing with each other more intimately at this crucial time was achieved by dealing with the presenting problem they brought in. Generally, the therapist can find a way of centering the therapy on the presenting problem while also achieving other goals the therapist thinks are important.

Another special situation is one in which a family presents a problem and the therapist finds out that the problem does not exist. For example, one family offered a young daughter as a problem because she was misbehaving and getting poor grades in school. The therapist checked with the school and found out that the daughter was behaving well and was getting good marks. In such a case, it is sometimes best not to confront the parents with this information. Presumably, the parents are not dumb, they know the daughter is not a problem, and they have some other reason for presenting themselves in this way. It is best to explore the situation tentatively and to learn what is behind it. In the case of this nonproblem daughter, the therapist found that the mother had an older daughter, by a previous marriage, who was due to leave a mental hospital. The mother was concerned about how to deal with her as well as with the problems that were arising in her marriage. By accepting the nonproblem presented, the therapist could resolve the other, pressing problems.

At times, a therapist must simply act as a wise advisor and not as a therapist in the usual sense. For example, some people bring a problem that is really not a problem; but in their inexperience of living they may think it is. For example, one young couple came in with their first child, a normal and cheerful four-year-old. They wished to be sure that their child was "sufficiently prepared intellectually for the academic program" at the nursery school. A first interview seemed to indicate that they were just uncertain young people who, like many couples today, did not have parents or older relatives to advise them in child rearing and so they came to the experts. They were assured their child was intellectually sound and ready for the nursery school program.

Ending the Interview

The first interview should end with the setting of the next appointment, which may involve several issues. It may have become clear in the interview that some family member who is not present is essential to the therapy. This member may be a grandmother living separately. Or it may be a separated or divorced spouse who is still involved deeply in the problem. Arranging for that person to come, and discussing how to get the person to come, is part of the ending process.

Some therapists who are directive in their orientation are skillful enough to have devised a directive by the end of the first session. This directive can be offered as homework for the family between interviews. It may be a simple task or it may be complex, but a simple task is usually better at this stage. If a directive is given, the family remains involved with the therapist between interviews.

In summary, for the average problem in the majority of families who seek therapy, a first interview can be conducted in a way that provides maximum information and begins a change. When a family arrives, the members do not quite know what is wrong but they usually think it is a particular person with a particular set of problems. Often they assume the problems have a cause in the past rather than in the present situation. The therapist meeting the family also does not know what is wrong but he does know something in the family situation is making the problem necessary. The first interview should clarify the family structure and provide some agreement between therapist and family about the nature of the problem and the goals of therapy. At this point, the therapist's task is to understand the problem and formulate it in such a way that something can be done with it. If he is to change the family, he must join the universe of the family and, from within that universe, bring about change.

The therapist joins the family in the ways he makes everyone feel at ease and involved in the social stage, has everyone contribute ideas about the problem in the problem stage, involves everyone with each other at the interaction stage, and includes everyone in specifying just what changes are desired from the therapy. Although some types of families cannot fit this format—such as families with infant problems, families only seeking testing for a child, or families erupting in a state of crisis—for most families the interview can easily go from stage to stage. How the therapist proceeds after the first interview will be determined by the particular problems. One must also expect that in the following interviews new problems may be presented and new goals must be established. The "presenting problem" is not only what is offered in the first interview but also what is offered as therapist and family become more involved with one another.

As the interview ends, usually the family and the therapist can manage a reasonably clear agreement, although sometimes more than one interview is necessary to clarify the issues. Some families would like an estimate of the length of therapy; it is best to respond that therapy will be as brief as possible to solve the problems. If a family is particularly resistant or doubtful about coming back, it is sometimes helpful to set a certain number of interviews. One can say, "Why don't we meet for six times (or three times) and then decide if more times are necessary."

Evaluating the Therapist

When observing a videotape of a first interview, one can judge whether or not the therapist properly conducted the stages of an interview outlined here. Besides such stages, there are a number of questions that might be asked about a therapist and his approach. With proper training and experience in interviewing, one can expect that a student will develop confidence. He or she should be able to approach an interview without trepidation, feel reasonably at ease with the family, and be able to talk to school teachers or probation officers or whomever is involved in the case. A therapist can be expected to be able to interview families of different social classes or colors. He should be able to interview in the office or in the home. One can also expect competence whether interviewing a large family group, a nuclear family, a mother and child, or one person.

When observing a first interview with a family, a supervisor can ask the following questions:

1. Does the therapist frame the interview situation so the family knows who he is, what the situation is, and why different kinds of questions are being asked?

2. Has the therapist organized the family in the room well so that business can be conducted, for example, by dealing with obstreperous children or chaotic interchanges?

3. Is the therapist sufficiently nonmoralistic so the family members are encouraged to talk about their problems?

4. Has the therapist shown the flexibility to shift his approach when one way of gathering information is not working?

5. Does the therapist show a range of behavior from being reflective to being confronting?

6. Has the therapist avoided pursuing a personal interest that is not relevant to the family problem?

7. Is the therapist able to assume the posture of an expert *while also* able to express ignorance when appropriate?

8. Does the therapist avoid offering solutions before the problem is clarified?

9. Does the therapist seem to know when to encourage dissent among family members and when to soothe them?

10. Does the therapist avoid siding with one family member against another or one faction against another (such as child against parents)?

11. Does the therapist avoid being too personally involved with the family?

12. Does the therapist avoid being too professional and detached from the family?

13. Is the therapist attempting to get *all* family members participating in the interview?

14. Has the therapist shown he can tolerate unpleasant material or strong feelings from the family members?

15. Is the therapist gathering information about significant other people not present in the interview?

16. Is the therapist learning whether other social agencies are involved with the family?

17. Is the therapist motivating the family members to change? Is he engendering hope and a willingness to make an effort?

18. Has the therapist been more positive in his approach than negative, in the sense of putting down the family?

19. Has the therapist shown the family that he or she has something to offer them and can bring about change?

2

Giving Directives

Irecall a young man in his late twenties who wished to be a great novelist but he could not bring himself to sit down at the typewriter and write. He was just unable to produce. The young man was also afraid of women. Although he could associate with prostitutes, he had never had an ordinary date with a woman. He came to therapy asking to solve both problems: he wished to write and he wished to have dates with women. The therapeutic strategy was obvious: when posed two symptoms, one should be used to cure the other. I asked the young man to specify how many pages per day he should write, and he said he should write one page per day of 250 words. I directed the young man to write six pages per week (he negotiated one day off). If he did not follow the directive, then the following week he had to ask young women for dates until he went out with three women that week. The next week if he did not write six pages, he must arrange three dates again. Rather than ask a woman for a date, the young man sprang to his typewriter and methodically wrote a minimum of six pages per

week. Later the problem of dating young women was resolved. By taking this approach, the therapist inevitably
wins: if the patient wrote, he solved one problem, and if
he did not write, he had to go out with women, and so solved
another problem. It is, of course, essential that a therapist
know how to give directives so that they are carried out. It
is a misfortune that most clinical training has not included
this skill. A therapist must largely learn it on his own unless
he meets a master therapist, such as Milton H. Erickson,
and can receive some instruction. Most of what is said in
this chapter on directives is derived from Erickson.*

Purpose of Directives

Giving directives, or tasks, to individuals and families
has several purposes. First, the main goal of therapy is to
get people to behave differently and so to have different
subjective experiences. Directives are a way of making those
changes happen.

Second, directives are used to intensify the relationship
with the therapist. By telling people what to do, a therapist
becomes involved in the action. He becomes important
because the person must either do or not do what the therapist says. If the directive is something the people are to
do during the week, the therapist remains in their lives all
week. They are thinking about such things as: What if we
don't do it? What if we only half-way do it? What if we
change it and do it in our own way? and so on. When they
come back for the next interview, the therapist is more
important than if he had not given a directive.

Third, directives are used to gather information. When
a therapist tells people what to do, the ways in which they
respond give information about them and about how they

---

*See J. Haley, *Uncommon Therapy: The Psychiatric Techniques of
Milton H. Erickson, M.D.* (New York: Norton, 1973) and *Advanced Techniques of Hypnosis and Therapy* (New York: Grune & Stratton, 1967).

will respond to the changes wanted. Whether they do what the therapist asks, do not do it, forget to do it, or try and fail, the therapist has information he would not otherwise have. In fact, in the preliminary talk about the task the therapist learns things he would not learn otherwise. For example, if the task is to do something at breakfast time, the therapist learns what happens at breakfast because the people will discuss that as they talk about how to do the task.

What Is the Directive?

Some therapists are uncomfortable about giving directives because they feel perhaps they should not take the responsibility for telling someone what to do. It is important to emphasize that directives can be given directly or they can be given in a conversation implicitly by vocal intonation, body movement, and well-timed silence. Everything done in therapy can be seen as a directive. If an individual or a family in an interview is talking about something and the therapist says, "Tell me more about that," he is giving a directive. If the therapist only nods his head and smiles, encouraging them to continue, that is also a directive. If someone says something the therapist does not like, he can tell the person not to say that anymore—and that is telling him what to do. If the therapist turns his body away from the person and frowns, he is also telling the person that he should not say that sort of thing.

Whatever a therapist does is a message for the other person to do something, and in that sense he is giving a directive. If someone says, "I feel unhappy," and the therapist replies, "I understand, you feel unhappy," the reply does not look like a directive. But it can be defined as one since the therapist is indicating that he is interested in such statements and the person should say that sort of thing, or that it is all right to say that sort of thing. Since the therapist may not have responded to something else the person said but has responded to this statement, his response tells the person that this statement is important. The therapist's response also implies there should be more talk about such important things. Once a therapist faces the fact that whatever he says or does not say is telling a person to do something, or is telling him to stop doing something, then the therapist will find it easier to accept the idea of giving directives. In fact, even when a therapist tries to avoid giving directives by pointing out to the client that the client is trying to get the therapist to direct him what to do, the therapist is directing the client how to behave.

There may be times when a therapist does not want the responsibility of directing someone's behavior. For example, someone might ask, "Should I quit my job?" or "Should I divorce my wife?" Here, it might be best to respond by saying, "That is something you have to decide yourself." However, if a therapist has any opinions about that decision, those opinions are going to be communicated to the person by what the therapist says or implies, by the tone he says it in, by the way he moves. But the therapist can still put the responsibility for the decision on the client if he does not want to take it himself.

The question of who is responsible for what in therapy is a complex one. A therapist may believe that he himself decided on a directive and was responsible for a course of action, but closer examination of the interchange may indicate that the client led him into that directive. Often, too, the responsibility taken by the therapist is given by the client in more direct ways. A mother may ask that a therapist bring up a sensitive subject so that she and her children can discuss it, and the therapist may choose to cooperate by taking the responsibility for bringing that subject up. At times, the therapist may want to relieve the client of responsibility, and at yet other times he may want to have the client feel that the therapist is accepting responsibility when in fact he is not. This chapter does not deal with the intricacies of who actually determines a course of action in a therapist-client encounter but rather how to give directives when the therapist assumes that he himself is initiating what happens.

Types of Directives

There are two ways of giving directives: (1) telling people what to do when the therapist wants them to do it, and (2) telling them what to do when the therapist does *not* want them to do it—because the therapist wants them to change by rebelling.

First, we will discuss giving directives when the therapist wants people to do what he says. The emphasis here will be on giving directives to whole families during an interview, but the procedures are essentially the same when interviewing a person alone and giving a directive.

When a therapist wants people to do what he says, there are two types of directives. In telling someone to stop doing something, the therapist is trying to change behavior in a family by telling one or more people to stop what they are doing. For example, if a mother intrudes when a father and son try to talk to each other, the therapist can tell the mother not to intrude. Whether the therapist puts it nicely or forcefully, the therapist is asking her to stop what she is doing.

To ask someone to stop doing something is one of the most difficult directives to enforce. It can be done, but it is not easy. Usually one needs high status or a reputation as an expert for someone to stop usual behavior simply because he is told to. With minor problems or educational situations such direction is easier. If someone drinks too much, sometimes it is a good idea to tell him not to drink. He might stop. But if the problem is severe, he is likely to drink more, and a therapist does not usually have the power to enforce the directive. In the same way, some mothers in families with minor problems will stop intruding on father and son if told to stop. But if the family problem is severe, the mother may very well not stop but rather may debate the therapist about how he does not understand or appreciate her. A directive to stop needs to be accompanied by other messages. A therapist may have to repeat the directive often, or magnify it by standing up and waving his hands at her to stop. Or he may have to put the mother behind a one-way mirror and have her watch father and son talk. Sometimes he needs to get the cooperation of the father and son by asking them to prevent her interrupting.

If the therapist tells someone to stop usual behavior, he must usually go to an extreme or get other family members to cooperate and change their behavior to support him in this task. Often it is like trying to stop a river from flowing; one can try to block it, but the river will go over and around the block and the therapist will drown.

In telling someone to do something different, the therapist is trying to change behavior in a family by telling the family members to behave in a way that is different from their usual behavior. The therapist is asking them to try new ways. Instead of trying to block the river, the therapist is diverting it into a new pathway.

There are two ways to tell people to do something different: (1) good advice and (2) directives to change the sequence in the family.

Telling people that they should treat each other better is usually not useful to them. For one thing, they have had good advice from other people and have not been able to follow it. For example, if a mother fights with her daughter about what time her daughter comes in at night, good advice to them is usually not helpful. The therapist may say, for example, that they should listen to each other with respect, be nicer to each other, and find some compromise they both like. In most cases the therapist gives this kind of advice when he thinks they have not realized they should do these things. The therapist thinks he is telling them something new. Actually, they know how they ought to behave; their problem is that they cannot behave that way. Every time they try to be nice and respectful they get into a runaway fight.

Unless the therapist is dealing with someone who is quite unintelligent, or unless the problem is a mild, educational kind, good advice is not usually helpful. If the therapist is tempted, he can ask the family a question like this:

"If I were to give you some good advice, what would I say?" The family members will then tell the therapist all the good advice that he has considered, that they have been given in the past, and that has not helped.

Giving good advice means the therapist assumes that people have rational control of what they are doing. To be successful in the therapy business it may be better to drop that idea.

The directives that will be talked about here are ones in which the goal is to change the ways the family members deal with one another by introducing action. There are many ways to accomplish this goal. For example, if a mother and daughter are in a continual fight with each other about when the daughter is to come in at night, one can direct the father to take charge of this problem. This directive will change the sequence in the family. Or one might use many other kinds of directives in this situation. How to give such directives so that they are followed is a matter of skill and practice.

Motivating a Family to Follow Directives

To motivate someone to do something means to persuade the person that there is some gain in it for him. When a therapist wishes to motivate family members to carry out a task, it is necessary to convince them that the task will achieve the ends they want for themselves individually, and for each other and the family. How to motivate a family will depend on the nature of the task, on the nature of the family, and on the kind of relationship the therapist has with the family. But one can talk about general ways to motivate people.

The direct approach, a common approach for persuading family members to do a task, is for the therapist to say to them that he knows they want to solve their problem and that he wants the same thing. When they agree on a goal, the task is offered in that framework of achieving what they want out of therapy.

When the family members are in conflict over their aims, it is sometimes necessary to find some gain for each of them in the task. For example, the therapist can say that the mother wants to be sure her daughter behaves properly, the daughter does not want this constant arguing with her mother, and the father does not want always to be called in as a referee. Therefore they should do the task.

In the direct approach, the therapist takes what has been learned about the family members in the session and uses what seems most evident and matter of fact as the basis for persuading them to do the task.

If it looks as if the family will not easily cooperate in the task, the therapist can go at the matter more indirectly. Often this indirect approach can be used first; later one can be more direct. In the indirect approach, the therapist leads the family members to talk about their difficulties in such a way that they are ready to listen to someone who can offer something to do. For example, the therapist may ask the members to talk about everything they have tried to do that failed to solve the problem. This discussion yields information about what has been tried, so that the therapist does not ask them to do something that has been tried before without success. Equally important, such a discussion gives the therapist the opportunity to emphasize what has failed before. As each failure is listed it can be emphasized as a failure by saying, "And that failed too." After the listing is done, the family members will notice that everything *they* have tried has failed, and so they are more likely to listen to what *the therapist* has to offer.

A similar approach can be used by encouraging the family members to talk about how desperate their situation is. Rather than reassure them it is not so bad, the therapist can agree with them that it is quite bad. If the situation is made to appear desperate enough, they will listen to the therapist and do the task he offers. That is, the therapist uses their desperation as a motivation by emphasizing it. He can even project their situation into the future and have them talk about how disastrous the future will be if something is not done.

However, one can take a quite opposite approach if family members are talking about how things have been improving. One can agree with them and go along with that assessment. Then one can ask them to do the task as something that will help them continue to improve even more, so that what one offers is seen as a small addition to help along an improving situation.

It is possible to motivate family members to do a task at home by starting them on small tasks during the interview. For example, if a mother is asked to help her child do something in the room, and this task goes well, then she is motivated to do what the therapist asks when he directs her to help the child at home during the week. Similarly, if the therapist asks a father to intervene and help the mother and daughter while in the room, to ask him to intervene at home during the week can be seen as merely a continuation of that initial intervention. In such situations, the task at home does not seem such a major event because in a smaller way it has already been done during the therapy session.

The therapist must fit the task to the people. As he interviews a family, he will observe what sort of people the members are and can fit the task to the family style. If the family members emphasize doing things in an orderly, logical manner, the task offered to them should be an orderly, logical task—they will be more likely to do it. If they form a casual, disorderly household, a casual framework for the task may be more appropriate. If they are concerned about money, the therapist emphasizes that the task costs nothing. One of the ways to get this kind of information is to ask the family members to do things while in the therapy room, such as move their chairs, or talk about certain subjects. The ways they go about doing such tasks will give the therapist information on how to frame the outside task most acceptably for them.

How the therapist describes the size of the task is important. For some families and for some tasks, the therapist may choose to describe the task as small. For families who seem resistant, sometimes it is best to define the task as a small thing being asked of them. Families who enjoy crisis or have a flair for the dramatic can be told that this task is a major thing being asked of them. That is, some families will feel a large task is too much for them, while others will feel that a small task is beneath them. The needs of both types must be met.

The therapist can exert authority in a number of ways. Generally, in motivating the family, the therapist should use his position as an expert on what should be done. If he acts as if he knows his business, people are more likely to do what he tells them. Usually people in trouble prefer to have a therapist know his business. Sometimes this preference can be used in an extreme way. If a family is the kind that bickers about things and unravels whatever is suggested, the members will continue to do so when the therapist tries to motivate them to do the task. In that situation, the therapist may tell the family, "I want you to do something, and I have my reasons but I'd rather not go into them. I just want you to do this in the coming week." The therapist can also get many tasks done by getting people to do the task in order to prove to the therapist that he is wrong or that his method will not work.

A variant approach is to say to a family, "I'm going to ask you to do something that you will think is silly, but I want you to do it anyway." Then debate is cut off, because the family cannot say the task is silly after the therapist has already said that it is.

Being Precise

After the family is motivated, the therapist should give clear instructions (unless for a particular reason he wishes to be confusing). The directives should be clearly *given* rather than *suggested*. For example, it is better to say, "I want you to do such and such" than to say, "I wonder if you've considered possibly doing such and such." If the therapist says, "Why don't you do such and such?" he is really asking a question rather than giving a directive. It is better for the therapist to be precise and clear and say exactly what he wants done. He should observe the family members as he gives instructions because he can usually tell from their responses whether they are clearly understanding what he is saying. The therapist should not be afraid to repeat himself. Being repetitious is better than not being understood. Sometimes people will think ahead about one part of the instructions and thus not listen to another part. If the therapist has any doubt that someone understands, he can ask that person about the instructions and even ask him to repeat the instructions.

One of the reasons for being precise is not only that the therapist wants the task done, but also that if it is not done he will want to be sure it was not left undone simply because the instructions were not clear.

However, in some situations the therapist may not want to be precise and detailed when giving a task. He may want, instead, to drop in an idea so that the family "spontaneously" thinks of doing that kind of task. Nevertheless, the therapist still must be precise in his casual dropping of the idea.

Involving Everyone

Just as the therapist should involve all the family members in an interview, he also should give everyone something to do in a task. (For special reasons he may leave someone out but exclusion should not happen accidentally.) A good task has something for everyone. Even if the therapist specifically asks someone to stay out of the task, this request is still giving the person something to do.

The task should be structured like any other piece of work. Someone is needed to do the job, someone to help, someone to supervise, someone to plan, someone to check to see that it gets done, and so on.

If, for example, the therapist should ask the mother and father to agree on something during the week, he should make this task quite precise. The time set aside to talk about it should be decided, what each is to bring up should be specified, and the children should be assigned something to do. One child can remind the mother and father that it is time, if that is necessary; another child can interrupt them when it is time to end; and a third can report the agreement to the therapist at the next interview.

The purpose of involving everyone is to put the emphasis on the total family unit, except in special cases where the therapist wants one part of the family to do a task and wants the others to stay out of it. The therapist must also be careful not to confuse hierarchy in the family by involving children in adult tasks. But, just as no one should be left out in the interview, no one should be left out of the action designed to take place in the home.

Reviewing the Task

In many cases, particularly if the task is very complex, it is a good idea to have the family members review what they are to do. If one member reviews, the others should be brought into the discussion by asking them to specify their particular parts in the task. This review, which can be done quite quickly with most families, is further insurance that the task is fully understood.

The therapist should anticipate difficulties while reviewing the task. When he gives family members a task, while he is talking they are sometimes thinking of ways to get out of it. If this situation seems possible, the review should be followed by a discussion of ways they think they might avoid the task. Usually, family members will bring up what they have thought about. If not, a few suggestions may be helpful. For example, the therapist can ask: "What if somebody forgets?" or "Suppose someone gets sick?" Such suggestions are helpful, particularly if family members have indicated that such things often happen. When the therapist does this, the family members have blocked themselves off from getting out of the task and are more fully committed to it.

Examples of Tasks

A few simple examples of tasks may be helpful at this point in the discussion.

1. In an actual case in which the grandmother is siding with her grandchild against the mother, the therapist sees mother and grandchild (a ten-year-old girl) together. The grandchild is instructed to do something of a minor nature that would irritate grandmother, and the mother is to defend her daughter against the grandmother. This task forces a collaboration between mother and daughter and helps detach daughter from grandmother.

2. In another case, a husband is asked to do something for his wife that she would not expect, and she is asked to receive it graciously. He cannot do something routine, which she would expect, and therefore he is encouraged to initiate something new in the marriage. He also must think about his wife carefully to decide on something she would not expect.

3. A father and son are asked to do a minor thing that the mother would not approve of. It will be difficult for the mother to arrange what they do when the thing must be something she does not want.

4. A mother who does not differentiate among children of different ages may be asked to set and enforce a different bedtime for each child, even if the times are only fifteen minutes apart. This task forces her to differentiate on the basis of age.

5. A father who is siding with his small daughter against the wife may be required to wash the sheets when the daughter wets the bed. This task will tend to disengage daughter and father or cure the bedwetting.

6. Among the many tasks that can be done inside the interview room are those that involve changing pathways of communication. Father and mother may be directed to talk without including daughter, or mother and son may be told to talk without father interrupting. A son may be physically moved to sit beside a male therapist while they observe

the women in the family making a decision about something, thereby drawing a sex boundary. A family in which everyone constantly interrupts may be told to pass a coat or hat around and only the person holding it may talk. Or a "speaker's chair" may be set and only the person sitting in it may talk. All these tasks shift the pathways of communication.

7. A mother and father who need an excuse to be affectionate with each other may be asked to show affection to each other in an obvious way at set times to "teach their child" how to show affection.

8. A husband and wife with sexual problems may be required to have sex relations *only* on the livingroom floor for a period of time. This task changes the context and so the struggle.

9. When there is an intense triangle between a mother, a teen-age daughter, and a father, the father may be asked to take the daughter out to a nice place for lunch to give her experience in behaving well in public. Mother can be asked to dress the daughter for the occasion or choose the place. Such a directive may seemingly involve father and daughter more intimately but actually draws a generation line in the result.

10. A man who is afraid to apply for a job may be asked to go for a job interview at a place where he would not take the job if he got it, thereby practicing in a safe way.

11. Among the many tasks a supervisor may give to a therapist is one to help him disengage from a family. The supervisor can have the therapist tell a couple near termination of therapy that they will probably have a major disagreement. The couple will be inclined not to want such a fight, and they will pull together against the therapist to avoid it, thereby extruding him.

12. When a mother is behaving helplessly with the children and so keeping the father involved but exasperated, the father may be instructed to educate the mother in how to deal with the children (beginning by practicing in the room). To get husband off her back, the mother will

become more effective with the children and the couple is then likely to begin quarreling more openly.

13. An individual or family may be told that during the coming week they will spontaneously get an idea that will improve their situation. They may be told they are at a stage where they are responsive now to ideas from within themselves. This task helps patients initiate changes.

14. To get more distance and objectivity between a mother and child, the mother may be asked to hide something where it will take the child no more than ten minutes and no less than five minutes to find. She must repeatedly attempt this task until she succeeds. The mother must think through just how her child thinks, and how he thinks differently from her, to succeed.

15. Some tasks involve compromises that satisfy everyone. For example, one husband was always concerned about his health, and he regularly took his temperature, even walking about the house with a thermometer in his mouth. His wife became angry every time he did this, and they would fight about it. They could not resolve the issue. The therapist agreed that the husband should be able to take his temperature when he felt it necessary. His wife should also not be provoked by her husband "forgetting" and walking through the living room with a thermometer in his mouth. The directive was that they break the oral thermometer that same day and purchase a rectal thermometer for his use.

16. When a husband or wife, or parent and grandparent, are at an impasse over who is correct in the way the child should be dealt with, a therapist can provide a behavior modification program. One person may be exluded by this arrangement, or they may be brought together. For example, the parent can say to the grandparent that this is a new procedure being learned at the clinic and so from now on parent and not grandparent is to be the authority on what to do with the child with this new procedure. Or, parents who have fought over different ways of dealing with the child can reach agreement on this new way and so resolve a parental conflict that has been maintaining a child problem.

17. With a depressed person, the therapist can require a series of tasks that require the person to activate. The more trivial the tasks, the more angry and less depressed the person will be. For changing the organization maintaining the depression, the therapist can require the family members to initiate and enforce the tasks to activate the person.

18. A task can be used to prevent something happening that a therapist does not want. For example, a mother who felt she was unable to control a 12-year-old boy said that she was reluctantly going to put him in military boarding school, because there was nothing else she could do. The therapist suggested that the boy did not really know what a military school would be like, and in fairness the mother should teach him about one before sending him away. The mother agreed, and under the therapist's direction she began to teach the boy to stand at attention, be polite, and make his bed every morning after rising early. It became a kind of game between mother and son to have her be the sergeant and him be the private. In two weeks he was behaving well enough so that mother did not think it was necessary to send him off to military school. Mother had found a way to deal with the son, and he had found a way to do what she asked.

The Task Report

When a therapist has given a task, he should always ask for a report at the next interview. Generally there are one of three possible results: the task has been done, it has not been done, or it has been partially done.

If the family has done the task, congratulations are in order and the interview goes on from there. If the family members have partially done it, an exploration is necessary of why they have not completed it. Sometimes there are practical reasons and they just could not complete it. At other times they just did not get it all done and have no good excuse.

When people have only partially done what the therapist has asked, he should not excuse them easily. If he lets them off, he is saying that what he tells them to do is not important. This message makes the therapist less important and also makes it less likely that they will do the next task he asks of them.

The problem is clearer when the family members have not done the task and they do not have a valid excuse. The therapist should not be forgiving about this situation. Once he has given a task, he has started something he has to finish. The best attitude for the therapist to take is that *they* have failed. It is not that they have failed the *therapist,* but they have failed *themselves.* That is, the therapist condemns them for having missed an opportunity. The therapist should not imply that he is disappointed in himself and has failed.

One way to deal with task failure is to tell the family members that the task was very important and that for their sakes it is too bad they did not do it. The therapist can tell them that now they cannot know how beneficial it would have been to them. If they say they did not think the task would do any good, the therapist can say they can never know that now, because they did not do it. Throughout the interview, when they bring up problems, the therapist can point out that naturally they have those problems because they did not do the task. His goal is to get them to say they would like to have the opportunity to try again and do the task. If they do say this, the therapist can tell them that opportunity is gone and can never come again —they cannot do the task now. In this way, he sets up the situation so that the next time he asks them to do a task they will do it.

Generally, a therapist should not easily forgive people who have not done what he has asked. Sometimes it is best to be hard on people for not doing a task and then later in the interview find a way to excuse them. But failure to do what a therapist asks, or only partly doing what he asks, should never be treated lightly.

Metaphoric Tasks: The Use of Analogies

Although the metaphoric way of directing someone will not be dealt with here in detail, it should be mentioned. It is not always best to make explicit what the therapist wants to happen in a family or what he wants the members to do. Sometimes people will be more willing to follow a directive if they do not know consciously that they have received one. Talking in metaphor is one way to give such a directive.

A metaphor is a statement about one thing that resembles something else. It is the analogous relationship of one thing to another. We say "high as a kite," meaning the way the person is "high" resembles the way a kite goes "high." Or we say "The way his mother talked to him it's like he was run over by a train." A play on the stage is a metaphor about life because what happens there resembles what happens in life. Often when a therapist wants family members to behave in a certain way, he gets them to behave in some other way that resembles the one he wants. Then they will "spontaneously" behave the way he wants them to.

As an example, in one case where a boy was reported to be afraid of dogs, the therapist learned that the boy had been adopted as an infant. The boy ostensibly did not know he had been adopted, and the parents did not wish to tell him. The therapist assumed the boy did know. The therapist wanted to get the family to take a dog into the home and also wanted to deal with the adoption issue. Therefore, he talked to the boy about "adopting" a dog who had a problem of being frightened. He then discussed with the boy various issues, such as the possibility that the dog might become ill and have to be taken to the doctor (which situation paralleled the adopted boy being taken to the doctor). When the boy said the family might have to get rid of the dog if he became ill and cost doctor bills, the therapist insisted that once adopted the family was committed to the dog and would have to keep him and pay his doctor bills no matter what. Various concerns the boy might have had about himself as well as the parents' concerns about him were discussed in metaphoric terms in relation to the proposed adoption of the puppy.

Metaphors are not only words but actions. The ways in which a therapist deals with the children in a room can influence the ways the parents will deal with the children even if he does not point anything out to them. By how he operates, the therapist is showing them how to operate without making an issue of it. This approach is showing something metaphorically; the therapist is saying something in action that resembles something else he wants to have happen.

Another example can illustrate this approach. Suppose that a therapist wants a married couple to enjoy sexual relations more than they do. He wants husband and wife to behave differently together and to have a more pleasant mood during sex. He sees that there is bad feeling and a sense of contest around sexual relations and he also sees that they (or he himself) have difficulty talking directly about their sexual activities.

If he decides not to approach this problem directly, then he begins to think of what other situations there are that a married couple go through together that have some processes resembling sexual activity, something that is permissible to talk about. One possibility might be for them to have a date together as they did in their courtship days. The therapist can talk about what is to take place on their evening out. Or there might be a game they play together. The therapist can talk about the way they should deal with each other during a session of the game.

One of the metaphors Erickson developed to use for this problem is to have the couple talk about eating together. The therapist can discuss how they have dinner together. Is there a time they have dinner without the children present, just the two of them? As the therapist asks the couple about this, he can talk about aspects of eating that resemble sexual relations. He can say, for example, "Sometimes a wife likes to have appetizers before dinner and start slowly, and her husband likes to dive right into the meat and potatoes." Or, "Some husbands compliment their wives on how nice everything looks, and other husbands just don't notice and so their wives don't put out any effort." As he talks about these things, if the couple appears to be connecting what he says with sex, he changes to a part of the subject that does not touch so closely on the sexual topic. He does not want them to make the connection consciously. Then he moves back again to talk about how some people like dinner with the lights dim and perhaps with candles, while others like bright lights where they can see everything they want to enjoy.

At the end of such a discussion, the therapist can move naturally toward a task about dinner together. They are to choose a night and together they are to prepare a pleasant dinner. They are to show appreciation for each other's differences in taste and are only to bring up pleasant things and not the troubles of the day. The wife is to try to stimulate her husband's appetite, and he is to do what he can to provide what will please her. If the dinner goes well, the odds are that the mood will carry over to sexual relations.

In this approach the therapist chooses a goal of changing some family activity. Then he selects an activity that resembles the one he wants to change, an activity easier for the family members to deal with. He talks about that area to gain information and to influence the way they think about it. Finally, he assigns a task in that area, a task that has the outcome he wants both in that area and in the area he is really trying to change.

Paradoxical Tasks

The directives up to this point have been the kind a therapist gives when he wants the family members to do what he says. There is another kind of directive in which he wants the members to resist him so that they will change. These tasks may seem paradoxical to family members because the therapist has told them he wants to help them change but at the same time he is asking them not to change.

This approach is based on the idea some families who come for help are resistant to help offered. The members are very good at getting a therapist to try and fail. The therapist is then pulling at the family members to improve, while they are resisting and provoking him to go on pulling. This situation is frustrating for both the therapist and for the family.

To some extent it is true of all families that they are resistant to change if they are in a stable state. If they are in a crisis and unstable with everyone upset, they will often follow directives easily because they are trying to stabilize. But if they are stable and a therapist asks them to change, he is asking for instability and something new and people can react against that. Yet all families who come for help are unstable enough to have sought assistance. So it is never simply one way or another.

Usually a family has stabilized around one family member being the problem. When the therapist moves to make a change in the situation of the problem person, he is moving to unstabilize the family and he will meet resistance in varying degrees. The paradoxical tasks are designed to deal with this problem.

There are two general approaches with a paradoxical task: (1) an approach to the family as a whole, and (2) directives that involve only part of the family.

The Approach to the Family as a Whole.   An example of an approach to the whole family is the case described in Chapter Five. The therapist expressed his concern about what would happen if the child was properly toilet trained and became normal. Within a framework of trying to change the family, the therapist restrained the members from getting better. The paradoxical approach always has two levels on which two messages are communicated: "change," and, within the framework of the message, "don't change."

As another example, a family may enter with a problem child who will not go to school. The therapist—within the framework of his job, which is to help the boy get back to school—can talk to the family about how perhaps the boy should not go to school. He can suggest that it might be better if the boy just stayed home and can offer various reasons for this, depending on the particular family. He might say that perhaps the family would get upset if the boy went to school like normal children and therefore it would be better if he stayed home.

Skill is required if this approach is used, because the therapist is communicating a number of different things at the same time. He is saying "I want to help you get better" and he is saying "I am benevolently concerned about you." He is saying things to the family that are on the edge of being insulting: he is saying he thinks the family members can really tolerate being normal, but he is also saying perhaps they cannot.

The dangers in this approach come about when the therapist does not communicate all these things at once. If he does not, the family members may feel merely that he thinks they are hopeless. Or they may feel that he is taking advantage of his position to be insulting. Or that he does not really care if they change or not.

When the approach is successful, the family members achieve the goal of the therapy to prove to the therapist that they are as good as other people. They "spontaneously" change. The therapist must accept the change when it happens and let the family put him down by proving him wrong. If he wants to ensure that the change continue, he might say to the members that probably the change is only temporary and they will relapse again. Then the family will continue the change to prove to him that it is not temporary. What he is doing if he talks about the change being temporary is blocking off a relapse. He can do the same thing by encouraging a relapse. This approach can ensure that no relapse will occur. He can say to the family, "I can see you've changed and are over the problem, but I think this has happened too fast. I would like you to have a relapse and this week go back the way you were before." Sometimes he can put it, "I want you to feel as miserable as you did when you first came in."* To make this directive reasonable to the

---

*Milton H. Erickson is, of course, the master at directive therapy and he has a particularly graceful way of encouraging a relapse. He

family members, the therapist might say that too fast a change is upsetting, or that they really need to understand how badly they felt before, or whatever else might seem reasonable to them. However, when he asks them to relapse, they will resist by not relapsing, which is the therapist's goal. (Even if they should relapse, the relapse is under his direction and so they are following his directives and cooperating with him and so he can then get them not to have a relapse again. But such relapses do not happen if the approach is done properly.)

Directives that Involve Part of the Family. Often a therapist will not want to use a paradoxical approach to the whole family, but only with a particular person or a particular pair. The procedure remains the same: he asks for people to stay the same, within a framework of helping them change.

For example, a mother may be overprotecting her child and hovering over him so that he has no freedom to make decisions or take responsibility for what he does. If the therapist tries to persuade her to do less for the child, she may respond by doing more, often saying that the therapist really does not understand how handicapped the child really is. One can take a paradoxical approach by asking the mother to spend a week hovering over the child. She is to watch over him, protect him, and do everything for him. A therapist might give different reasons for this directive, depending on the mother. For example, he might say she should do this so she can find out how she really feels in this situation, or so that she can observe herself and the child. To use this approach well, the therapist should ask for more extreme behavior than the mother has been showing. For example, she should not only hover over the child, but she should also set aside a definite time to spend a whole hour warning the child about all the dangers in life (an hour is a

---

will say, "I want you to go back to that time when you felt miserable, feel as you did then, and see if there is anything from that experience you wish to salvage." Since there is usually a nostalgia for lost symptoms and problems, as well as relief, such a suggestion fits particularly well.

long time). Or the therapist should take some other aspect of her behavior and make it more extreme. If this approach is done well, the mother will react by rebelling against the therapist and hovering over the child less. She will not like to do what she is doing because someone is telling her to do it. She also does not like to do more of it, particularly when she also feels that too many demands are made upon her by the child already. She will begin to emphasize that the child should do more for himself and take more responsibility. That is, she will begin to move to the position the therapist would really like her to go to. Usually it is necessary to pursue this approach. If the mother hovers over the child less the therapist should not congratulate her but should push her to do more. This approach is one way of disengaging a child from a parent without using another family member.

The same approach can be used with couples who are always fighting in an unproductive way. The therapist can ask them to go home and have a fight at a set time and for a certain period, such as three hours. His goal is to get them to fight less. People do not like to fight or make themselves miserable because someone tells them to do so.

Similarly, if a child is provoking his parents, the therapist can ask him to do that for a full week. If he provokes them, they will react differently because they have heard him asked to do so. If he does not provoke them, the therapist has changed a pattern in the family, which is what he is after.

To use the paradoxical approach a therapist must develop skill and must practice. He also needs to be able to think about problems in a gamelike or playful way even though he realizes that he is dealing with grim problems and real distress. He also needs to tolerate the emotional reaction of the family toward him, since this approach forces them to deal with him in ways they have never dealt with a helper before.

The design of a therapist's directives in this approach is relatively simple. He observes how the family members deal with each other and directs them to behave in that way.

How he gives the directive, how he makes it seem reasonable, and how he reacts to a change and follow-through can require more innovation than the design of the task.

Stages of a Paradoxical Intervention. To summarize the paradoxical approach, the proper stages can be illustrated with a case example. A nine-year-old boy was referred to a clinic for a problem of compulsive masturbation. He masturbated at school and at home in front of his mother and sisters. The problem was so severe that he had worn holes in the crotch of his pants, and his mother reported he had been hospitalized for blood in his urine. The problem had existed since the boy was five years old. A child therapist had worked with the problem for a year and a half with no improvement. He had tried insight into the problem, had tried some rewards and punishments, and he had met regularly with the boy's mother. He referred the case hoping that family therapy would help. The family was on welfare and the father had been dead for several years. There were three older daughters in the family, two of them living outside the home. The twenty-year-old daughter had two small children who were also in the home.

The stages of the paradoxical approach can be summarized. First, as in all directive therapy, one must establish a relationship defined as one to bring about change. This definition is usually implicit in the framework when someone asks for therapy, but it can be emphasized. Second, one must define the problem clearly. In this case the problem was defined as public masturbation. Third, one must set the goals clearly.

The goal was not to stop the boy from masturbating but from masturbating in public and without pleasure. Setting goals clearly is particularly important if one is using an effective therapeutic technique.

Fourth, one must offer a plan. It is helpful to offer a rationale to make a paradoxical directive reasonable, although one can also leave the plan implicit and merely give the directive. In this case the first step in the plan involved the mother and other family members and the second plan involved the boy. The therapist asked the mother to let him deal with the problem with the boy privately, although he also wished to see the whole family together at times. The mother agreed. In this way the therapist attached the boy to himself and made the problem an issue between two males. Later, when he saw the boy alone, he offered the rationale that his paradoxical request for an increase in the masturbation was to prevent the boy from doing it on days when he did not enjoy it.

Fifth, one must gracefully disqualify the current authority on the problem. The authority of the problem may be a spouse or a mother or some other family member. Usually someone is trying to help the person solve the problem, and that someone must be defined as not doing the right thing.

In this case, the mother had taken the boy from doctor to doctor for years to solve the problem. The therapist suggested that she would become upset when the boy improved. The mother did not like that idea. The therapist asked her what she might do with herself when the boy was over the problem. She thought she could find something else to do with herself. A purpose in dealing this way with the mother is to encourage her to prove that she will not get upset when the boy improves. The only way she can prove this is to help the boy become normal and show she is not upset. Therefore she is working at home to improve the boy while the therapist is working in the office to improve him and they are working together. In the therapy the mother was, of course, seen alone to interest her in school and work so she would have more in her life than this problem son (and an even more problematic daughter).

Sixth, the therapist must give the paradoxical directive. As part of defining the problem, the therapist asked the boy to make a baseline chart on how often he masturbated. The boy came in the following week and reported the number of times. He said that he enjoyed it most on Sunday. The therapist gave the paradoxical directive that the boy do it more on Sunday when he enjoyed it and not on the other days when he enjoyed it less. He was asked to do it eight times on Sunday, twice as often, perhaps getting up early to get it done.

Seventh, the therapist should observe response and continue with encouragement of usual behavior. The therapist should not relent for rebellious improvement or if the person is upset but reemphasize the rationale and the plan. If the person improves and does less, the therapist should define that as not cooperating because the request was for more problem behavior.

In this case the boy had done his masturbating on Sunday, but he had also done it on Monday when he was not supposed to. To punish himself, he was asked to do it twelve times on the next Sunday. Masturbation was also made more of an ordeal by requiring him to undress completely, fold up his clothes, and so on.

The next week the boy came in without the baseline paper, had joined a hockey team, and was more cheerful. The therapist insisted more on the masturbation. By the fifth interview the boy had rebelled and masturbated less than required on Sunday. The therapist condemned him for not cooperating and, as punishment, required him to masturbate once each day in the livingroom in the presence of his mother and sisters. It had taken five weeks to arrange that the boy do exactly what he had been doing as a presenting problem. Now it was to be done as a punishment. (Some clinicians would have difficulty being this punishing, but given the severity of the problem, and the fact that the boy was only being asked to do what he was already doing, this therapist did not find it difficult).

Eighth, as change continues, the therapist should avoid credit for it. Accepting credit means that relapses occur in relation to the therapist. Although a therapist might want to "share" with a client and explain what he is really doing, the risk is a relapse caused by the therapist's need for comfort. A way to avoid credit is to be puzzled by the improvement.

In this case, the therapist recessed for two weeks. The first week he required the masturbation program. The second week he left unclear what the boy was to do. This omission allowed the therapist to judge the amount of spontaneous change (rather than a methodical extinguishing of the behavior). If the boy gave up the public masturbation, the therapist would drop the issue. If he had not, the procedures would be reinstituted.

In two weeks the boy reported that he had done little or no masturbating the second week and seemed to have lost interest in it. The therapist dropped the matter and talked to the boy about going to camp (which had not been previously allowed by mother).

The therapist continued the therapy focused on the mother and daughter problem, with the boy present but not involved around the issue of his symptom. A few weeks later the masturbation was inquired about, and the mother said at times the boy provoked her by putting his hands in his pants while watching television. This action was not made an issue, and in a followup a few weeks later the problem was gone.

The mother was allowed to show that she did not get upset when the boy improved, and the boy's general manner became more mature in a matter of a few weeks. He even made some trouble with a friend at school, which he had never done before because he was a quiet boy and a good student. The therapist and mother defined this kind of trouble as normal for a boy that age. The teacher confirmed that he was changing.

It should be emphasized that in this case the paradoxical maneuver was used within a family context. The therapist dealt with the boy about other issues, such as sports and girl friends. He also dealt with the mother about other interests in her life. When the boy improved and became less obedient, the mother showed that she did not get too upset about the change. The shift to the daughter's problems allowed the mother to be less focused on the boy. All these aspects were part of the therapy and not merely of the paradoxical maneuver. There were also stages to the therapy and not merely an encouragement of the symptom and a backing off when improvement occurred. It was necessary to follow through in a systematic way.*

Designing Tasks

When a therapist first gives tasks to families, designing tasks may seem difficult. With practice and experience design becomes easier. A few guidelines can be offered.

Whatever the task, it should be simple enough so that the family can do it (unless the therapist has a special reason for wanting them to fail). He wants successful achievement and so he should only ask people to do what is possible for them to do in their situation. He should be able to say with confidence, "This is something you can easily do." The task should also be adapted to the financial and time situation of the family.

Although the goal is to design a task the family can do, getting the task done can be less important than the negotiations around the task. For example, if the therapist says he will not assign a task until all the family is present, he is setting up the task properly but he is also using the task to get the family to organize itself in a new way by the members taking charge of getting everyone to the session. Sometimes the arrangements to do the task, when accomplished, solve an organizational problem without requiring the task. Sometimes, too, a threat of a task will force changes. With the directive approach, the directive becomes something for the family to talk about instead of about their problems or their past. It provides an issue for therapist and family for discussion.

A task can be a simple one if the primary goal at that stage is to intensify the relationship with the therapist. Asking family members to make a list of problems, or to observe certain behavior during the week, or to talk together at a set

---

*The use of paradoxical interventions is complex and an approach in itself, so the subject is merely touched upon here. With Cloé Madanes, I am preparing a book called *Paradox in Therapy*, which will deal with this subject more extensively.

time all will serve the purpose of getting families involved with the therapist.

When the primary goal is to bring about an organizational change, the task to be given requires more thought. The best task is one that uses the presenting problem to make a structural change in the family. For example, if the therapist wants mother and problem child more involved and wants a parental child excluded, and the problem child is a fire setter, the therapist can ask the mother to teach him how to set a safe fire with matches for a certain period each day. If a child is afraid of dogs and the therapist wants to disengage mother and child and have the father intervene, father and child can be asked to select a particular kind of puppy.

With this approach, the focus is on respecting and utilizing what the family considers important, the presenting problem, and what the therapist thinks is important, an organizational change.

The steps in designing a task are to think about the presenting problem in terms of the sequence in the family and to find a directive that changes both. For example, a common problem is a child who declines to go to school. The families differ in many ways from each other, but the most typical sequence is the following.

The child refuses to go to school. The father insists the child go and in the morning pushes the child to go. The child manifests anxiety, illness, vomiting, or runs away. The mother steps in and insists the father is too hard on the child and the father backs off. After a while the parents agree the child must go to school. The father insists the child go, the child manifests involuntary behavior, the mother intervenes, and the father stops insisting.

There are many variations to this sequence. It may be the mother who insists the child go and the father who becomes upset. It may also be that some physical problem overwhelms the mother as child and father get into altercations over the school issue. The explanations for why the child stays at home vary, but they usually include the idea that if the problem is not at school the child is necessary at home for some function in the life of one or both parents.*

When this problem has become clear in the first interview, it is necessary as a first step to be sure that the problem is not a school situation where for good reasons the child should not go.

To get the mother and father to work together it is necessary to motivate them by having them agree that the child must go to school and is falling behind. Drawing them out about a child's future if the child does not attend school is also helpful. Usually parents agree that something must be done, that is why they are there. It is best to review with them all the ways they have tried to get the child to go that have failed. An important part of this motivating stage is to join the parents within their difficult problem. It is very important to avoid interpretations about why they have failed or what might be "really" behind the problem.

At this point it should be made explicit that whether the child goes to school should not be up to the child but up to the parents. The therapist needs to pull the parents together in relation to the child.

The directive designed must take the usual sequence into account. Various directives are possible. The responsibility might be put on the father to take the child to school, or it might be put on the mother. Or the therapist may say that mother must see that the father does it. Or it could be

---

*The description here is necessarily oversimplified. All families are unique and their variation must be taken into account. There is one pattern that requires special consideration when it exists. Most families with a child problem have one parent "overinvolved" with the child in an intense dyad, and the other parent more peripheral. One can use the peripheral parent to disengage the bond between the overinvolved parent and child. However, at times there is a family in which both parents are overinvolved and form an intense dyad with the child. Sometimes they alternate, one being so at one time and the other at another time. When this double bonding exists, as it does with most severely disturbed young people, simple procedures cannot be used. One cannot simply shift and have the more peripheral parent more involved because he or she already is. In a school case like this, when it is a double-bond arrangement, either parent can be firm about the child going to school or soft in the sense of interfering when the other is firm. The pattern goes on, the parents being interchangeable in maintaining it.

appropriate, if logistically possible, that both parents escort the child to class.

In a straightforward task such as this, the crucial issue is anticipating what will happen. The therapist must review with the father how he will take child to school. The parents are then asked to discuss how the child will behave—temper, upset stomach, anxiety, vomiting, or whatever might happen. The mother is asked what she will do when child becomes upset. Her concern that the father and child might kill each other can be examined in terms of its validity. The parents should anticipate that the child might be innovative at the moment when success is about to occur and say something like, "I won't go to this school but I will go to some other." How should the parents respond? Generally it is best to agree that the child could finish the term in this school and then perhaps transfer to another, but they should not let the child deflect them from their task.

The therapist should keep in mind, when discussing this task, that the goal is both to get the child into school *and* resolve the difficulties between the parents to which the child is responding to by not going to school. These difficulties need to be defined in terms of the child's problem. For example, if the parents say they get so upset with each other's way of dealing with the child that they think about separating, the therapist should not discuss separation. He should say that separation is an important issue but whether they separate or not, the child must go to school and they must solve this problem together. Later, when the child is going steadily to school, the parents may bring up separation. At that time it is appropriate to deal with separation since it is a real issue and not merely part of the previous sequence.

The therapist may want the parents to review with the child in the therapy interview what is to happen on the morning designated for going to school. Perhaps the therapist will want them to practice the task. He can have the father insist and the child get upset and mother try to save child. If siblings are involved, they should be given something to do in relation to the task.

When the family reports what happened, the therapist finds that the family has succeeded or not, or it has partially succeeded. Each alternative leads to different results. If the family has succeeded, the therapist should see the family for a period to stabilize them with the child in school and deal with the marital and other issues involved. If the family has partially succeeded by getting the child to school but he left school early, or some unanticipated difficulty arose, the task can be repeated. If the family has not done the task for no excusable reason, the therapist must deal with this seriously, mourning this misfortune, and then offer an alternative. He can begin, for example, the set of procedures around making it more uncomfortable for the child to be at home than at school. For example, the child is to get up at school time, get dressed, and stay in his room reading during the school hours. No television or entertainment, and so on. Often the parents will do this task since they failed at the other. After succeeding at this task they can again push the child toward school.

A way to view the approach is to give directives going directly to the goal, such as getting the child to school. For those families in which a direct approach is not effective, the therapist falls back on an alternative plan that will motivate the family toward the goal. If that alternative is not effective fall back on yet another alternative plan. In all of these cases one is changing the sequence and so is changing the structure between the parents and child as well as drawing a generation line, clarifying paternal functions, and differentiating those functions from husband–wife issues.

When one uses a directive approach it is essential that a clearly defined presenting problem be negotiated. The better tasks use the presenting problem as leverage for inducing change. The more ambiguous the problem, the more unclear the design of a task. Similarly, if the goal is not clear, a task cannot easily be designed. The therapist must specify his destination if he is to introduce a directive to arrive there. As therapists learn to clarify problems and to set goals, designing directives becomes easier.

3

Communication as Bits and Metaphor

The two most important questions in therapy are whether a person has changed after therapy more than he would have without it, and whether one therapy approach is more effective than another. When investigating such questions, clinicians often do not agree on how to describe the therapy situation. At one extreme are the behavior modifiers who wish to use a rigorous description and quantitative measurements. They would like to classify the therapy problem as the presence or absence of acts that can be listed as discrete items. Many other clinicians at the opposite extreme object to this approach and argue that no act is independent of another act because both acts are connected through different meanings. Clinicians at each extreme argue that the other misses the point of the therapy experience. They cannot agree on procedures and results because they have not agreed on the language for describing a therapy problem.

When a therapist listens to a complaint in a first interview, or when he investigates his results after therapy, he must classify in some kind of language what is happening. The ways he describes what he hears and observes will be determined by his point of view and by his training. Some therapists classify what people say as symbolic communication. Others listen to the frequency of some type of behavior. Others will be hearing what happens as a sequence of interpersonal action in an organization. To formulate problems and to answer the question whether therapy has been successful or not, one must clarify the different languages in which the problem situation is being defined.

Suppose that a woman enters therapy reporting that she washes her hands many times a day and would like to recover from this affliction. The behavior modifier might describe such a person by focusing on her behavior and counting the number of ritual washing acts performed per hour. Therapy would be defined as a set of operations to reduce or eliminate the number of inappropriate acts. The premise of this approach is that this person's behavior can be described in terms of "bits" of behavior. A traditional dynamic clinician might describe the same person by saying she is expiating guilt with this compulsive washing. The therapeutic task would be to offer a human encounter that would resolve the person's guilt and change her perception of the world. The ritual washing would not be described as a "bit" that could be counted. It would be a metaphor, an analogy, about her life.

Digital and Analogic Ways of Communicating

The fact that there are two such extreme ways of describing human beings may be based on the fact that the human being is capable of communicating in two different styles, or languages. Sometimes a person communicates in precise and logical ways and sometimes he expresses himself in the language of metaphor. When he is being logical, his behavior can be described in a logical, scientific language just as a scientist might describe plants or mollusks. Yet when a person is not communicating in terms of logical categories, no descriptive system made up of logical categories can encompass what he is doing. The "map" is not appropriate for the territory. Describing him in logical categories would be like counting the words in a poem. Conversely, when a person is communicating in terms of discrete categories, to describe him in terms of metaphors is not appropriate.

One way to characterize the two different modes of human communication is in terms of *digital* and *analogic* communication.* Digital communication consists of that class of messages where each statement has a specific referent and only that referent. Something happens or it does not happen; there is *one* stimulus and *one* response. It is possible to make a computer classification of such communication because each message fits into a specific category. In this mode, behavior appears to be as logical as the object-linguists would like it to be: one can say, "If *A*, and only if *A*, then *Z*, and only *Z*." Each message is about *one* thing and not about something else as well.

It is because human beings can communicate in digital language that they are able to build computers, reshape nature, and function in complex organizations. The use of digital language to describe human behavior appears most appropriate when the subject is the study of a human being dealing with the environment—when a person is building bridges. This language begins to be problematic when it is applied to human beings dealing with one another. To use digital language to describe people talking with one another, we must expect them to communicate in logical, rational ways, speaking words that have specified, previously defined referents. From the digital view, the description of a man pounding a nail and the description of a man fighting with his wife should be synonymous descriptive problems. In both cases it would be a matter of phrasing the description in a precise language of single referents. Yet describing an

*G. Bateson and D.D. Jackson, "Some Varieties of Pathogenic Organization," in D.D. Jackson (Ed.), *Communication, Family and Marriage,* (Palo Alto, Calif.: Science Behavior Books, 1968, pp. 200–215).

interchange between husband and wife in digital language may leave out the essence of the interchange. The fight a married couple may have over who is to pick up whose socks does not necessarily have socks as a referent but rather what the socks have tended to mean in the context of the relationship. If one tried to program the interchange into a computer, each message of the quarrel could not be placed in a single category but would need to be coded for all the multiple referents.

When a message has multiple referents, it is no longer a "bit" but is analogic, in that it deals with the resemblances of one thing to another. It is a language in which each message refers to a context of other messages. There is no single message and single response but multiple stimuli and multiple responses, some of them fictional. Analogic communication includes the "as if" categories; each message frames, or is about, other messages. Included in this style of communication are "play" and "ritual," as well as all forms of art. The analog can be expressed in a verbal statement, as in a simile or verbal metaphor. It can also be expressed in action—the showing of how something is by acting it out. A message in this style cannot be categorized without taking into account the context of other messages in which the message occurs.

If there were a continuum from digital behavior to analogic, the problem could be more easily resolved. But there appears to be a discontinuous change from one style of communication to another. This change forces a dichotomy. To illustrate the problem of discontinuity, we can take as an example a television picture or a halftone newspaper photograph. Both are composed of a series of dots or "bits" of information. Yet the newspaper picture is more than the sum total of the dots that make up the picture. If we build such a picture by adding dots, they continue to be dots until a certain point at which the picture becomes recognizable as a representation of something, such as a scene or a person's face. At the point where the shift takes place from bits to scene, the change from digital to analogic communication is discontinuous. Information theory and the theory of quantification of bits of behavior can easily deal with the dots, but these approaches cannot as easily relate the scene of the picture to the original scene or describe what is being communicated to the reader by the photograph. If the picture has a caption, the problem is the same. It is merely a group of letters, or digital bits, but at the point the bits form a recognizable word, the communication has shifted from digital to metaphoric. The problem is not one of extremes of a continuum but rather a dichotomy between two types of communication. Problems of description arise with these two styles of communication whenever one is talking about human action, and particularly in the field of therapy and its evaluation.

Therapy and the Use of Analogies

One of the more interesting aspects of the attempts to change people is the fact that the use of analogies, or metaphors, seems especially central to the procedures of therapy. Quite different schools of therapy have in common a major concern with the use of analogic communication. It is not simply that the behavior modification approaches concern themselves with "bits" and the dynamic clinicians with analogies. Behaviorists do tend to be digital in their descriptions of problems and when evaluating outcome, but their actual therapy can be described as both digital and analogic.

Psychoanalysis was a procedure that encouraged patients to talk in analogic style. The request for "free association" was a directive to the patient to temporarily abandon the digital style of communication and say whatever came to mind, no matter how irrational it seemed. Speaking in this way, the patient offered a series of analogies about his life. The analyst also requested dreams, and when the patient was reporting a dream the style was again analogic. The analyst's task was to apply analogies of his own by interpretations and to explore the connections between the various metaphors that the patient was communicating. The dream metaphor was exposed to free association, which led to a description of an event that was in turn discovered to be a metaphor about other aspects of the patient's life.

Rather than have the patient offer the analogies, some behavior therapists offer analogies when attempting to change the same type of patients. The patient is asked for a list of "anxiety" situations and he ranks them in order from those that make him least anxious to those that make him most anxious. Then he is asked to relax while the therapist offers a series of analogies about those situations. For example, if the person is afraid of blood, the therapist first describes a scene where there is a little blood and increasingly emphasizes wounds and bleeding as the scenes progress. The patient responds only by a digital indication whether he is "anxious" or not as he listens to the metaphor. He does not offer analogies himself, except in describing his problems and in casual discourse with the therapist, but he has veto power over the analogies offered to him by the therapist. When the patient indicates he is "anxious," either by a word or by a movement, the therapist stops offering analogies or shifts to a milder kind.*

In an opposite approach, rather than avoid making the patient anxious by carefully paced metaphors, as in behavior therapy, Thomas Stampfl developed implosive therapy, a procedure of helping people become less fearful by asking them to be fearful.† He forces the patient to be "anxious" by building extreme metaphors. For example, if the patient says he is afraid of bugs, the therapist will tell him that he is surrounded by bugs, the bugs are getting bigger and approaching him, they are overwhelming him, and so on. In this kind of therapy the patient has no veto power, since becoming anxious only increases the extreme nature of the metaphor offered. He can only "recover" by not being anx-

*J. Wolpe, *Psychotherapy by Reciprocal Inhibition* (Stanford, Calif.: Stanford University Press, 1958).

†P. London, *The Modes and Morals of Psychotherapy* (New York: Grune & Stratton, 1964).

ious, often by laughing as his fears are reduced to absurdity in the analogies offered by the therapist. Paradoxical intention therapy follows a similar procedure.*

Verbal conditioning therapy operates in a way opposite from Wolpe's behavior therapy and from Stampfl's procedures even though all of the approaches are derived from conditioning theories. Instead of the therapist offering analogies while the patient responds with digital signs, the patient describes his life in analogic style and the therapist offers digital responses. From the therapist's view he is "reinforcing" certain parts of the patient's communication, with these reinforcements being nods of the head or encouraging words. For example, if the patient says something like "My life is a drag," the therapist does not respond, but when the patient says, "My life sometimes looks bright," the therapist smiles or nods his head to encourage further metaphors of this kind.

A neglected aspect of research on therapy is the fact that it is not uncommon for a therapist to offer analogies about life, often in the form of examples of his own experience or reports about patient's experiences. This use of analogy is not usually considered a focus of the therapy, but is done in passing, during informal interchanges with the patient. A surprising number of therapists tell their patients jokes. Some employ a systematic use of anecdotes with patients. Milton Erickson has developed this procedure more fully than most people. He tells the patient a story that is formally parallel to the patient's problem and he views therapeutic change as related to the shift in the patient's analogies provoked by the analogies he is receiving.†

---

*Frankl, Viktor E., "Paradoxical Intention and Dereflection," Psychotherapy 12 (1975): 226–237.

†J. Haley (Ed.), *Advanced Techniques of Hypnosis and Therapy: Selected Papers of Milton H. Erickson* (New York: Grune & Stratton, 1967, pp. 229–312). See also J. Haley, *Uncommon Therapy: The Psychiatric Techniques of Milton H. Erickson, M.D.* (New York: Norton, 1973).

Analogies in Family Interviewing

The procedure of interviewing whole families has made evident a level of analogy that is also implicit in all forms of treatment. Family therapy consists of many approaches by different schools, but usually the whole family is seen together and typically the therapists ask the family to offer verbal analogies about their problems. Simultaneously, as the family members deal with each other in the interview, they are performing an analogic portrait of their life together.

The verbal descriptions by the family are examples of what is happening that is analogic to other things happening, and the therapist responds with metaphors about the family or about other families. However, in addition to the verbal exchange, many family therapists actively request changes in behavior of the family members either in the room or outside of it. It becomes more evident when one observes this style of therapy that in all therapy the relationship of patient and therapist is analogic to whatever is being communicated in the therapeutic sessions. For example, the therapist may note that a father only talks to his son through the mother. The therapist's intervention may be to ask the mother to sit over to one side while father and son move their chairs so that they face each other and have a talk. Sometimes this request is phrased as being necessary "to see how father and son talk to each other." This interchange between father and son is then a metaphor about their relationship with each other, but when the therapist makes this arrangement he is also acting out an analogy about many aspects of the family, including how the mother should remain out of the interchange. Whether interviewing one person or several, each act by a therapist is also an analogy about how to behave. This relationship analogy or metaphor is *meta*, or "about," the content of the discussion. If therapy were merely a matter of offering digital bits of information to patients to give them understanding, the relationship would not be particularly relevant. However, the change in the behavior of the patient occurs as an aspect of the analogic changes in the relationship with the therapist.

When we recognize the multiple levels of analogic communication that occur in therapy, we can face the complexities in the process of inducing therapeutic change. Each statement by a patient is multiply coded. It refers at least to his previous statements, to his context of interpersonal relationships, and to his current relationship with the therapist. That is, his statement "fits" a complex set of situations by resonating analogically to these multiple facets of his context. The patient appears peculiar, that is, neurotic or psychotic, when his statements are of a deviant kind because they must "fit" a deviant context. For example, if a psychotic patient says to a therapist "My stomach is full of cement," with no cue that indicates he is speaking in metaphor, the statement is an analogic expression of a complex context. He is metaphorically speaking about the hospital food and expressing an analogic statement about his relationships in the hospital. By providing no cues as to how his statement is to be received, he is indicating his distrust of the therapist. Simultaneously, the statement is also a metaphoric response to a previous comment by the therapist. When the patient is "cured," he might communicate in a more normal way by saying something like, "The food in this place is terrible, and the way I'm treated makes me sick to my stomach anyhow." Then he would be properly labeling his metaphor. He still would be speaking analogically but would be using a more "normal" analogy. Change in the patient would be shown by the patient's shift in the style in which he indicates the kind of situation he is in with the person to whom he is talking.

When we examine the question of how a therapist induces a patient to change his communicative style, it would seem evident that insofar as the patient's communication is adaptive to his context, then that context must be changed for his communication to change. The life situation of the patient, and his relationship with the therapist, must shift if the way he communicates to the therapist is going to shift. The patient's style cannot be changed by "working on his communication," but only by making organizational changes in the situation to which he is adapting.

A Problem as a Metaphor

Let us take an example to illustrate the use of analogy in therapy. A man enters therapy because, he says, he is afraid he is going to die of a heart attack. He has been assured by a number of doctors that his heart is functioning well, but he still fears that his heart will stop at any moment and he will die. The therapist is faced with the task of changing this patient's style of communication.

If the physician takes the patient's analogy as a digital statement about his heart, he is likely to reply with a digital answer: "Your heart is all right." The patient then proceeds to the next doctor even if the physician supports his reassurance with impressive scientific instruments for examining the heart.

Some therapists will receive the patient's communication about his heart as an analogy—a statement that means something about something else. They will ask a series of questions to gather information about aspects of the patient's life that are analogic to his statement about his heart. These questions typically are "Can you tell me more about that?" (to increase the flow of analogies); "How do you feel about that?" (to encourage more specifically analogic material); and "Do you have similar fears about other things?" (to bring out related analogies).

The kind of analogies that interest the therapist will depend on his particular theory about the "cause" of the patient's presentations. The psychodynamic therapist as well as the behavior therapist is interested in metaphors about the past because of an assumption that past traumas lead to present difficulties. For example, should the patient say, "My fear came on about the time my brother died of a heart attack seven years ago," both kinds of therapists show active interest even though their therapeutic procedures will be different. The psychodynamic therapist will begin to make "interpretations" to help the patient connect the analogies about his own fear of death and his feelings about his brother. The behavior therapist will have found an area of anxiety, the trauma of death, to be deconditioned. He might deal with the present rather than the past in his therapy, but his causal explanation will be oriented toward the past.

A family-oriented directive therapist will have quite a different view: he will assume that the patient's statement about his heart is analogic to his current situation. He will inquire how the client relates to his wife, about his job, about his children, and so on. The therapist will also want the wife present in a session so that he can examine how they deal with one another and how the complaints about the heart are used in the ongoing interchange between husband and wife. When he interviews husband and wife together, the therapist will take an interest in the wife's response when the husband is feeling better and when he is feeling worse. For example, he might note that she communicates depression when the husband is emphasizing the better aspects of his life and health and that she appears more involved and animated when he discusses his heart problem. The family-oriented therapist will construct a theory that the husband's communication about his heart is a way of stabilizing the marriage. The kinds of data he will seek are those that reveal how the heart analogy is built into the person's ecology, or interpersonal network.

For example, the family and work life of a person with this kind of presenting symptom is organized around this analogy. The children must be quiet or it will upset father, who fears for his heart; trips and recreation are determined by the state of father and his heart; the kind of job he has and his task performance on the job are regulated by his heart. Often the problem is both the focus of fighting and the way of avoiding conflict in the marriage. For example, sexual relations must occur only under circumstances determined by the man who is concerned about overtaxing his heart. Conflicts about sex between the couple can be avoided when the heart is such a convenient issue. One also finds, in such cases, that husband and wife fight in the morning because he says he cannot go to work because he might die if he exerts himself, while his wife insists he must go or he will lose his job. Often one finds that the days the husband stays home because of his heart are those days he is most worried about his wife's state of mind and is afraid to leave her alone.

What Causes Change?

When we turn to how to bring about change in a person who communicates this kind of analogy, we must make a distinction between how different therapists understand such a problem and what they do about it. All therapists, whatever their schools, are attempting to change a metaphor in such a case—they wish to change the patient's communication that he expects to die of heart failure at any moment. Many therapists would not see it as a problem of changing the patient's communication. They would postulate something inside him that has to be changed such as a conflict, a fear, an idea, or an incubus. However, the definition of successful change would be that the person no longer communicates a statement about dying of heart failure.

By the nature of their approach, most therapists would not reassure the man that his heart is all right, as many physicians, wife, and friends have done. However, implicit in all of their communication to him is the message "There is nothing wrong with your heart and your statement is an analogy about something else." By not responding to him as a "real" heart problem, their metacommunicative behavior indicates to the patient that his heart is all right. It is important to emphasize that this framework exists, in order to make it clear that even if a therapist should take literally the metaphor about dying of a heart attack, he does so within a framework that indicates there is nothing wrong with the person's heart.

There are two approaches that appear to succeed with this problem more often than they fail. The first approach defines the problem as a one-person situation and the subsequent therapy attempts a shift in perception. The second approach assumes it is a multiperson problem and the therapy is family oriented.

The first approach is a paradoxical intervention that includes taking literally the person's metaphor about dying of a heart attack. Typical exponents of this way of working are Victor Frankl and Stampfl. The procedure is to advise the person that he is not only going to die of a heart attack but he should drop dead right now. If this procedure is used improperly, it merely dissuades the person from returning for another session of such treatment. If it is used properly, it brings about a transformation that includes abandoning the communication that he is going to die of heart failure. The proper approach includes, first, establishing a trusting relationship with the person. This step involves defining the relationship as one in which the therapist is being helpful and is on the side of the client. It must also include the communication that there is nothing wrong with the person's heart. In the second step the person is encouraged to fall dead of a heart attack at that moment. This approach takes the person's metaphor about his heart absolutely literally: since he has a heart that will fail, it should fail now. The person's communication is not received as an analogy about something else, but as a digital statement about his heart.

Both aspects of this procedure must be included: the framework of helping the person over the problem with an indication his heart is all right, and the statement that his heart is failing and he should drop dead right now. When the therapist is successful, the patient abandons his analogy about his heart, often laughing at some point in the procedure. The procedure is repeated at every instance of the expression of a fear about the heart.

Although this approach can be successful, it does not take into account the consequences within the person's family of the change when the heart analogy is abandoned.

Predictably the wife and other members of the family will become at least temporarily upset. Marital uproar may occur and may lead to a separation. One cannot change this kind of communication without changing, often unpredictably, the organization in which the person lives.

A Family Approach

A procedure that is similar in that it also takes literally the metaphor about the heart but that also takes the family into account has been developed by Milton Erickson. Rather than himself take the metaphor about the heart literally, Erickson arranges that the wife do so. In such a situation the wife usually believes the doctors who say that her husband's heart is normal, but she also responds to her husband's behavior by fearful concern that he might indeed have something wrong with his heart. Essentially, she oscillates between condemning her husband at one moment for his illusion and sympathizing with him at the next moment for his heart condition. This kind of oscillation is typical of the intimates of people who show various kinds of severe psychiatric symptoms.

Erickson establishes a trusting relationship with both husband and wife, which is essential in this approach. This approach includes assisting the wife with her problems that are avoided by the communication about the heart. When this relationship is set, and the wife is ready to have her husband give up this metaphor, Erickson arranges that the wife encourage the husband to die of his heart attack. He may have her do so in various verbal and nonverbal ways, including having her respond to each complaint as if it is a real heart attack, calling for an ambulance or other proper medical assistance. An even more effective procedure he has used is to have the wife visit various funeral parlors and collect their literature on funerals. Each time the husband expresses his fear of dying of a heart attack, the wife quietly distributes the funeral literature throughout the house. This procedure rapidly resolves the problem.

To say that the problem is "resolved" with such an approach is to say that the metaphor has been blocked and the couple is forced to develop other ways of communicating with one another. In all those areas of encounter between husband and wife where the heart metaphor was previously used, other styles of behavior must now develop. The system has been forced into instability. One might think the husband would substitute another incapacitating metaphor, such as a fear of cancer. However, this substitution does not occur in actual practice. The alliance of wife and therapist forcing the change in the heart metaphor also seems to force a change in that *class* of metaphors. Typically, the husband becomes angry and speaks more straightforwardly about various situations with his wife where the metaphor was previously used, such as sex life, recreation, and so on. The wife in turn expresses herself with another metaphor besides depressive behavior, and in the process the two of them work out changes in their behavior with each other and more "normal" marital communication.

This example is similar to other kinds of metaphors that are expressed with bodily sensations and in which the bodily sensations change when a different kind of communication becomes necessary. For example, the wife with a "real" pain in the neck that has no organic cause can be described as a woman expressing analogically her opinion of her intimates. Similarly, the pain in the head, the pain in the stomach, the nausea, and so on, can be understood as metaphors about family life and so treated. Some people seem to be able to say, "You give me a headache," and not have the headache. Others must actually develop a headache, using themselves as an analogic tool to express a statement about their system. Often patients who use the headache metaphor can be taught in therapy to say verbally they have a headache when they have not, so that the verbal statement continues to serve the purpose of the metaphor without the pain. Usually this approach leads to the patient's abandoning both the somatic and verbal metaphor.

Whatever therapeutic approach the clinician uses, he is distinguished from other students of human behavior by his particular interest in analogic communication. When social scientists insist he is "soft" in his approach and should deal with facts, the clinician says they misunderstand and are overlooking the importance of metaphoric communication.

Assessment of Therapy

When we turn to the question of change in therapy and how change can be described and evaluated, one problem seems immediately apparent. Most evaluations of therapy have attempted to evaluate change by focusing on digital communication. Evaluating a change in a metaphor is a problem with an undeveloped methodology.

Most evaluations of therapy in recent years have attempted to be scientific by gathering factual information before and after therapy with similar information gathered from some contrast group such as prospective patients on a waiting list. The methodology used relies largely on the self-report of the people involved. Two factors are usually emphasized: Is the problem the patient originally presented still there or has it been relieved? Has the patient sought assistance from other people after the termination of therapy? The investigator gathers this information by self-report from the patient, the therapist, and perhaps family members, and looks for responses that can be coded as "bits" for quantifiable measurement. The responses must be in a "yes or no" form, or in the form of a scale involving "no change, some change, great change," and so on. For example, if the patient presents the problem of a fear of dying of a heart attack, some classification of severity is made at the beginning of therapy. At the end he is asked whether he still has the fear or not, and if so, he is asked to classify its severity. Whether a phobia, a depression, or whatever, the attempt is to make the problem a "thing" that is either present, not present, or partially present.

Serious questions can be raised about self-report. Clients who have invested a great deal of money in therapy, or who like or dislike their therapists, will report "facts" biased by that context. Similarly, therapists are hardly objective observers of a task in which they have a large personal investment. The supposedly disinterested investigator also has his interests and works within a context that influences what happens. For example, a patient may exaggerate the problem to an investigator at the beginning of therapy even though the investigator will not be treating him, because the patient may believe that whether or not he is treated depends on the investigator's opinion. However, the problem is not merely one of bias and unreliability. It is also the fact that self-report is metaphoric as well as digital. Insofar as what the patient or therapist says is "biased" by the experience and context of the treatment, each is communicating analogically about that context even if he ostensibly responds in digital form. Communication is a metaphor from the person to the investigator, which not only has as its referent the problem, and whether the problem exists or not, but also carries an analogic statement about the relationship with the therapist, with family members, and with the investigator. The problem thus becomes one of evaluating a metaphor that is cast in digital terms.

It is also possible to approach the problem of evaluation as one that necessarily involves changes in the patient's analogic style of communication. When symptoms are seen as metaphors, the question is whether the metaphor has changed. One might use projective tests before and after therapy to determine changes in metaphors, but the reliability of these tests is most doubtful. A clinician would not stake his reputation on the outcome of a projective test, partly because the test must be interpreted subjectively and partly because the influence of the tester enters into performance. A more self-evident reason is that the projective test produces metaphors that are a communication to the tester—and the patient does not live with the tester but with his intimates. For example, a person is likely to give a different response to an ink blot if he is talking to a tester than if his mother is administering the test. The relationship is different and so the style of communication is different. What is relevant to change is whether the patient has changed his style with those people with whom he lives (unless the particular symptom involves a problem of relating to strangers).

The importance of doing even digital evaluation of change in therapy is granted. But when there is such a focus by clinicians on analogic communication, it seems evident that evaluation must deal with analogy. Such an evaluation necessarily should include observation and measurement of the way the "patient" communicates with other people, including his wife, children, employer, and therapist. Since analogic communication has multiple functions in an interpersonal network, the network must be examined for change. Self-report about this kind of communication is not adequate. There must be actual observation of the behavior of the patient with his intimates. For example, after therapy does the man still take his pulse when his wife looks at him amorously? Does he fight with his wife about other matters than his heart? The difficulties of research in this area are being explored with studies of films and with family testing, but the development of rigorous measurement has hardly begun. Without this exploration of change in analogic communication, most clinicians would feel that evaluation of therapy is incomplete and misses the point. (However, the difficulty in evaluation does not mean that therapists should be excused when they avoid evaluating the outcome of their therapy. The difficulties are a matter of degree. Certainly a therapist can keep track of his successes in helping clients get over their presenting problems while still accepting the more complex aspects of change.)

From the viewpoint offered here, therapy is an intervention by an outsider into a tightly structured communication system in which symptoms are a style of behavior adaptive to the ongoing behavior of other people in the system. Whether the problem is defined as a phobia, a depression, a character disorder, acting out, or whatever, the communication is functional within the system. The act of intervening, whether it is called *individual therapy* or whether the therapist brings together the intimates of a patient in an interview and so calls it *family therapy,* is an intervention into a family system. The therapeutic process may consist of easing the persons out of the metaphors they are using into more appropriate ones, or the metaphors can be blocked so that others must be developed. When therapy is done effectively, the total system in which a person lives undergoes change so that more normal communication is possible from everyone involved. Determining whether the change has happened is a more complex problem than the preliminary therapy evaluation studies would indicate.

To summarize, it is possible to describe symptoms as communicative acts that have a function within an interpersonal network. The symptom is not a "bit" of information but is an analogy that has as its referents multiple aspects of the person's situation, including his relationship with the therapist. From this view, the goal of therapy is to change the communicative behavior of the person—to change his metaphor. Insofar as his behavior is a response to his situation with his intimates, that situation must change if his communication is to change. Various forms of therapy can be described as ways of responding to the analogies of the patient in such a way that the analogies change. Evaluation of outcome should include not only the presence or absence of a "bit" of behavior by the patient but also an evaluation of the changes in the system to which the patient is adapting by his special form of communication.

4

Communication: Sequence and Hierarchy

Research investigators require complex theories; clinicians need simple ones. The researcher must account for and reflect on innumerable variables. The clinician must choose key variables and act. The situation is incredibly complex when several people deal with each other in organized ways. The researcher who examines slow-motion films to study body movement, linguistics for vocal intonations, and semantics for the meaning of the verbal content finds himself in a world with an almost infinite number of variables. Fortunately, clinicians are more free to simplify; the problem is to choose the important variables most relevant to change.

Power and Organization

When one is observing people who have a history and a future together, one sees that they follow organized ways of behaving with one another. If there is any generalization that applies to men and other animals, it is that all creatures capable of learning are compelled to organize. To be organized means to follow patterned, redundant ways of behaving and to exist in a hierarchy. Creatures that organize together form a status, or power, ladder in which each creature has a place in the hierarchy with someone above him and someone below him. Although groups will have more than one hierarchy because of different functions, the existence of hierarchy is inevitable because it is in the nature of organization that it be hierarchical. We may dream of a society in which all creatures are equal, but on this earth there is status and precedence and inequality among all creatures. In many societies, one does not even speak the same dialect to a superior as to an inferior, and everywhere the messages that creatures interchange in their repeating ways are messages that define positions in organizational hierarchies. If a group attempts to organize on the basis of equal status among the members, some members become more equal than others as organization develops.*

Before proceeding further with a discussion of hierarchy, it might be best to clear up a possible misunderstanding that can occur when power and hierarchy are discussed. Although one must accept the *existence* of hierarchy, that does not mean one needs to accept a *particular* structure or a particular family hierarchy. One need not accept the status quo either in terms of the economic structure of society or the issue of a particular unfortunate hierarchy. Everywhere

---

*A possible objection to the concept of hierarchy is that there are alternative ways to describe an organization. The "pecking order" we observe may be a product of our thinking and not of the nature of organization. For example, when horses enter a barn we note that they assume a certain order and maintain it each time they enter the barn. We may not describe this pattern in terms of one creature being superior and one secondary. What we observe is a pattern in which the animals behave in a sequential order. The description scheme we choose will depend on our purpose in making the description. If our focus is on how to change a malfunctioning organization, then a description should clarify how organizations malfunction and offer ideas about how to produce change. The concept of hierarchy, or levels of status and power, seems most appropriate as a description for therapeutic purposes.

there are hierarchial arrangements that are unjust. One economic class suppresses another. Women are kept in a subordinate position in both family and work groups merely because they are female. People are placed in subordinate positions because of race or religion. Children are oppressed by their parents, in the sense of being restricted and exploited in extreme ways. Obviously, there are many wrongs that need righting that involve hierarchial issues, and any therapist must think through his ethical position.

It is crucial that a therapist not confuse the existence of an unjust hierarchy with a strategy for changing it. If one sees a child being oppressed in a family, that does not necessarily mean one should join that child against the parents to "save" him. The result could be an unhappier child as well as unhappier and more restrictive parents. By attacking the parents directly the therapist may feel morally justified, but the goal of therapy is not the moral justification of the therapist and it is usually the child who pays for such an attack. To attack parents merely because they are the authorities and part of the establishment is naive and can easily lead to the failure of therapy.

Not only do all animals form hierarchical organizations, but it is important to note also that the hierarchy is maintained by *all* the participants. Those of higher status enforce their status by their actions, but those of lower status will act to enforce hierarchy if a higher-status creature does not enforce his status. When animals or humans step out of order, the reestablishment of hierarchy is a group effort with those below as active as those above. (The cooperative behavior of those below has often aroused the despair of revolutionists.)

When we look at the family in terms of hierarchy, the organization includes people of different generations, of different incomes, and of different degrees of intelligence and skills. These complex hierarchical lines are related to the many different functions of a family. The most elementary hierarchy involves the generation line. Within the family there are intricate involvements of uncles, aunts, cousins, and others in the kinship system. But at the most simple level it is parents who nurture and discipline children, who in turn nurture and discipline children as the generations proceed over time. At any one moment there are, at most, four generations operating. Most commonly there are three: grandparents, parents, and children. These three generations can be simplified into three levels of power, or status. In the traditional family, as still is evident in Asia, the greatest status and power resided with the grandparents; the parents were secondary and the children lowest in status. In the western world, particularly in this time of rapid social change, the status and power position of the grandparents is less. In the nuclear family living arrangement, the power often resides with the parents, and the grandparents are moved to an advisory, if not superfluous, position. Professional experts tend to replace the grandparents as authorities.

Yet whatever the arrangement, every family must deal with the issue of organizing in a hierarchy and rules must be worked out about who is primary in status and power and who is secondary. When an individual shows symptoms, the organization has a hierarchical arrangement that is confused. It may be confused by being ambiguous so that no one quite knows who is his peer and who is his superior. It may also be confused because a member at one level of the hierarchy consistently forms a coalition against a peer with a member at another level, thus violating the basic rules of organization.

When the status positions in a hierarchy are confused, or unclear, there will be a struggle that an observer would characterize as a power struggle. If the observer has a theory of innate aggression or of a need for power, he may say the participants are satisfying an inner drive by struggling for power. Yet it would seem more useful to characterize such a struggle as an effort to clarify, or work out, the positions in the hierarchy of an organization. When a child has temper tantrums and refuses to do what his mother says, this situation can be described as an unclear hierarchy. In such a case the mother is often indicating that she is in charge while simultaneously treating her child as a peer and so the hierarchy is confused.

If there is a fundamental rule of social organization, it is that an organization is in trouble when coalitions occur across levels of a hierarchy, particularly when these coalitions are secret. When an employer plays favorites among his employees, he is forming coalitions across power lines and joining one employee against another. Similarly, if an employee goes over the head of his immediate superior to a higher authority and joins him against the superior, there is difficulty. If a manager sides with an employee against a foreman in the middle, trouble will occur. When such a coalition happens occasionally it is a minor matter. But when sequences of this kind become organized so that they repeat and repeat, the organization is in trouble and the participants will experience subjective distress.

Since therapy includes the art of keeping the kind of relationship ambiguous, it is not surprising that power struggles often appear in a therapy context. For example, when a therapist defines himself as an expert by taking money for his assistance and then declines to be an expert and even asks the patient what he feels should be done, the hierarchy is confused. An effort will be made by the patient to clarify the relationship. An observer might call the resulting action a "working through" of resistance, but it can also be seen as an organizational problem. To say that a therapist and patient struggle for control in therapy does not imply that they have a "need" for control but that the relationship is ambiguous because of the nature of the therapeutic process.

Sequences

One of the ways we can map out a hierarchy is by observing the sequences that occur in an organization. If we see that Mr. Smith tells Mr. Jones to do something and Mr. Jones does it, that may be an isolated act. If the act occurs again and again, we deduce that Mr. Smith is higher in the hierarchy than Mr. Jones. A structure is composed of repeating acts among people. What has revolutionized the field of therapy is the realization that a goal of therapy is to change the sequences that occur among people in an organized group. When that sequence changes, the individuals in the group undergo change.

A therapeutic change can be defined as a change in the repeating acts of a self-regulating system—preferably a change into a system of greater diversity. It is the rigid, repetitive sequence of a narrow range that defines pathology.

People seem to have a difficulty, in fact a reluctance, to observe and describe repeating patterns in a chain of three or more events. This difficulty is particularly great if we ourselves are involved in those events. For example, a therapist may notice that a wife repeatedly provokes him. Perhaps he will even recognize a sequence of two actions by noticing that she provokes him after he has criticized her husband. Yet, it seems more difficult to notice that the child was rude, the father disciplined the child, the therapist reacted against the father, and then the therapist was provoked by the wife. Our cognitive attention spans seem to have difficulty with such sequences. In fact, it is possible, as Braulio Montalvo has suggested, that we have built into ourselves necessary amnesias for overlooking parts of sequences. It is when we record interaction on videotape that we observe sequences for the first time and think about them in new ways.*

Let me give an example of a way to think about sequences as they have been thought about within the developing child guidance movement. There were progressive stages: first it was assumed that the problem was a child who had something wrong with him. It was hypothesized

---

*This idea about the function of amnesia was first suggested to me in a personal communication and is expressed in a videofilm of a therapy session edited by Montalvo: "Constructing a Workable Reality."

that he was responding to past experiences that had been interiorized.

Later, the mother was emphasized and it was said the child had a problem of the relationship with his mother. For example, it was said she was helpless and incompetent and the child was adapting to that behavior. To explain why the mother was that way, it was hypothesized that she was responding to past experiences and partially to the child.

Later yet, the father was discovered. It was suggested that the mother's behavior was explained by her relationship to the father. For example, if the mother behaved competently with the child, the father withdrew from the family; but if she was helpless and incompetent, he was involved. It was also hypothesized that her ineffectiveness with the child was a way of supporting the father when he was under stress and depressed. If the mother was helpless, the father would pull himself together to help her deal with the child.

Finally, it began to be recognized that a system was involved with all participants behaving in a way to keep the sequence going. The father's state of mind was a product of his relationship with mother and child, who were also as they were because of sequences established with him and with each other.

To clarify a sequence further, a simple description can be made of a repeating cycle. The sequence can be absurdly simplified to three people each capable of two "states." There is father, mother, and child and each of them can be either competent or incompetent (the child can be said to behave or misbehave). Since the sequence repeats in a circle, there is a series of steps each leading to the next and so back to the beginning again. One can start such a description at any point in the circle.

Step 1. *Father—Incompetent.* The father behaves in an upset or depressed way, not functioning to his capacity.

Step 2. *Child—Misbehaving.* The child begins to get out of control or express symptoms.

Step 3. *Mother—Incompetent.* The mother ineffectually tries to deal with the child and cannot, and the father becomes involved.

Step 4. *Father—Competent*. The father deals with the child effectively and recovers from his state of incompetency.

Step 5. *Child—Behaving*. The child regains his composure and behaves properly or is defined as normal.

Step 6. *Mother—Competent*. The mother becomes more capable and deals with child and father in a more competent way, expecting more from them.

Step 1. *Father—Incompetent*. The father behaves in an upset or depressed way, not functioning to his capacity, and the cycle begins again.

The therapeutic task is to change the sequence by intervening in such a way that it cannot continue. Making family members "aware" of the sequence by pointing it out to them does not change it and can raise resistance, causing failure. It would also appear that changing any *one* of the steps, or the behavior of any one of the three people, is usually not sufficient to bring about change in the sequence. At least two behaviors must be changed. It is also assumed that as change occurs with the child, there will often, but not always, be conflict between the parents as one of the stages of therapy.

A way to think about a sequence of this kind is to see it as an example of a malfunctioning hierarchy. Mother and father are not relating as peers with each other in an executive capacity. Their difficulties with each other, including the ways they protect each other, prevent them from defining a clear hierarchy within the family. As a therapist encourages them to deal jointly with the child, the issues between them that prevent their joint action become more evident. It also seems clear that if the therapist joins the child against them by attempting to rescue the child from them, he is not changing the sequence and is confusing the hierarchy even more.

A Note on Normality. These descriptions of human interaction are offered as a way of thinking for purposes of therapy. They are not offered as a model for what normal families *should* be like. When a clinician examines the context of a symptom, he may find a confusion of hierarchical levels in a family. Such a finding does not mean that to raise normal children one should not have a confusion of hierarchical levels in a family. It might or might not be so. Where there is a problem child, one can describe a certain organization in the family, but it is an error to deduce from that description how to raise normal children. I have observed over 200 normal, or average, families in research settings, and the patterns are so diverse that to talk about a "normal" family seems naive. How to raise children properly, as a normal family should, remains a mystery that awaits observational longitudinal studies with large samples. How to think about the organization of a family when planning therapy is a different issue. As an analogy, if a child breaks a leg, one can set it straight and put it in a plaster cast. But one should not conclude from such therapy that the way to bring about the normal development of children's legs is to place them in plaster casts. A clinical description that is used to plan for a change and a research description of ordinary situations are not synonymous.

Malfunctioning and the Family. A therapist should be able to think in terms of three steps in a sequence, at least, and three levels of a hierarchy. Once he puts together sequence and hierarchy, he is in a position to devise strategies for bringing about change in a rational rather than merely in an intuitive way. His simplest goal is to change a sequence by preventing coalitions across generation lines. When he changes a sequence of father consistently joining child against mother, the family will begin to function differently and the individuals in the family will give up their subjective distress. The goal can be presented in this simple way, but achieving that goal requires ingenuity and skill.

Although three levels of a hierarchy do not seem many when describing the complexity of human life, even that number creates sufficient permutations to be awesome. For example, if one thinks in terms of a triangular unit—such as mother and father and child, or mother-in-law and husband and wife—one can calculate how many triangles there are in the average family if we think in terms of three levels of a hierarchy. In a family with two parents, two children, and four grandparents there are only eight people, but in terms of triangular units there are 56 triangles (and this count does not include uncles, aunts, neighbors, employers or therapists). Each person in the family is involved in 21 family triangles, and every one of the 21 triangles of parents and children carries the possibility of a coalition across generation lines and so the possibility of a malfunctioning structure.

Summarizing the hierarchical idea offered here, there are certain characteristics of a malfunctioning organization if one thinks in terms of three levels and a triangular unit.

First, the three people responding to each other are not peers but of different generations. By *generation* is meant a different order in the power hierarchy, such as parent and child or manager and employee.

Second, the member of one generation forms a coalition across generations. In a two-generation conflict one person joins another against the other's peer. In a three-generation conflict, the person at the top forms a coalition with the person on the bottom against the person in the middle. The term *coalition* means a process of joint action *against* a third person (in contrast to an "alliance" where two people might share a common interest not shared by the third person).

Third, the problem is most severe when the coalition across generations is denied or concealed.

In this scheme it should be emphasized that an organization is not malfunctioning because of cross-generation coalitions but because such coalitions are repeated again and again as part of the system. A woman must save her child from her husband at times, but when this act becomes a way of life the family organization is in trouble.

Three-Generation Conflicts

The therapist should keep in mind that the "map" in his head will never be identical with the "territory" that he is offered when a case walks in the door. The clients just will not present their problems in the properly contextual way. For example, a woman might come in complaining about her daughter being irresponsible, and she will add that her daughter drinks and leaves the child alone at night. Or a mother might bring in a twelve-year-old child complaining that he steals from her, which upsets her and his grandmother who lives around the corner. A noncontextual therapist might see the child as sullen and deprived with a poor self-image and who feels unloved. When a therapist watches his colleagues at work or lives in an inpatient institution, he will observe at times that a patient becomes obstreperous and "acts out." The staff may decide that the patient is "acting out" an internal conflict and may put him in a group to express himself. They may also discuss him as spoiled, rebellious, regressed, and so on.

A therapist must examine such presenting problems in terms of the hierarchy and the sequence that is being followed that requires people to behave as they are doing. All these examples of presenting problems can be seen in the following sequences.

One of the most common problem sequences met by a therapist is the one involving three generations. The classic situation is made up of grandmother, mother, and problem child. That is the typical one-parent family situation among the poor and among the middle class when a mother has divorced and returned to her mother. In the classic example, the grandmother tends to be defined as dominating, the mother as irresponsible, and the child as a behavior problem.* The typical sequence is as follows:

1. Grandmother takes care of grandchild while protesting that mother is irresponsible and does not take care of the child properly. In this way grandmother is siding with

---

*"In this type of family the grandmother is allocated executive power, while the mother and grandchildren function as one vaguely differentiated subgroup." See S. Minuchin and others, *Families of the Slums* (New York: Basic Books, 1967), p. 364. The authors also point out that in some cases a grandmother and mother may struggle in such a way that the child is simply neglected.

the child against the mother in a coalition across generation lines.

2. Mother withdraws, letting grandmother care for the child.

3. The child misbehaves or expresses symptomatic behavior.

4. Grandmother protests that she should not have to take care of the child and discipline him. She has raised her children and mother should take care of her own child.

5. Mother begins to take care of her own child.

6. Grandmother protests that mother does not know how to take care of the child properly and is being irresponsible. She takes over the care of the grandchild to save the child from mother.

7. Mother withdraws, letting grandmother care for the child.

8. The child misbehaves or expresses symptomatic behavior.

At a certain point, grandmother protests that mother should take care of her own child, and the cycle continues, for ever and ever. Included in the cycle, of course, is sufficient misbehavior or distress by the child to provoke the adults to continue the cycle.

When one thinks of generation lines as hierarchical lines of power, it is evident that the classic three-generation conflict can take place with an expert substituting for the grandmother. In long-term child-oriented therapy, the sequence is as follows:

1. The therapist deals with disturbed child, implying that mother has not raised the child properly and so the expert must take over and free the child from internal conflicts. Insofar as the therapist is an expert, he is higher in the hierarchy than mother, and by attempting to save the child from mother he is forming a coalition with child against mother across generation lines.

2. Mother withdraws, letting the expert take responsibility for the problems of her child, feeling that she has been a failure or this intervention would not be necessary.

3. The therapist runs into difficulty with the child, and he also realizes he cannot adopt the child and so protests that the mother should do more for the child and care for him properly.

4. Mother begins to involve herself more with her child.

5. The therapist protests that the mother is not dealing with the child correctly. Taking over more, the therapist insists the child must be saved from mother.

6. Mother withdraws, letting the therapist take care of the problems of her child.*

This sequence continues until the child becomes an adolescent and graduates to a therapist who treats adolescents.

It is possible for clinicians to have this kind of three-generation conflict in relation to each other and not only to family members. Typically, student clinicians in training have a supervisor above them and a patient below them in the hierarchy. In the class structure of any agency, the same situation applies with clinicians who are not students. For example, a psychiatrist can be supervising a therapist staff member with patients. The typical sequence is as follows.

1. The supervisor disagrees with the way the student or staff therapist is handling a case and wishes to save the patient from the student. Sometimes the patient has come to the supervisor with a complaint, initiating this sequence, and sometimes it is merely apparent in the discussion between supervisor and therapist. As the supervisor insists on a particular way of dealing with the case, disagreeing with the therapist, he is forming a coalition across generation lines by siding with the patient against the student.

2. The student withdraws, either letting the superior handle the case or asking for excessive help from the supervisor.

3. The patient misbehaves or makes an extreme demand.

---

*B. Montalvo and J. Haley, "In Defense of Child Therapy," *Family Process 12* (1973): 227–244.

4. The supervisor protests that he cannot treat every case in the clinic and the student should be more autonomous and take responsibility for his own patients.

5. The student begins to deal with the patient in his own way.

6. The supervisor protests that the student is not dealing with the patient properly and takes over, insisting that he must save the patient from the student.

This sequence continues and the patient becomes part of the chronic caseload in a clinic. It is also typical of in-staff conflicts in a mental hospital setting.

The Parental Child.   In some families, particularly one-parent families with many children, there is a third generation that is not clearly a "generation." There is a mother and her children, but in between there is an older child who functions as a parent for the younger children. He or she is not of the adult generation but is a child, and yet the child functions as an adult insofar as he or she is taking care of the younger children.*

The position of this parental child is often quite difficult because he has the responsibility for the younger children but not the power. Therefore, he is caught in the middle between misbehaving children and a mother who does not delegate full power to him. What typically happens is that the mother sides with the children against the parental child when there is trouble. She insists the parental child be in charge while not giving sufficient autonomy to deal with the situation.

The sequence is very much like the grandmother, mother, and child conflict, but with different personnel. The indicators of this situation are an older child speaking

---

*The idea of the parental child is described in S. Minuchin and others, *Families of the Slums* (New York: Basic Books, 1967). One of the better presentations of this concept as well as a therapeutic approach to it is shown in a therapy training film, "A Family with a Little Fire," by Braulio Montalvo (for information inquire at the Philadelphia Child Guidance Clinic, 34th and Civic Center Blvd., Philadelphia, Pennsylvania 19104).

for the younger children in a family session, protecting them, and often dealing with quite serious problems without letting the mother know about them.

In clinical organizations, this hierarchy is evident wherever there are paraprofessionals. Usually, the hierarchy includes a professional in charge, a paraprofessional who actually takes charge, and the clientele. The paraprofessional is not really at the staff level and yet does the actual work with clients and is blamed by the professional if there is trouble. Often there are secrets between client and paraprofessional just as there are in families with parental children. This hierarchy is also typical in mental hospitals where the aides or attendants function as parental children because they are not professional staff members and yet are not at the level of patients. They have the responsibility but not the power and so must deal with the patients secretly on many issues, including on disciplinary issues.

Two-Generation Conflicts

It is arbitrary to differentiate one-generation from two- or three-generation structures, since all situations involve multiple generations. Yet for practical reasons it can be helpful to focus on one set of levels rather than on another. There are two typical patterns that appear as two-generation problems.

The Overwhelmed Mother. In some families with many children there is a mother who is in charge of everyone with no hierarchy among the children. The center of whatever happens, like the hub of a wheel, the mother has each child go through her to deal with any other child. Such a mother appears overburdened by constant demands from the children. This structure can be seen if one asks the children to do something, such as draw something on the blackboard, while the therapist talks to the mother. The children will constantly interrupt to ask the mother something, show her what they have done, ask her to settle arguments, and check with her before doing anything. Such a structure is typical of organizations where an administrator cannot delegate authority and so remains in charge of everyone.

One Parent against Another. The most typical two-generation problem is where one parent sides with a child against the other parent. The "child" can be two years old or forty years, since the problem is not age but organization. A depressed woman with several children may still be functioning as a child in the relationship with her parents. The sequence can also take place when the parents are separated, if they are still at odds over the child.

The typical sequence in this situation is as follows.

1. One parent, usually the mother, is in an intense relationship with the child. By *intense* is meant a relationship that is both positive and negative and where the responses of each person are exaggeratedly important. The mother attempts to deal with the child with a mixture of affection and exasperation.

2. The child's symptomatic behavior becomes more extreme.

3. The mother, or the child, calls on the father for assistance in resolving their difficulty.

4. The father steps in to take charge and deal with the child.

5. Mother reacts against father, insisting that he is not dealing with the situation properly. Mother can react with an attack or a threat to break off the relationship with father. The threat to leave may be as indirect as "I want a vacation by myself," or as direct as "I want a divorce."

6. Father withdraws, giving up the attempt to disengage mother and child.

7. Mother and child deal with each other in a mixture of affection and exasperation until they reach a point where they are at an impasse.

This sequence can continue forever and ever as mother (or father) crosses generation lines and sides with child against the other parent. Another way to describe it is as an intense involvement of one adult and child that regularly includes and excludes the other adult.

The fact that change in the child is followed by a chasm developing between the parents, or even a threat of separation and divorce, has led to the family theory that a child with symptoms is always holding a problem marriage together. It would be better to think in terms of the sequence—the threat of separation occurs at a certain point in a sequence that includes a change in the child.

As a sequence of this kind continues, the focus on the child becomes a way of dealing with issues that arise in marriage. In that sense it seems justified to say that the symptoms of the child have a function in the marriage. Many problems between a couple that cannot be dealt with directly may be communicated about in terms of—and therefore through—the child. The child becomes the communication intermediary and so stabilizes the marriage. For example, at those moments when mother comments on how the child is threatening to run away, she may be indirectly threatening to leave her husband. By discussing the child, the couple can deal with the marriage issue without making it explicit and therefore without making irreversible decisions.

The two-parent sequence is seen most clearly in a family where one parent is a step-parent. For example, an unmarried woman with several children may marry, partly to have a man's help in raising her children. When the new husband begins to discipline the children, or perhaps show affection to them, the mother may react against him by saying he does not truly understand these children. She may even suggest that the marriage was a mistake. The husband will withdraw, not wanting to upset his marriage. Then the children will have a problem that the mother will have difficulty with. She will call upon her husband again, and the sequence will repeat. Such a situation can continue for many years, since it is independent of time.

The Problem in a Clinical Organization.   This situation, of a person of the parent generation siding with a child against the other parent, is typical in staff conflicts in agencies and mental hospitals. The situation occurs whenever a therapist is dealing with a patient and a fellow staff member is in charge of that patient and many others on a ward. The typical sequence involves:

1. An "intense" relationship, a mixture of affection and exasperation, between a therapist and a patient on the ward.

2. At a certain point the patient misbehaves, or requests something special, such as some privilege or freedom from discipline for some misbehavior.

3. The ward administrator insists on dealing with the patient as one of many who does not deserve anything special and he tries to persuade the therapist that this approach is best.

4. The therapist reacts against the ward physician, saying he does not truly understand this patient.

5. The ward physician withdraws, giving up the attempt to intervene between therapist and patient.

6. Therapist and patient continue in their intense relationship, with therapist joining patient against ward doctor by attempting to save him from the doctor who does not understand him.

This organization situation and others like it are inevitable in the nature of mental hospitals. The pattern may explain why so many patients and doctors become chronic members of such institutions.

Variations.   The marvelous complexities of human life have been simplified here to three generations and a short sequence, which is rather like describing a human being as a skeleton without flesh. These different sequences have also been presented as if they occurred independently. However, one may also find a two-parent family in which mother and grandmother are in the central struggle over the child and the father is outside the sequence. One may also find a situation in which the grandparents are crossing generation lines, the parents are in conflict over a child, and a parental child is saving the child from the parents. That situation is sometimes called a *psychotic family*. It is probably true that an individual is more disturbed in direct proportion to the number of malfunctioning hierarchies in which he is embedded.

The Therapeutic Problem

The goal of any clinical description is that it should lead to ways a therapist can think about what might cause change and what might not. The sequences have been oversimplified here, but even in this form it becomes possible to think about how change may be induced. What would *not* bring about change seems evident. If a person is caught up in a sequence of this kind, expressing his emotions is not likely to cause change.* Similarly, if a person discovers "why" he is behaving as he does, through some explanation in terms of his past history, change is not likely to occur. From this point of view he is behaving as he does because of the ways other people are behaving, not because he was programed by his past. Whether in terms of catharsis or insight into his unconscious, the theory of repression is a handicap if one is thinking about how to change sequences.

It is tempting to believe that if a person only "discovers" he is part of a sequence, that he can change—that if a mother could only "learn" that she is regularly including and excluding her husband from caring for their child, she would be able to stop such a sequence. However, the evidence indicates that such learning, or discovery, does not usually lead to change but rather becomes a rationale for continuing the sequence. When such insight is offered by a

---

*When a person expresses his emotions in a different way, it means that he is communicating in a different way. In doing so, he forces a different kind of communication from the person responding to him, and this change in turn requires yet a different way of responding back. When this shift occurs a system changes because of the change in communication sequence, but this fact has nothing to do with expressing or releasing emotions in the sense of catharsis. For example, if a man gets red in the face and is silent every time his wife criticizes him, the therapist may arrange for the man to express his anger in words instead of by changing the color of his face. If the man does so, the wife must respond differently and a new system is being generated. Asking "How do you feel?" about something is the least likely way to bring out emotion; the client simulates it in words. It is better to provoke him to more anger, perhaps by sympathizing with him, to shift the way he is communicating.

therapist, the mother may "discover" that the therapist is just like her husband and does not truly understand her special child. She may exclude the therapist as she does her husband, only to bring the therapist back again when she has difficulty with her child. The therapist may develop a theory of resistance to explain why his insightful approach is not producing change.

If expressing emotions or having insight does not produce change, what does? A few general ideas guide this new way of thinking about the therapeutic problem. The first and primary idea is that change occurs by the therapist joining the ongoing system and changing it by the ways he participates within it. When dealing with a governed, homeostatic system that is maintained by repeating sequences of behavior, the therapist changes those sequences by shifting the ways people respond to each other because of the ways they must respond to the therapist.

At the most general level, the therapist should not side consistently with anyone in the family against anyone else. But that does not mean he should not temporarily side with one against another, because that is in fact the only way he can induce change. If he only places his "weight" in coalitions equally, he will continue the sequence as it was. In the same way, if he only joins one person against another, he may maintain the system as it was by simply becoming part of the deadlocked struggle. That task is more complex: the therapist must temporarily join in different coalitions while ultimately not siding with anyone against anyone.

With situations in which a family has a severely disturbed member, it is necessary for the therapist to join in multiple coalitions simultaneously. He must, for example, side with the parents in their executive function in relationship to a disturbed young person while at the same time siding with the young person in terms of his ultimate goal of helping the young person out of that disturbing situation. With skill gained by experience, a therapist can learn to skate among coalitions, being partially involved at one moment and firm at another. He must retain the freedom to join in whatever coalition is appropriate at any particular time.

It is also necessary at times to cause a crisis in a situation by siding only with one person for an apparently indefinite period of time. When a husband and wife are stable and miserable, the therapist can induce instability by joining one or the other and saying that person is completely right. This temporary firm coalition can later be balanced by shifting to a coalition with the other person, but at any moment in time the coalition can appear permanent.

The most typical way to proceed when balancing within different temporary coalitions is to proceed in steps. The first step is to determine the type of sequence that is maintaining the presenting problem. The second step is to specify a goal. If grandmother is joining child against mother, the goal is to have the mother in charge of her child and the grandmother in an advisory position to the mother. If mother or father is too intensively involved with a child in a coalition against the other parent, the goal is to have the parents involved with each other and the child more interested in associating with peers than with parents. The goal in all cases is to draw a generation line and prevent consistent coalitions across it. By the ways the therapist forms coalitions from his higher status as an expert, the therapist prevents the family from forming coalitions across generation lines. The third step involves a new idea. It is improbable, if not impossible, that a system can go from "abnormal" to "normal" in one step. Change must occur in stages, and the first step should be to create a different form of abnormality.

The idea that therapy has stages is relatively new. Possibly the first clinician to introduce stages systematically was Joseph Wolpe with his reciprocal inhibition technique.* Another early designer of stages was Murray Bowen. He reports, in a personal communication, that the way he once began family therapy was by seeing an individual alone and

*See J. Wolpe, *Psychotherapy by Reciprocal Inhibition*, Stanford, Calif.; Stanford University Press, 1958.

asking that person to take a stance in relation to his family that he had always wished to take but had not. As the person takes that stance, stages follow: first the family members attack that person as disloyal, and secondly they threaten to divorce or expel the person. If the person holds out against them, then the third stage is Bowen interviewing the whole family together.

Although specific stages for most therapy methods have not usually been worked out, a variety of therapeutic approaches do assume that the therapeutic process is such that one cannot go *directly* from the problem at the beginning to the cure at the end. The process takes different forms. There is a class of therapeutic situations in which the problem presented must be redefined as another problem before it is resolved, because the kind of abnormality has been redefined as another kind. Sometimes this shift occurs routinely as part of the initial negotiations to select a solvable problem and sometimes it occurs later.

For example, a case of "mental illness" may be redefined as one of bad behavior. The family of a psychotic might be asked to put him in jail rather than in a mental hospital. "Crazy" and "bad" should not be confused as one category if the therapist is thinking of shifting from one to another. Similarly, criminal behavior is sometimes solvable if it is redefined as an "illness" problem. (This approach has nothing to do with the philosophical issue of whether crazy people are bad or criminals are mentally ill. It is a tactical therapeutic issue.)

In more minor form, it is not unusual for a clinician to define the psychiatric or medical problem of a child or an adult as a misbehavior problem. For example, anxiety attacks might be redefined as manipulative and so misbehavior. In the case of a child starving herself, her not eating can be redefined as not minding. The problem shifts from a child who is ill to parents who should pull together to make her mind.*

* S. Minuchin, "The Use of an Ecological Framework in Child Psychiatry," in J.E. Anthony and C. Koupernick (Eds.), *The Child in His Family* (New York: Wiley, 1970).

In all forms of therapy there has been a tendency to take whatever the patient says as something that needs to be redefined as a different problem. The patient who is too emotional needs more cognition, and the overly intellectual patient needs more emotion. The patient who concentrates on details needs to generalize, and the one who consistently generalizes needs to be more concrete. The client who talks about his "misbehavior" needs to have that behavior redefined as something he cannot help and therefore an "illness." The "ill" psychiatric patient needs to take responsibility for his actions and therefore his "illness" is redefined as "misbehavior."

Whenever the therapist prescribes a symptom and so offers a paradoxical directive, he is requesting a different abnormal situation by exaggerating the presenting abnormal situation. This approach is clearest with the procedure of "flooding" someone. An abnormal situation is made into a parody of that abnormal situation, and so into a new one, when someone who is afraid of bugs is forced to think about bugs crawling about everywhere. In most of the behavior therapies, the presenting problem is redefined as a different one. Some behavior therapists translate the presenting problem into a frequency count of certain behavior and this new definition of abnormality is then resolved. Wolpe transforms a presenting problem into a list of anxiety situations that are items for which he can set up a procedure to cure.

When we turn to the schema of pathological systems outlined here, it becomes evident that one way to think about designing a strategy and planning the stages of therapy is to think about shifting from the presenting system to a different abnormal one. This different abnormal system may be the presenting system of some other family. The following examples serve to present this idea (further examples are given in Chapter Five).

A mother may be too central to her children, so that there is no hierarchy in the family and all the children function through her as if she were the hub of a wheel. In such a case it may be appropriate to create a system where an older child relieves the mother by taking charge. Essentially, this change creates a parental child hierarchy. From this new abnormal state, it is possible to shift to a more reasonable hierarchy in the family so that all children can participate with different responsibilities.

Conversely, if the family comes in with a parental child system, one possibility is to make the mother overly central as the first stage. This change frees the parental child, and from this new abnormal hierarchy it is possible to go to a more normal one.

If the sequence involves a grandmother who is crossing generation lines and siding with the child against the mother, one can follow the procedure suggested in Chapter Five in which full responsibility is given to the grandmother. One can then go from this abnormal stage to another abnormal one in which all responsibility is given to the mother and the grandmother cannot discipline the child at all. From this abnormal state one can go to the more normal one.

If mother and child are in an overly intense relationship and the father is peripheral, the first stage can be one where the father takes total control of the child and the mother is excluded. This is an abnormal system, and from it one can move to a more normal one. It might also be possible to use an older sibling as a parental child to disengage mother and child, thereby introducing a parental child system as the first state. Similarly, one might introduce the grandmother and create that hierarchy as a first stage.

In summary, one of the reasons for failure of some therapies has been that they assume one can go from an abnormal state directly to a normal state. It is more productive to think in terms of stages between abnormality and normality. Faced with a malfunctioning system, one can think of how to transform that into another malfunctioning system that can then be shifted to normal.

Sequence and Hierarchy

It is in the ways that repetitive sequences define hierarchies that systems theory and hierarchy come together. The hierarchy is shaped by the behavior of the people involved, and insofar as the behavior is repetitive and redundant it is a governed system that is error-activated in that deviance activates a governing process. If the person deviates from the repeating behavior and so defines a different hierarchy, the others react against that deviation and shape the behavior back into the habitual pattern.

Pathological behavior appears when the repeating sequence simultaneously defines two opposite hierarchies, or when the hierarchy is unstable because the behavior indicates one shape at one time and another shape at other times. For example, if the parents at one point take charge of a child and at another point accept the child as the authority in the family, the hierarchy is confused.

A parallel can be drawn here between levels of communication and levels of hierarchy. The "double bind" was a concept derived from the paradoxes that occur when messages are on multiple levels and are conflicting.* For a therapist to ask another person to disobey him, or to direct someone to behave spontaneously is to produce a paradox. The person cannot behave spontaneously if he has been *instructed* to behave in that way.† In the organizational description offered here, the same principle applies to a larger unit. If a person directs another to disobey, he is defining the hierarchy in two incompatible ways. The person directed is lower in the hierarchy since he is being told what to do, but he is also equal or higher in the hierarchy since he is being expected to disobey or to behave spontaneously. Two incompatible definitions of the hierarchy are offered simultaneously by communicating paradoxical messages. Just as everyone cannot *not* communicate with other people—even

---

*G. Bateson, D. D. Jackson, J. Haley, and J. Weakland, "Toward a Theory of Schizophrenia," *Behavioral Science* 1 (1956): 251–264.

†J. Haley, *Strategies of Psychotherapy* (New York: Grune & Stratton, 1963).

trying to avoid someone is communication*—so must everyone deal with the issue of hierarchical position in relation to the other person. When a therapist indicates he is not superior to a patient (by being "human" with him or even asking him what might be done) while accepting an expert's fee from the patient, he is offering incompatible positions in a hierarchy: he is a paid expert and therefore higher in the hierarchy since he is a helper paid to help the other, while he is also asking the other's advice on what to do. Quite possibly the nature of therapeutic change centers in the ways the hierarchical issues are kept unstable in the therapeutic relationship either by being ambiguous and confused or by being defined in shifting and incompatible ways.

A changing definition of a hierarchy may develop as part of a sequence. For example, when a mother asks her husband's assistance with a child, she is defining the hierarchy as one in which two parents are joint authorities over a child. When the husband responds by dealing with the child, and the mother reacts and condemns him for not understanding the child and joins the child against him, the definition of the hierarchy has shifted. She is now defining it as one in which she and the child have the authority over father's behavior.

It is the task of the therapist to change the sequence and so change the hierarchy of the family. It is also his task not to be caught up in a sequence in such a way that he is perpetuating the problem he is supposed to resolve. If the goals of the therapist are clear to him, he is less likely to be caught up helplessly in the ongoing process.

*It should be emphasized that most of the ideas about communication in this book derive ultimately from Gregory Bateson. I participated in his research project for ten years, along with John Weakland and Don D. Jackson and William F. Fry. An idea such as the one that people cannot not communicate predates that project since it was published by Bateson with Jurgen Ruesch in *Communication, the Social Matrix of Psychiatry* (New York: Norton, 1951). For a collection of Bateson's writings, see *Steps to an Ecology of Mind* (New York: Ballantine, 1972).

Certain consequences of a theory of systems as a model for therapy are sometimes not thought through by members of the profession. If we assume that a family is a system we must accept the premise that behavior will repeat and also the premise that movements toward change will activate the governing processes that have been keeping the system stable. Granting these premises, once therapy has begun and the therapist has become part of the system, we must assume that when change occurs he will react to keep the system as it was during therapy. That is, we must assume that the therapist, the change agent, will resist change once the therapy is an ongoing process. Some professionals are willing to accept the idea that treatment institutions, like mental hospitals, resist change, but do not think through the fact that this idea must apply also to the therapist. Given this view of the therapeutic situation, the supervisor, who operates more on the periphery of the system than does the therapist, has the function of helping the therapist move past change as well as helping him disengage from the family. (The supervisor too is part of the system, but is less involved in terms of the immediate feedback processes exchanged by therapist and family.)

To put the matter another way, therapy involves changes in relationship between the therapist and his clientele. If a therapist and family accept a helping contract, they are agreeing that the therapist should help and that the family should receive the help. All messages are in that framework and define the relationship in that way. Yet it is impossible to cure someone by helping him if the cure involves arranging that the client no longer need help. The more help the therapist offers, the more he is defining the person as needing help. The more the person accepts help, the more he defines the relationship as a helping one. The goal of the therapy is to have the therapist and person achieve a relationship as peers in the sense that the client does not need any more help than does the therapist. Once the helping relationship is established, if either party moves toward changing the relationship, the other will react to stabilize the relationship they have.* Not only does the patient resist change in a relationship, but so does the therapist. The art of therapy includes shifting from one type of relationship to another while being part of a stabilized system. The supervisor can help in this situation by the use of a variety of techniques, including the use of recesses in the therapy, such as meeting in a month rather than next week, and even the encouragement of controlled relapses.

Once it was thought that clarifying communication in families would not only bring about togetherness and harmony but would also cause basic change in family structure. But such clarification, when it involves pointing out to family members how they are communicating, seems to produce little change. At the opposite extreme was the idea that the therapist should individuate family members from one another and so provide more autonomy and less togetherness. With experience it has become more clear that the autonomy of a person is dependent on how other people behave. Even the definition of autonomy can only be in relationship to other people. Of course, at times both the effort to clarify communication and the emphasis on achieving autonomy can inadvertently break up habitual sequences in families and so produce change. It has merely become more evident in recent years that the therapist can focus directly on changing those sequences and so more quickly and efficiently produce change.

The particular strategy of a therapist will vary with the unique family, the context of therapy, and it will also be influenced by the stage of development of the family since families change over time.† As children mature and parents and grandparents age, sequences and hierarchies change. In the family life cycle, there is an extraordinary reversal of hierarchical structure. Children shift from being taken care of by their parents to becoming peers of parents as

---

*J. Haley, *Strategies of Psychotherapy* (New York: Grune & Stratton, 1963).

†J. Haley, *Uncommon Therapy: The Psychiatric Techniques of Milton H. Erickson, M.D.* (New York: Norton, 1973).

fellow adults to taking care of parents in their old age. It is now being assumed that "spontaneous" change is related to developmental processes in families. Sometimes therapy is given credit for a change when a natural process has accomplished it. Yet often families do not develop and change over time, but remain fixated in a problem sequence. The therapist must intervene to make a change and cannot depend on a natural process to do his job.

5

Therapy in Stages

The first obligation of a therapist is to change the presenting problem offered. If that is not accomplished the therapy is a failure. A therapist should not let himself be distracted into other matters so that he forgets this primary goal. Moreover, by focusing on the symptoms the therapist gains the most leverage and has the most opportunity for bringing about change. It is the presenting problem that most interests the client; when the therapist works with that he can gain great cooperation. If a person with symptoms is offered as a problem, the therapist may believe that changes must take place in that family system before that person can change. Yet he should not try to persuade the family that the *real* problem lies in the family and not in the person. Such a distinction is artificial. The therapist may fail to achieve his ends if he engages in pointless debate with the family about the cause of the problem, attempts to educate them about family communication, or tries to persuade them to accept "family therapy." The goal is not to teach the family about their malfunctioning system, but to change the family sequences so that the presenting problems are resolved.

When dealing with a symptom, the approach must vary depending on whether it is a one-parent or two-parent family, on what the class and ethnic background of the family is, as well as on the age of the children involved. A wealthy middle-class family must not be dealt with in the same way as is a lower-class family on welfare, just as one must adjust the approach to accommodate either an Italian Catholic working-class family or a German Lutheran farm family. How the therapist approaches the family will be determined by many factors—the emphasis here will be on a schematized structure that can apply to many families.

When a child, whether small or adolescent, is brought to a clinic by a family, he is a problem or the family would not have taken the trouble to come. (At times a family presents a child as a supposed problem when actually he is not and they really have other purposes in coming, but the emphasis here is on the usual situation.) From the family standpoint, the child is the problem and they may even be puzzled when the therapist asks the whole family to come for the first interview. It is not necessary to persuade the family that they have family problems, but they do need to be persuaded to cooperate in doing what the therapist asks to help them get over the problem they present.

If the therapist is thinking in terms of dyads, or two-person units, he is considering the child's symptoms as a response to one other person who is making the symptom necessary. The therapist might think of how to change the symptomatic behavior of the child or how to change the reciprocal responses of the other person so that the child's symptomatic behavior cannot continue.

If the therapist is thinking in terms of triads, he seeks out the triangle involved in the problem and the sequence that requires the symptomatic behavior. He assumes that, when a child has symptoms, at least two adults are involved in the problem and that the child is both a participant and a communication vehicle between them. If there is only one parent in the family, the therapist inquires into the relationship with some other adult, such as a grandmother or a divorced or separated parent. If there is no other adult at the parental level who seems to be important and there is a grandparent involved, the problem will be seen as a three-generational one. (Sometimes, of course, the problem may not even be in the family but in the school or neighborhood, or in the relationship between the family and some other institution. The emphasis here is on problems within the family.)

Case Examples

When the therapist has conducted the first interview properly and so has learned the sequence of the family problem, he then seeks out the most appropriate strategy for bringing about change. It is best if he assumes that change should occur in stages and that he cannot jump from the problem stage to the cure stage in one leap but must have other stages in between. Usually he must go from a problem stage to a new problem stage before he can go toward the normal system. Some case examples will be offered here to indicate the kinds of stages that can be used.

The Intrusive Grandmother. One family presented the problem of a ten-year-old boy who was generally misbehaving as well as wetting his bed. In the family interview, the grandmother reported that the mother mishandled the child and did not appreciate him. The mother reported that whenever she attempted to discipline the child, the grandmother intruded and protected him. The therapist had mother and grandmother agree that the goal was to have the boy mind properly and stop wetting the bed, so that the destination of the treatment was clear.

In the approach to be described here, only the key moves in the therapy are emphasized. The work on relationships is taken for granted. For example, it is assumed that the therapist explores the boy's ideas about the problem, and that he develops an undersanding relationship with both mother and grandmother.

Since grandmother and mother explicitly stated that they disagreed about how to handle the boy, it was possible to persuade them to experiment with a new approach for a short period of time. The grandmother was asked to take full responsibility for the boy for two weeks. She was to deal with all matters of discipline and with the bedwetting, including the washing of the sheets. The mother was not to discipline the boy but simply to enjoy him. If he misbehaved, she was to report that misbehavior to the grandmother, who would take care of it. All negative communication between boy and mother was to go through the grandmother, who would be central. The family agreed to this two-week experiment.

Essentially, this stage is the creation of a malfunctioning structure. It is not appropriate that a grandmother have full charge of a child while the mother is peripheral.

The family was interviewed during the first two-week period, and the grandmother's difficulties and exasperations were discussed. The mother was warned to continue to leave everything to the grandmother. At the end of two weeks, the therapist required the family to reverse itself. The mother was to take full charge of the boy, and the grandmother was merely to enjoy him. All communication of a negative kind between grandmother and boy was to go through the mother.

This stage too creates an abnormal arrangement insofar as grandmother is completely shut out of the boy's problems, even to the point of not being allowed to offer advice to mother about what to do with him. By having the grandmother put in charge first, it becomes easier for her to stay out of it when the mother is put in charge.

By the end of the second two weeks, it is possible to have a session discussing which arrangement proved best. In most cases the grandmother prefers that the mother take charge of the work of the boy, since the grandmother is older and has already raised her children. She will also agree to communicate through the mother to the boy rather than side with the boy against his mother. She agrees partly because she is threatened with having full care of the boy if she intrudes. The child's symptoms usually disappear when the hierarchy is correct. In some cases the family can decide that the grandmother should continue to be the one in full charge of the child. If this arrangement is agreeable to all, it becomes a functioning system but tends to be an unstable one over time as grandmother ages.

In this approach the therapist does not go from the malfunctioning structure to the functioning one, but as a first step creates a different malfunctioning system. This system is only partially different, however, since the grandmother is asked to take charge when she has already been taking charge. However, she is put *fully* in charge. If the therapist attempts to go to the more normal system first, by having the mother take full charge, usually the grandmother will continue to intrude, demonstrating that the mother is not adequate to the task.

The Parental Child.   One working mother called and reported to a therapist (Braulio Montalvo) that her eight-year-old daughter had set a fire in their apartment. An appointment was set and the whole family came for the first interview. It was a low-income, black family containing a twelve-year-old boy, the eight-year-old problem girl, and three smaller children. There was no father in the home. The incident that precipitated the crisis was a fire in a mattress set by the small girl. The older boy, who was responsible for the children, managed to get the mattress into the bathroom and put the fire out. He did not call the mother because he did not wish to disturb her at work. When asked about the fire, the girl only cried. It became apparent in the first interview that the older boy was a parental child. In the room he hovered over the problem girl, answering questions she was asked, and seemed to be more motherly with the child than the mother was.

The first step in this type of case can be to create an abnormal situation by making the mother central, with all communication going through her. This step is abnormal insofar as it does not allow organizational hierarchy among the children, which is necessary in families, particularly in a family with a working mother, where an older child is needed to take charge at times. To make this step it is necessary to block off the parental child and make the mother central.

Both in the room and in the directive for a task at home, the therapist blocked off the parental child and forced the mother to talk to her daughter about what happened. When the older boy intruded, the therapist quieted him and physically moved the boy over beside himself. He placed mother and daughter side by side to talk.

The therapist gave the mother and daughter a task to do at home. He defined the task as something only for this girl and her mother, not for the other children, who were put temporarily in charge of the parental child. The mother was to spend five minutes, timed with an egg timer, teaching the little girl how to use matches. At this point in the session, the parental child wished to demonstrate how he could use matches, but he was blocked off.

In the following session, the therapist had the daughter demonstrate that she could safely use matches by lighting a small fire in an ash tray. He then had her teach a younger sister how to do it, showing how the mother had taught her, while the mother observed. By this second session, the mother was blocking off the parental child from intruding on her activities with the daughter so that the therapist no longer needed to do so.

At this point it was necessary to reorganize the family in a more normal way. Rather than have him be overburdened as a parent when only a child, the twelve-year-old boy was moved out as the only pathway of communication between the mother and the children. He was therefore delegated responsibility for the children when the mother was away, but the therapist emphasized that mother was in charge and that the boy was not a fellow parent. The boy was also encouraged to go out with peers, and the therapist worked to overcome the mother's reluctance to give him freedom because of evil companions on the street. Making friends outside the family weakened his parental child position within the family.

The mother was also encouraged toward activities outside the home so that she was not sacrificing her personal life for her children. The fire setting vanished with the change in organization.

The Two-Generation Problem

Although several generations can be involved in a problem with a family with two parents, the most simple way to think about a child problem when one thinks in triads is in terms of one parent siding with a child against the other parent. The typical situation is an overintense parent–child dyad that alternately includes and excludes the other parent. When the sequence is seen in this way, the therapist can select among different approaches. He can enter the family through different doors, either through the father–child relationship, the mother–child relationship, or through the mother–father relationship. The following examples illustrate these different approaches.

Approach 1: Using the Peripheral Person. When a therapist interviews a whole family presenting a child problem and sees the mother and child as overinvolved and the father more peripheral, he may decide to use the father to break up the intense relationship between mother and child. Whether or not to use this approach will be determined by the unique situation of each family and by the therapist's judgment of how workable a relationship he can establish with the father. In the sequence of this type, the father usually has attempted to deal with the child and has met opposition from the mother as the mother reclaimed the child from him, often protesting he does not understand the child. Often, too, the father has criticized the mother for her overprotection of the child, antagonizing her and persuading her that he does not either understand her or the child. Therefore, to activate the father to intervene between mother and child may require skillful persuasion.

If a therapist chooses this approach, he must be careful not to imply that the father is being brought into the situation because the mother has failed. Such an indictment of the mother may not only antagonize her and risk her taking the family out of treatment, but may also exacerbate the bad feeling between the mother and father. The child may thus be freed from the intense involvement with the mother, but bringing the parents together may be made more difficult.

There are different ways of making the situation acceptable to the mother. For example, if the problem is a male child, the therapist can say that the child has now reached an age where he should be more involved with men and therefore the father and son must do certain activities together. In this way the overprotection by the mother in the past is not condemned; the child has just reached an age where, according to an expert, different behavior is appropriate. If the problem is a female child, the mother can be persuaded that she has an obligation to see that her daughter understands men, and therefore she must be encouraged to be involved with her father as part of her education.

If this approach is used there are three stages before the goal is achieved. In the first stage, father, son, and therapist become involved in an activity while mother is shifted to the periphery. This stage creates a new abnormal organization. In the second stage, mother, father, and therapist are intensely involved, while the child drops out of the adult struggle and is free to join his peers. He may or may not need guidance into peer activity. In the third stage, the therapist must disengage and get out, leaving the parents involved with each other and the boy involved with friends.

When the therapy goes well, these stages flow logically one to another. For example, when the mother is excluded at the first stage, she is motivated to become involved. As she is blocked off from being involved with the child, she becomes involved with the father. This change occurs naturally when she objects to the way the father is dealing with the child. When the therapist focuses the parents on each other and excludes the child, the second stage is underway. The therapist must then disengage, entering the final stage, ensuring that the child will not be brought back to replace him.

A typical case can illustrate the stages. One is briefly presented here and described in more complete form in the case report presented at the back of this volume. A family with an eight-year-old boy and a four-year-old girl presented the problem of the boy's lifelong fear of dogs. After a year of individual therapy with no improvement they were referred to the Philadelphia Child Guidance Clinic and the case was assigned to Dr. Mariano Barragan. The whole family was interviewed in the first session and their history and situation was discussed. A treatment strategy was planned in a strategy seminar.*

In this family, the mother and son could be described as intensely involved and the father more peripheral. The mother was the authority on the boy's fear and took the boy wherever he needed to go because of his fear of dogs. The mother and father associated little together, with the father holding down two jobs. The therapist decided to use the father to intervene, to disengage mother and son from each other. The stages follow.

In the first stage, the therapist arranged that the father teach his son how to deal with dogs, since the father was a mailman and so an authority on them. The mother was shifted to the periphery since she was not an authority on how to handle dogs. The father and son were also assigned to find a puppy that was afraid of people and the boy was to cure the puppy of that fear.

In the second stage, the mother and father and therapist became intensely involved when the therapist directed the parents to go away for a weekend vacation alone together as a reward for their son improving. The mother expressed her resentment of her husband, and the couple finally re-

---

*The participants in this strategy seminar were Curtis Adams, Mariano Barragan, Joanna Chapin, Lee Milman, Braulio Montalvo, and Frances Ziegler.

vealed that the husband had done something in the past that cut off communication between them. The mother said to the therapist, "It's like you said, we've used our son to bridge a gap between us." Actually, the therapist had not said this, since he was not interested in interpretive therapy. The therapist gave directives to improve the marriage while the boy continued to go out alone and make friends.

In the final stage, the therapist disengaged, leaving the parents involved with each other and the boy involved with peers. A two-year followup showed the improvement as stable.

The therapy of this particular family proceeded easily from stage to stage, partly because the family was ready to change and partly because the therapist was skilled. The therapist made change easy by negotiating rather than difficult by interpreting hostilities or problems between parents. Obviously, not all families change so easily. They may become stuck at different stages. Sometimes the peripheral person just cannot become involved successfully with the child, or retreats when the marital issue comes up. (This pattern is typical of fathers of severely disturbed adolescents; in such cases, special therapeutic techniques are required.) The child then relapses. Sometimes the therapist himself cannot shift to the next stage and continues to focus on the child when he should be working with the marriage. At other times a therapist cannot disengage himself, continuing treatment when it is no longer necessary and so preventing the final change that frees the child and leaves the parents dealing with each other without him. All therapy works best if the therapist can become intensely involved but can rapidly disengage, being willing to give credit to the family rather than to himself.

Approach 2: Breaking up the Dyad with a Task.   At times the peripheral person cannot be successfully used in the problem of disengaging an overinvolved mother-and-child dyad. If a therapist decides that is the situation, he may choose another approach. There are a variety of ways to intervene between mother and child so that they become

less involved with each other. It is not useful to make interpretations to the mother about how she overprotects the
child and that she has unconscious needs to do so. Such an
approach typically antagonizes the mother and prevents
change. A successful way is to guide the mother in helping
the child achieve more competence. Another is to divert the
mother to activities more appropriate than hovering over
her child. In situations where her husband is providing her
with little satisfaction, this diversion may be difficult, because what little satisfaction she receives is from the child.
Sometimes a program of work, education, or community
action outside the home can divert her, particularly if this
change is accompanied by arranging activities for the child
that require his association with peers and not with adults
in some natural activity (rather than an artificial activity
like group therapy).* As mother and child become occupied
in different directions, they become less involved with
each other.

A quite different approach is to provide a task that appears to encourage the mother's helpful protection but that
in actuality disrupts the relationship because it is unbearable
to continue in the same way. The following case example
illustrates such a task.

Erickson reports a case† that provides an example of
entering the family through the overinvolved dyad. A twelve-
year-old boy was wetting the bed every night and his mother
was excessively concerned about him. The father was not
concerned and did not think the boy should be treated for
the problem. The therapist interviewed the father, found
him a difficult and uncooperative man, set him aside, and
focused on mother and child. Erickson reports:

---

*Getting the mother involved with her own mother, or with other
members of her family network, is a procedure advocated by Murray
Bowen and can be seen as another way of disengaging her.

†J. Haley, *Uncommon Therapy: The Psychiatric Techniques of Milton H.
Erickson, M.D.* (New York: Norton, 1973, pp. 207–208).

As I sized up the situation with mother and the boy, it was apparent that Johnny was utterly hostile toward his mother about this bedwetting. He was angry and in a struggle with her about it. I told Johnny that I had a remedy for him that he wouldn't like. It would be an effective remedy, absolutely helpful, absolutely certain to get him over the problem, yet he would not like it—but his *mother* would *dislike* it more. Now what could Johnny do? If his mother would dislike it more than he did, that would be fine. He could put up with anything that made his mother suffer more.

I proposed to Johnny that his mother could get up at four or five a.m. in the morning, and if his bed was wet she could rouse him. She didn't have to wake him up if the bed was dry. However, if his bed was wet and she roused him, he could get up and sit down at his desk and copy so many pages from any book he chose. He could put in the time from four to seven o'clock or from five to seven o'clock, copying material. His mother could watch him do that and watch him learning to improve his script. The boy's handwriting was really terrible and needed improvement.

To Johnny it sounded horrible to get up at four or five in the morning—but Mother had to get up first. It sounded unpleasant to have mother sit there watching him improve his script, yet he only had to do that on mornings when his bed was wet. Nothing more disagreeable than getting up at that hour of the morning—to improve your handwriting.

They began this procedure, and it wasn't long before Johnny didn't have a wet bed every morning. He began skipping mornings. Pretty soon he had a wet bed only twice a week. Then a wet bed every ten days. Mother still had to get up every morning and check.

Finally it was a wet bed once a month, and then Johnny reoriented himself entirely. He developed the first friendships he had. It was during the summer and the kids came over to play with him, he went over to play with the kids. His marks in school that following September were greatly improved. His first real achievement.

Now that was playing mother against son and son against mother. It's the simple approach of "I've got a remedy for you, but you won't like it." Then I digress to the fact that mother will hate it even more. Johnny wants me to come to the point of what is the remedy? Then he's all for it. Improvement in handwriting becomes the primary goal, a dry bed becomes an incidental, more or less accepted thing. It's no longer the dominant, threatening issue at hand.

Mother, watching her son improve his handwriting, could take pride in her son's accomplishment. The son could take pride in it. When the two of them brought the handwriting to show me, it was just an eager boy and an eager mother showing me this beautiful handwriting. I could go through it page after page and point out this letter "n," this letter "g," this letter "t," and discuss the beauty of the script.

Since Johnny has a dry bed, his father has played ball with him—coming home early from the office. The father's response when the boy stopped wetting the bed was surprisingly complimentary. He told the boy, "You learned to have a dry bed faster than I did, must be you're a lot smarter than me." He could afford to be generous, since he felt it wasn't the psychiatrist who solved this problem, but the superior brain power he had bequeathed to his son. In the family it became a joint achievement which was blessed by the father, and the boy got recognition and acceptance for his accomplishment.

Approach 3: Entering through the Parents. The most typical family therapy approach is to begin with the child's problem and shift to the marital struggle in which the child is involved. Ordinarily this shift occurs in the first family interview. The parents report the problem and the therapist draws out each family member about it. The parents appear in agreement in the beginning, but as they discuss the situation, differences between them appear. The therapist teases out that difference, but he will find it best if he does not deal explicitly with the issues in the marriage until he gets improvement in the child, the presenting problem. Rushing to the marriage as a problem can make therapy more difficult later. Often there is a change in contract during some phase of treatment so that the treatment is agreed to as a marital problem rather than a child problem. Or the therapist may continue the involvement of the child so that if the conflict between the parents becomes too overt the focus can shift to the child. In this approach the overinvolved dyad is broken up by shifting directly to a more intense involve-

ment between the parents. Then, the last stage of therapy
is the disengagement of the therapist from the family, leaving the parents involved with each other and the child with
his peers.

Although this family therapy approach is routine, the
ways therapists deal with the family are quite varied. Some
therapists confront the parents with an interpretation that
the problem is really between them. Other therapists will not
make such a confrontation but will change the marital relationship by ostensibly continuing to focus on the child problem. Some therapists will offer directives, and some will not.

In this approach the therapist often forms and changes
coalitions without the awareness of the participants. For
example, with an overinvolved mother and a peripheral
father, a male therapist may relate to the mother in what is
essentially a flirtatious way, thus provoking the father into
a more intense involvement with his wife. A female therapist
may do the same in relation to mother. At other times the
therapist may support what the father is doing with his child,
thereby making a coalition that excludes the mother until
she moves to protest her husband's behavior with the child.
(This approach is essentially the same as Approach Number
1, described previously, but without directives.) Many family
therapists do not have clear stages of therapy in mind but
do what they intuit should be done next, often thinking
within a conceptual orientation of the individual needs of
family members.

In the following example, the focus of the treatment
was on the parents, but in an indirect way without exploring
their problems with each other. The family shifted from the
overinvolved mother to the marital situation to the disengagement of the therapist quite rapidly.

A family arrived for treatment with a five-year-old boy
who had never been toilet trained and who several times a
day had a bowel movement in his pants. He had never gone
to the toilet. There was also a younger brother who was
properly toilet trained. The family was seen for three diagnostic interviews by a child psychiatrist who focused on the

child. After evaluation, the family was transferred to Curtis Adams for treatment. Adams was participating in a strategy seminar, and the members of the seminar decided to treat this family by doing only one thing—restraining the family from improving. He would adopt the posture of being benevolently concerned about what would happen to the family if the child became normal, and would not do anything else.

The family was interviewed as a whole family in the first interview. The parents were a young, middle-class couple very concerned that they might do the wrong thing with their child. The boy was quite bright and articulate, saying such things as, "I poopy in my pants, and sometimes I get into my pajamas and I poopy in my pajamas." He was also able to talk with wonderful imagery if a therapist was interested in exploring that. The mother was an attractive, nervous young woman who was keenly alert to what the therapist thought of her. She was overinvolved with the child and benevolently exasperated with him. The father was an engineer who often worked or studied at night, and who stayed on the periphery. However, when he was home, he helped the mother clean up the child.

At the end of the first interview the therapist asked the parents what consequences there would be if the child began to go to the toilet normally. They replied that it would be wonderful. He expressed doubt and suggested they go home and think about what changes in their lives would occur if their child became normal and they were normal parents. The therapist's attitude expressed the idea that he could do something about the problem they presented, but that he would rather not until he was sure of the consequences to the whole family.

When the family returned the following week the parents had not been able to think of any adverse consequences if the boy went to the toilet normally. This reaction is typical for such a directive. The therapist himself had listed thirteen or fourteen consequences, but in the treatment he only needed to utilize three or four. He first approached the dyad of mother and child, raising the question whether the mother could tolerate being a mother who successfully solved her child's problem. He pointed out that some women can tolerate success, while other women cannot.

Although the therapist planned to do only one thing— restrain the family from improving—it is clear that there are multiple messages involved in any one act. To raise the question whether the mother can tolerate being successful is to restrain her from changing. However, no woman likes to think she cannot tolerate being successful and so there is a second message involved. There is also a framework, deliberately established by the therapist, that he thinks she can tolerate success, but that he wants to be sure. In this way the woman is not merely condemned as someone who cannot stand being successful, but she is supported in the idea that she *can* stand it, while being motivated to *prove* it. Each of these consequences emphasized by the therapist has the following levels: (1) that he thinks the person can tolerate success; (2) a benevolent concern about the person; and (3) a suggestion that the person finds intolerable.

The mother responded by indicating that she thought she could stand being a successful mother. She seemed uncertain whether the therapist was joking or not, as did her husband, but the therapist gave no indication. He asked whether becoming successful might not make her more successful as a mother than her own mother, and perhaps she could not tolerate that. The woman replied that she could certainly stand being more successful than her own mother, and began to discuss her difficulties with her mother and her alcoholic father. She also discussed her mother's feelings about her not having the boy toilet trained. (In this approach, the family members usually bring up more relevant material than they do if interpretations and inquiries are made. The problem for the therapist here was how gracefully to turn off the mother on issues of her history with her mother.)

The therapist shifted to the question of what the mother would do with herself during the day if the boy was over the

problem. Much of the mother's time was occupied washing
the boy's clothes, putting him on the toilet without success,
and keeping him near her rather than outside so that he
would not be playing with his pants fouled. It was revealed
that the mother kept the boy on the toilet many hours a day,
even putting the television in the bathroom so that he might
happen to have a bowel movement in the toilet while distracted. Clearly, she would have much more time to herself
if the boy were over the problem, and she considered seriously what she would do with that time and what she would
think about if she did not have the problem to worry about.

After exploring the mother-child dyad, the therapist
shifted to the similar consequences if father was a successful
father. Then he dealt with the consequences between the
couple if they became a normal married couple. They had
never had a baby-sitter and gone out together, because of
the child's problem. Where would they go if they could go
out, and who would decide? This approach was not emphasized as a way of exploring their struggle but as a new
decision area they would have to work out. The father
thought they could tolerate going out together if they just
had the chance. So did mother, mentioning how often she
had wanted to go out but never did.

A similar discussion of consequences was centered on
what the couple would talk about in the evening if they did
not have this problem to discuss. Each evening there was a
report on the mother's difficult day with the problem. At
the dinner table the focus was on the boy, since he would
get a faraway look in his eye and leave the table, and they
would rush to put him on the toilet—without effect. Husband and wife decided they could find something to talk
about beside the child's bowel movements.

This discussion of consequences is in a framework of
benevolent concern, which makes it difficult for the family
to get angry at the therapist. Yet from their point of view
the therapist is a successful husband and father who can
tolerate being normal, and he is suggesting that possibly they
cannot. It is a provoking situation for the family. Typically,

they become highly motivated to solve their problem to prove that they can tolerate being normal.

Another aspect of this restraining technique should be emphasized. When the therapist talked with the couple about having a normal husband-wife relationship and being able to tolerate going out together, he was provoking them about their ability to be attractive to each other. In the process he could be said to be establishing a pseudo-courtship relationship with the wife that was provoking the peripheral husband to reclaim her. Although the details of what happened were not explored, apparently the husband sat down with the child one evening after the second interview and firmly told him that if he did not have his bowel movement in the toilet he would be given castor oil and seated on the toilet until he did. The next day the boy went to the toilet properly. This action could be described as the father "spontaneously" intervening between an overinvolved wife and child.

On the day of the third scheduled interview, the mother called and said they would rather not come. The boy had gone to the toilet properly the day before and they did not want "to rock the boat." Whereas previously the mother had talked in a helpless way, this time she was quite firm and assertive in her statement.

The family returned the following week at the scheduled time and reported that the boy was now regularly using the toilet every day and had not had a bowel movement in his pants again. The mother mentioned that she was able to enjoy the time to do other things with herself. Both husband and wife talked about having gone out together and enjoyed it. They indicated to the therapist, without explicitly saying so, that they could tolerate being normal.

The therapist began his disengagement process by saying that he was puzzled that the problem had resolved itself and that he was pleased they had done so well. Credit was given to the family for the change. An appointment was set for two weeks later to be sure that everything was all right. In two weeks the family returned, reporting that all was well. The therapist deliberately shifted from a helping relationship to a social one in a brief interview. His task was to shift to a peer relationship with the parents and move out of the expert-client relationship. Such a shift can be calculatedly achieved in brief therapy.

This restraining approach can be used as a main therapeutic approach or as a different type of intervention when therapy is not going well. It can also be used when there is competition between a therapist and parent and directives are not being followed. The following case illustrates the use of this technique when a mother and female therapist are approaching an impasse.

A family presented the problem of a 15-year-old girl who was defying the mother, refusing to do what she asked, answering back rudely, and so on. The mother was a stepmother to this girl and to her 8- and 9-year-old sisters. She also had a two-month-old baby that was her only child with this father.

In the first interview, the daughter cried and would hardly talk, the stepmother was angry and complaining, and the father was busy explaining that the daughter had suffered a miserable childhood with an alcoholic mother. It had taken the father years to finally separate from his first wife, and he felt guilty about what the girl had experienced.

In the first interview the therapist attempted several tasks for the family that would involve mother and daughter in some way. The mother objected to every single task and refused to do anything with the daughter. Her attitude was that she had enough of the girl and the clinic could take her or give her to somebody else who would straighten her out.

The interview was supervised "live" by Cloé Madanes who began to believe that the problem was the relationship between the mother and the therapist. They were both in their early twenties and it appeared the mother was refusing to accept instructions from a female therapist of the same age who obviously had little experience, but who was a professional person while the mother was not.

Having suggested the previous tasks and watched them fail, Madanes called the therapist out of the room and suggested to her that she use an approach of restraining the family from changing. When the therapist returned to the family, she said she could probably help them solve the problem with the daughter, but she was not sure she should, because she was concerned about what consequences there would be if the problem was solved. When the family said there would be only positive consequences, the therapist pointed out that the father had been very close to his daughter through very difficult times, and he was also close to his wife. If mother and daughter became close to each other, father might feel excluded and jealous and be unable to tolerate such feelings. Father assured the therapist that he could tolerate his wife and daughter being closer. The therapist also pointed out that the two little girls might become jealous, and she ended the interview suggesting that the family think about the consequences for the next time.

During the week, the therapist and supervisor prepared a list of possible consequences that the therapist memorized. When the family returned, the therapist pointed out that a possible consequence would be that the mother would be a better mother than her own mother if she solved this difficult problem of three stepdaughters and a new baby. She suggested that some mothers could not tolerate being better mothers than their own mothers. The mother said she could certainly tolerate that. A few other consequences were mentioned by the therapist, such as the reaction of the mother's mother, how the change would affect the new baby, and so on. The family denied there would be any problem. The daughter began to talk a little. A week later mother and daughter came in reporting they had gone shopping together. The mother had bought a miniskirt for the daughter against the father's wishes. The daughter had cleaned the house and done all the laundry. The therapist pointed out that the mother was siding with the daughter against father over the miniskirt issue, and that this was an example of what the therapist feared. Perhaps the father could not tolerate this change. The father said he certainly could. The therapist suggested the relationship between mother and daughter had not really changed because, although they were doing their duty towards each other, there was no real friendliness and no real pleasure in each other. Therefore it was important that for the next week they still think about the consequences of a change.

The next week the family reported that the father had been on a night shift and that the mother and daughter spent the evenings together playing monopoly and card games and enjoying themselves. They were getting along well together. The therapist expressed her pleasure with this situation and apologized because she had not been able to help the family but the problem had somehow disappeared. The therapist apologized in a rather embarrassed way, and the mother reassured her in a rather patronizing way that she had done her best. They separated with the agreement that the therapist would call in a few weeks to see how they were doing, and the family would consult if another problem came up. A follow-up several months later showed they were doing well and there were no other problems.

This approach, restraining the family from changing, is effective with sensitive, overconcerned middle-class parents but is not as effective with workingclass or poor families. The family must be keenly attuned to the therapist's opinion of them.

In summary, the process from the beginning point at which one parent is overinvolved with a child to the end point at which the adults are involved with each other and the child is attached to peers cannot be made in one leap. There are a series of stages that will be determined by the approach. If the approach is through the use of the peripheral person, there will be a stage of coalition among therapist, peripheral person, and child. Then a stage of involvement between therapist and adults, and finally a stage of the therapist disengaging from the adults. If the approach is through the overinvolved person and the child, there is a stage of intense involvement between that adult, therapist and child, and then a disengagement of therapist from both of them.

When the entrance of the therapist is through the married couple, there is first a focus on the child, then a focus on the marriage, and finally a separation of the therapist from the couple.

When families are treated from this point of view, certain rules will make the therapist more effective. He should not oppose or confront the family members with what they are doing wrong but must "accept" what they are doing and within that framework make a change. The therapist should not make interpretations to help them understand why or how they are behaving. He should use interpretations tactically to motivate the family members to do what must be done. The therapist should not explore the past but should focus on the present situation and organize the family to change what is happening. The therapist should not seek long-term involvement but, rather, brief, intensive intervention and rapid disengagement.

6

Marriage Therapy as a Triangle

All clinicians deal with marriages in some way, but their points of view about marriage vary widely. For some therapists a married couple is "the basic building block" of the family and the most important entity. For other therapists the marital dyad is one of several subunits of the family. For yet others, the married "couple" is actually a triad because it is defined in terms of the inclusion or exclusion of someone else. With this latter view it is possible to see different stages of marriages. For example, a therapist may observe that the husband and wife spend the early part of their marriage differentiating from their parents. As this task is accomplished, they produce children that become part of the marriage. At no point do they form a distinct dyad. Of course, the issue is one of definition. If one is thinking in units of three people, a marriage does not exist as an independent entity. The description must include an observer, a therapist, a friend, parent, child, or some other third person.

The clinical question is how to think about the marital situation in a way that is most productive for bringing about change. At one time in the development of marital counseling a couple was viewed as two individuals associating with one another and they were interviewed individually. The therapy success with that approach has a reputation of being poor. Marital counseling also did not develop theoretical contributions. Instead, counselors simply accepted psychological theories of individuals and applied them to married couples. For example, when individual behavior was explained in terms of past causes, a wife or husband was said to be behaving as she or he was because of the influence of their pasts. Each spouse was supposed to be projecting into their current marriage the ideas of his or her parents' marriage or of introjections of mothers and fathers, and so on. During this period the idea of "neurotic choice of partners" was used to explain a man's choice of a wife who was like his mother (despite the possibility that his family, particularly his mother, chose his wife, which would be a more than two-person description of mate selection).

As family therapists began to accept views that were more social, they began to interview married couples as well as whole families together. During this period couples began to be described as dyads. Therapists were trying to break free of individual descriptions. Couples were viewed as interacting systems, as rule-governed entities, or as conditioning systems in which what one person did reinforced what the other did. It was observed that couples followed sequences of behavior that they could not seem to change when they tried as if they had interpersonal reflexes.

In describing rule-governed behavior, an example of how a couple follows rules is in the way the two people deal with an issue in terms of maximizing and minimizing it. When some partners talk together they will tend to balance each other out. Whatever they are talking about, whether work or sex or problems with children, one of them will say the problem is serious and the other will say it is not. As one spouse minimizes a problem, the other spouse must maximize it to compensate. This compensation in turn requires the first to minimize even more in response to an exaggeration. If a therapist believes that making partners aware of their rules will cause change, he can point out what they are doing. Often in such a case the wife will agree that it is a serious problem that they follow that rule, while the husband will say it really is not a problem. Should the therapist use directives, one spouse is likely to take the directive seriously and the other spouse will not. As therapists discovered the interpersonal power of rule-governed behavior, they found themselves with increasing doubts about free will. Often clinicians would behave as if they believed a person could choose his acts while privately suspecting that it was not so. For therapeutic effectiveness, it is often best to expect people to choose what to do, but a research view tends to be more deterministic.

When therapists observed that what one spouse did provoked the other, who provoked the first in turn, they began to see that a dyad was unstable and that it required a third person to prevent a "runaway." For example, if two spouses competed over who was most ill, total collapse could only be prevented by pulling in of a third party. Rivalrous quarrels that amplified in intensity required someone outside the dyad to intervene and stabilize it.* If a third person is regularly activated to stabilize a dyad, the unit is in fact not dyadic but is at least a triad. With this view, the unit becomes a unit of three people. Similarly, if a husband and wife regularly communicate to each other through a third person, the unit is three people instead of a married "couple." The observation that a child with a problem stabilizes a marital dyad led to the idea that the basic unit of family therapy should be parents and child. Typically, in family therapy it is assumed that a shift will take place from the unit of parents and child to the married couple. Some therapists who make that shift will change from thinking in a unit of

---

*For a description of this issue in a native culture, see G. Bateson, *Naven* (Palo Alto, Calif.: Stanford University Press, 1958).

three to thinking in a unit of two, as in the husband–wife relationship. Yet if one is consistent in thinking in terms of triads, whether one is dealing with parents and children or with a husband and wife, the unit is three, not two. In fact, one can note that the therapist replaces the child with the couple and thus stabilizes the dyad. Then the problem becomes one of how the therapist can exit without the couple unstabilizing and without bringing in the child again.

At this time many clinicians are learning to think in the unit of three and giving up the dyadic unit even when doing marriage therapy.* As a way of commenting on this complex subject, the social context of marital therapy can be emphasized.

The first idea to accept is that a marital "problem" is not only unique to that couple, but that it differs depending on how the couple came to the door of the therapist. The three main ways that couples arrive to present a problem are through a symptom of an individual, through a child, or through a request for marital counseling. Each situation requires a different therapeutic approach.

Symptoms as Presenting Problems

When a therapist deals with symptoms effectively, if the client is married, he necessarily finds himself involved in marital issues. As an obvious example, when a wife has anxiety spells that irregularly incapacitate her, a therapist is interested in the function of such spells in the marriage. He may find, for example, that she is anxious whenever her husband wants her to do something that she would rather not do. Or he may find that the wife becomes anxious whenever her husband becomes depressed, and that he comes out of his depression to help her when she is anxious. Some

---

*I have written about marital therapy largely from a dyadic view in *Strategies of Psychotherapy* (New York: Grune & Stratton, 1963). I have also presented the different stages of marriage over the life cycle in *Uncommon Therapy* (New York: Norton, 1973).

therapists will try to persuade the couple that the real problem is a marital one. Others will continue to focus on the symptom while dealing with the marital problem. After an improvement, these latter therapists may make a new contract to deal with the marriage.

Whenever a married person has a severe symptom it inevitably has a function in the marriage, and there will be consequences in the marriage when a symptom is cured. For example, if a wife has headaches that incapacitate her several days a week and if those headaches are cured, she and her husband will face a different marital relationship than they had previously. The man who cannot do certain things because of an exaggerated fear of some kind usually has a wife who both benefits from this problem and is exasperated by it. To resolve the "fear," it is best to deal with the marriage. Treating an individual for symptoms is like assuming a stick has one end.

A Child as the Presenting Problem

In most therapy with disturbed children, it can be assumed that if the parents could easily concede their marital difficulties the child would not be expressing the problem. Some married couples appear to be able to have savage battles without involving their children, while others center the marital struggle on the child. When a therapist helps parents exclude a child from their struggle, often they will exclude the in-laws from their marital struggles. Similarly, if a mother-in-law problem can be resolved, the parents seem to deal with each other without triangulating with the child. That is, if the married pair draw a generation line in one direction by holding together in relation to the children, they also seem to hold together in relation to the in-laws.

It should be emphasized that a child may be part of a marital struggle even if the couple is divorced: the war can still continue through the child. When a divorced mother offers a child as the problem it is essential to inquire into the involvement of the divorced father. Dealing with the divorced couple to have them reach agreement about the child is not marital counseling but postdivorce counseling, which usually requires that the therapist decline to deal with any issues except the child.

When the child is an adolescent or young adult and has reached the age of leaving home, the parents are actually entering on a new marital contract. The therapist faced with that kind of problem must assist them in working out a new set of issues.

Another way a therapist finds himself dealing with marriage is when the presenting problem is a family crisis. When there are threats of violence, suicide, or family behavior that arouse the community, a therapist is often called on to do something. The approach to marital issues at this time requires action rather than reflection, and the therapist must often take responsibility and make decisions for people who are in no state of mind to do so themselves.

Some family crises happen only once. But there are also marriages in which a crisis happens regularly, as part of a cycle. There may be threats of beating or suicide, and then amiable behavior, and then beatings and suicide threats erupting again. The marital therapist needs to bring the partners together and change that eruption cycle, or to help them really separate without an unfortunate consequence. Typically, the therapist tries to bring them together. If that does not work, he must move decisively to separate them. When he makes such a move, he must deal with his own uncertainties about how and whether he should have such influence on the lives of people. When there are threats of violence or suicide, the therapist himself also faces risks.

It is in crisis times that the most can be done with a couple, and that the most is asked of the therapist. A crisis means instability, and working with a couple at such a time can be emotionally upsetting for the therapist but most beneficial to the couple. If the therapist uses medication, tranquilizing partners when they are upset, he may prevent change and delay the resolution of issues until the next crisis.

The Marriage as the Presenting Problem

When a couple presents a marital problem, the therapist's views can depend on who is interviewed. If the therapist sees the wife alone, he or she may sympathize with her for having such a problem husband. When such an interview is followed by an interview with the husband alone, the therapist usually discovers that there were a number of things the wife neglected to mention and that the husband has a justified point of view too. When seeing them together, the therapist discovers patterns of action between them that show the marriage to be quite different from what either spouse described. With experiences of this kind, the therapist learns not to naively take sides with one spouse against the other and learns the value of seeing how people actually deal with each other rather than listening to their reports about how they do. When the couple is seen within the larger family group, a different understanding of the marriage is added because it is seen in context.

Usually a couple present a marital problem as an attempt to stay together. Otherwise, the couple would not come together to present the problem. Sometimes one of the spouses is determined to separate but has not revealed this decision to the other. For example, a husband may want a separation but not want to upset his wife. Therefore he will appear in marital counseling supposedly to work out problems but actually to arrange an amiable divorce. This intent can be learned only by seeing the spouses alone, since it will not be revealed in the conjoint interview. Also, sometimes the only way to learn certain kinds of information (such as an involvement in an extramarital affair) is through an individual interview.

When the spouses describe their marital problems they sometimes characterize each other as being mean, vicious, hostile, and so on. It is better if the therapist does not think of their actions in that way. Underlying most marital problems is a protectiveness that keeps the problem going. It is the benevolence that is often most difficult to change. The wife who viciously insults her husband can be seen as a villainess, but one can also think of her behavior as a way of helping her husband. If he is in despair and she provokes him, he comes out of his unfortunate state and becomes angry at her, thereby feeling better. Similarly, a love affair can be seen as a betrayal and a way of attacking a spouse, but it can also be seen as a way of protecting a spouse by helping him or her to avoid sex or to maintain a safer distance. Whatever is being said, there are always things not said because they would be too harmful.

When one examines a presenting marital problem, it is evident that the couple is following habitual rules of behavior and that the problem is at the level of those rules. For example, the wife may say the problem is that her husband is irresponsible with money and does not do what he should. The husband may protest that his wife is too prudish and never wants to enjoy herself, so he seeks his pleasure elsewhere. From the therapist's viewpoint, the couple is following a number of rules that make this kind of behavior appropriate. One rule may be that the wife is to behave responsibly and the husband irresponsibly. Why they have that rule, or how long they have had it, is probably unknowable. Changing the rule requires the therapist to intervene in such a way that they cannot continue with such behavior.

Whatever rules a couple is following, the therapist is part of the rules. For example, a couple with a rule about responsibility will follow it in therapy. The husband will behave irresponsibly about the therapy and the marriage, be reluctant to come, miss appointments, and so on. The wife will responsibly bring the husband to the therapy, insist upon bringing out all the issues, and so on. The therapeutic leverage comes in the way the therapist changes that rule as it is used in relation to him (not by objectively commenting on it to the couple).

One should also keep in mind that when rules are followed, the participants are sometimes replaceable parts. For example, when the wife is responsible and the husband irresponsible, a shift can sometimes take place so that the wife becomes irresponsible and the husband takes on the responsible position. The marriage relationship has not changed, the positions have just reversed.

In the complexity of the millions of messages exchanged by a married couple from moment to moment, there are multiple rules at multiple levels. There are not only rules about how to behave with each other, how to relate to outsiders, and so on; but also there are rules about how to negotiate rules, and rules about who is to establish the rules. Much of a marriage therapist's time may be spent patiently negotiating agreements over specific issues that can generalize to the larger situation of the couple. Given the nature of therapy, the therapist must be simplistic and focus on issues that seem crude compared with the complex richness of conceptualization involved in a research investigation of a marriage.

One of the ways to think about marital difficulties is in terms of flexibility. When the rules of a marriage are too rigid, the partners are distressed because they cannot adapt to changes. In a successful marriage, it appears that the two spouses are able to be equals in some areas and the wife can also take care of the husband and he of her. A couple that is limited in range can follow only one pattern. For example, the wife may be able to take care of the husband, but they cannot shift, allowing the husband to take care of her. Therefore, if the wife becomes ill, the husband must become more ill so that she can continue to take care of him since that is the only behavior pattern they have. Or the two people may take care of each other, but being equals is against the rules. Therefore, the partners can never function as peers, and so decisions made by equals are not part of their repertoire. One of the functions of marital therapy is to enlarge the possibilities of the two people so they have a wider range of behavior. Just as one way to see the goal of all therapy is to introduce complexity, so in marital therapy the opportunities of the partners are greater if their relationship has more complex possibilities.

When doing therapy with a couple, it is best for the therapist to consider that whatever the partners do in relation to each other is also in relation to the therapist. That is, the therapist should consider the triad whether he explains that context to the couple or not. If the therapist is male, he is in one set of coalitions that are different from those of the female therapist. If the therapist is older, the response of a young couple or an older couple will be different in his presence. If the male therapist is admiring of the wife, he must accept the fact that the husband will have a response to that. Should the therapist side with the husband, he must take into account what consequences this coalition will have for his relationship with the wife. There is no "objective" data in marriage therapy. A comment by the therapist is not merely a comment but also a coalition with one spouse in relation to the other or with the unit against a larger group.

Where the coalition becomes most important as an issue is with those therapists who are "growth" oriented and primarily concerned about the individual. Often the therapist may feel that the wife outgrew the husband and it is therefore appropriate that she divorce him, or that the husband "outgrew" the wife who is "only a housewife." Sometimes therapists who are supporting a feminist position encourage a wife to assert herself whether the husband likes it or not. Or a therapist may feel that one spouse is willing to work on the problems and the other is not and so separation should take place. A fundamental assumption should be that if the couple separates while in therapy, and did not come in with separation as the presenting problem, the therapist is part of that separation and has contributed to it by coalition behavior.

Although a therapist need not take the position that separation and divorce should never occur—obviously such a position is not sound—the issue is whether the therapist is being responsible. A therapist who thinks in threes will not naively break up a marriage because of ignorance about being involved.

One further note on separation. Sometimes a couple wishes to live separately while "working on" their marriage. To do therapy on the marriage of a separated couple has been a waste of time, in my experience. There are too many forces leading them apart when living separately, and the sessions tend to be conversations about problems rather than attempts to solve those problems. It is best to force the issue by requiring them to live together if marriage therapy is to be done.

When working with a couple the therapist should organize what is said and done so that the therapy has specific destinations. As a therapist intervenes, he or she finds that a philosophy of life and marriage is necessary as a guide. The therapist must think through the issues of separation and divorce as well as responsibilities within the family group. Simply not giving advice to a couple will not avoid the issue, since what the therapist thinks will be communicated somehow. It is preferable to clarify one's own thinking so that the marital problem of a couple does not meet an expert too confused and uncertain to be helpful.

Often a marital therapist may feel like a labor negotiator, or a diplomat involved in conflictual issues. If he joins one side against the other, he becomes part of the problem rather than part of the solution. Yet inevitably he is personally involved in whatever the issues may be; and so he may find himself taking sides whether he likes it or not. What is so appealing, and yet so stressful, about marital counseling is the way the action draws on the feelings of the therapist. His own biases about men and women, and his own attitude about marriage, are forced out into the open as he struggles with the marital issues. He usually finds out his own marriage undergoes changes in response to his experience with couples. Sometimes these changes are unpredictable. As he helps a couple clarify some positions, obscure others, and negotiate compromises, he also tries to stabilize the beneficial changes with the couple—while in his own life there may be changes not so beneficial, which must not interfere with his work. Yet if successful therapy is defined as solving specific problems so that there is more variety and complexity in the life of an individual, the opportunity for the therapist to achieve that goal in his own personal life is extended more through marital therapy than any other type.

Guidelines for the Therapy

How the therapist approaches a marital problem will be determined by many factors. What to do will be determined by the unique nature of the particular situation, although one can apply a few general rules. One way to approach the issue here is to emphasize what not to do as a way of presenting common difficulties. The following discussion points out some things to avoid when dealing with a marital couple.

The therapist should *avoid minimizing problems.* Whatever the issues between the couple, in the beginning of therapy the therapist should not try to soften the problem by minimizing it. The couple might respond politely, but they will feel he does not understand the severity of their situation. If the wife does not feel her husband treats her with respect, the therapist should explore that issue in detail. If the husband thinks his wife acts bored with his friends, the therapist should emphasize that as an important problem. A problem may seem trivial, but will represent a larger issue. Dismissing it will dismiss the larger problem. A small problem may be an analogy for a large one.

The therapist should *avoid abstractions.* It is better, whenever possible, to require the couple to focus on specific behaviors rather than on larger issues. The intellectual wife who is protesting about the rights of women may hesitate to state her objection to picking up her husband's underwear, but that situation may be where the larger issue manifests itself. The husband who protests that his wife is not affectionate can be focused on how he wishes to be received when he comes home from work. The therapist needs to search for specific behavior so that he can devise a directive that will lead to change.

A good therapist will *avoid consistently being in a coalition.* Although at times a therapist will side with a wife and at times with a husband, the art of therapy is to avoid the consistent coalition. One should join a spouse against another spouse only in a calculated way for a specific purpose. If a man says he will not allow his wife to work and the therapist is female, she may find herself wanting to save the wife from that villain of a male. Such an approach will lose. The therapist's problem is how to keep her own biases from intruding into the changes sought by the couple. Similarly, if a husband is giving up a fine career opportunity because his wife will not move away from her family, the therapist should not automatically side with the husband because he thinks he needs to join him against the wife on this issue. A therapist must always find ways to monitor his or her behavior to determine whether a covert coalition has happened. A colleague placed behind a one-way mirror is a help, if available.

To avoid coalitions it helps to keep in mind that one can be trapped by a spouse by either seductive or provoking behavior. It is not just happenstance that issues important to the therapist come out, because the spouses will test what is important to that therapist. One should also not assume a simple situation but expect more complex issues. A husband who "won't allow" his wife to work may have reasons the therapist does not know about. For example, the therapist may not know that the wife has arranged that the husband say just that.

Insofar as the therapist is an expert, he is higher in the hierarchy than either spouse, and if he joins one spouse against another he is crossing generation lines and can be causing the problems he is trying to change. As a general rule, when one is caught in such a coalition, it is best to interview alone the spouse one has been joining against. Whenever one sees a person alone, the tendency is to join that person against others. Therefore, if a woman therapist is siding with a wife against a husband, seeing the husband alone can help. However, one must balance the situation by seeing that the other spouse is not neglected.

Another solution is to bring in more people at that time—either a colleague behind the mirror, or the couple's children or parents. A larger group will shift coalition patterns.

In certain situations a therapist may want to *un*stabilize a marriage to produce change. Sometimes the marriage may be stable but miserable. An effective way to unstabilize the marriage is to join one spouse against the other and simply hold that position. Whatever is said, the therapist sides with one spouse and defines the other as wrong. It can be either spouse. The therapist must appear to be intending to hold to his coalition permanently, even though he may intend to switch later. This procedure, perhaps best developed by Minuchin, will bring out emotions and action in a stable couple. However, it requires skill and should not be used lightly by the average therapist.

The therapist should also *avoid debates about life*. Some couples will wish to discuss the meaning of life with a therapist; they should do that with other people. When philosophical issues come up, the therapist should shift the couple to more concrete issues. The task of the therapy is not to have the couple persuade the therapist to change his ideology or for the couple to be educated about life by him; it is to have the two people deal with each other in more productive ways.

It is a good idea to *avoid the past*. It has become a cliché to say one should focus on the present rather than the past in therapy, yet many therapists continue in different ways to involve themselves in past issues. This problem is greater with a marital couple than with other types of client situations because marital partners are experts at debating past issues. They often see their situation as a product of what has previously happened, may quarrel about who was right about what, and may end with bad feelings and no resolution. They can then blame the therapist for letting the quarrel happen. No matter how interested a therapist is in how people got to the point where they are, he should restrain himself from such explorations.

Sometimes, of course, something about the past can be used to motivate a couple in the present, for example, by finding some time in the past when they were getting along fine and so this is possible. Past ways of solving problems can also sometimes be used again. However, when there are unforgiveable things in the past, the therapist should not explore that past but find something to do in the present that allows forgiveness, so the couple can move on to better times. A task that is an ordeal for a couple can sometimes help them go beyond a bitter experience. For example, a Puerto Rican faith healer may resolve the problem of a wife having had an affair by taking the two steps that are often used by traditional marriage therapists with this problem. First, he persuades the couple that the wife was not really responsible for the affair, it was a ghost of another woman (other therapists might say the wife is not responsible because of an unconscious acting out). He sends the couple a long distance to a remote place, to a particular tree, to perform a specific ceremony to exorcise the ghost. Such an ordeal provides a ritual for ending the issue and gives both partners an investment in its ending. (A similar ordeal can be paying for expensive individual or marriage therapy.)

In a first interview with a married couple, some exploration of the past may be necessary, but by the end of it the therapist should have shifted to the present context. Various ways of dropping the past must be developed. A "fresh start" is a phrasing that is appealing; and it is always best to start the couple on a new agreement that they will attempt a change. In extreme cases it might be necessary to simply forbid a couple to discuss anything that happened prior to a week ago. However, one should try to avoid arguing with a couple about dismissing the past and simply shift the topic to the present and future.

The therapist should also *avoid thinking that problems are identical.* It is disrespectful to believe that a problem enjoyed by a married couple is the same as the therapist's own problem, even when it appears to be. If, for example, a couple never goes out together, and neither does the therapist and his or her spouse, these are not the same problem. Just as each snowflake is different, why one couple does not go out and what to do about it is different from why another couple does not go out, because their ecology is different.

When a therapist is young, he should not try to appear wiser than he is. The beginning therapist is often young and even unmarried. Faced with a couple married for twenty-five years, the beginner may be tempted to act as if he understands that stage of marriage as well as they do. It is not so. Instead, the therapist should find a stance to work from that is acceptable to an older couple. For example, the beginner can say, "Obviously you know more about marriage than I do since you've been married a long time, and certainly you know more about your own marriage than I do. But as an outsider, I can offer you an objective view of some of your problems."

A therapist should *avoid leaving goals unformulated.* It is often more difficult to formulate goals for marital problems than for other kinds. Yet out of negotiations with the couple should come goals. If a therapist does not have a destination, his path to get there is likely to meander.

The therapist should *avoid forcing a couple to ask explicitly for what they want from each other.* Because of unfortunate ideas about "working on a problem" or "clarifying communication," some beginning therapists tend to ask a couple to say everything right out in the open. This approach is an abnormal way of communicating. Saying to a wife, "Ask your husband for what you want," may be asking her to behave in a way she would rather not. She might feel that if she asks for something directly, it would be unwifely or it might risk shaming her husband if he could not deliver. It is sometimes better to request more indirection. For example, the therapist can say, "I want you to ask for what you want from your husband in such a way that it takes him awhile to understand what you mean."

The therapist should *avoid crystallizing power struggles.* Although for research purposes it may be useful to think of a marital problem in terms of a struggle for control, that is not the best way to think about it for clinical purposes. One should think in terms of clarifying issues rather than in terms of power struggles. Suppose, for example, that a wife complains that her husband spends too much time in his business and not enough in the home. The husband may respond that it is up to him to decide what is necessary in his business. If the therapist thinks of the problem in terms of a struggle for control, he does not see as many options as he would otherwise. For example, he might overlook the possibility that the wife wants to share more in the business. To talk about control or power as a way of clarifying issues can actually crystallize the issue in such a way that change is more difficult. By emphasizing power, one can be limited to one or the other person winning, and other alternatives can be blocked off.

Multiple therapists can make the situation more difficult to change. One therapist can do therapy more successfully than two, and one is more economical. Usually cotherapy is set up for the sake of uncertain therapists, not for the case.

A problem occurs when one of the spouses is in "individual" therapy with someone else while they also want marriage therapy. Usually this combination is not wise. For example, a husband may be in therapy and the individual therapist may feel the therapy is not getting anywhere but does not wish to give up the patient. So he suggests adding marital therapy, hoping that might make some kind of change. The marriage therapist then starts under a handicap. The husband is talking to his individual therapist about what happens in the marital sessions, thus livening up his therapist. But the wife has only the marital therapist and no one to talk about the situation who is exclusively on her side. Usually she insists at some point on individual therapy for herself. At that point the couple either drop the marital therapy or else each has an ally outside the marital therapy. This coalition structure makes change in the marriage more difficult. It is better not to combine couple and individual therapy. Even at the risk of antagonizing a referring therapist who wants to hold his patient, it is better to suggest that for the period of the marital therapy the couple only have therapy together.

Finally, the therapist should *avoid allowing irreversible positions.* Although at times it may be necessary to force a situation where there is no turning back, in most situations it is extremely important to keep a husband or wife from stating a position they cannot change. The therapy should not allow free expression by the couple but only expression that will achieve a purpose. If a husband is saying something that the therapist can see will make the man look like a sap, or will force him to defend an indefensible position, the therapist should intervene and not allow it. If the wife is going to state something she will not be able to undo, then the therapist should distract her. The goal should be to allow room for change, negotiation, and flexible alternatives in the life of the couple.

In summary, the marital therapist must take problems seriously, focus on specific issues, form deliberate coalitions to tip balances, not allow free expression of ideas that might cause irreversible harm, formulate goals, and not always require that couples talk explicitly about problems. Most important, the marital therapist should not assume that one couple or one problem is identical with another.

7

Problems in Training Therapists

Until quite recently a therapist could graduate from a clinical training program and be considered trained even though none of his teachers had observed him do therapy or even seen him conduct a single interview. It was also possible that a student never watched anyone do therapy so he could see how it might be done. Even more curiously, the student's success or failure with cases was never examined because therapy outcome research was not part of a clinical curriculum. Unobserved in his work and unexamined on his results, it is perhaps not surprising that the average therapist is not particularly skillful according to therapy evaluation studies.

With the introduction of one-way mirror rooms and videotape equipment, clinical training is changing. Many programs now focus sharply on training in interview skill. They also examine outcome. However, therapy training only changes when theories of how to do therapy change, not because of technical advances. One-way mirrors and audiotape have been available since the 1950s. Yet many clinical programs continue unchanged as if a need for observation

169

had not been suggested. An entirely new approach to therapy, such as therapy with a family orientation, has even been introduced into the field and yet the training continues in a traditional manner.

As clinical training programs change it is being discovered that a theory of therapy and a theory of training are often synonymous. If a teacher believes that insight causes therapeutic change, he trains a student therapist by giving the student insight into himself and his personal problems. If a therapist thinks that change occurs because of an increase in positive reinforcements, he trains his therapy student with positive reinforcement procedures. Some of the parallels between the premises of therapy and the premises of training will be offered here as current training issues.

Selecting an Orientation

Any therapy training program must make choices about what therapy *is* and how it should be done. Sometimes there are no choices because traditional procedures continue unexamined or because the setting determines the training. For example, psychologists find it difficult to learn how to do family-oriented therapy if they have only undergraduate college students as clients, because training thus takes place in universities isolated from cities. Psychiatric residents may learn little about therapy if they are forced into a framework of medication and custody because they function as agents of social control in mental hospitals.

Within the limitations imposed by a setting, the faculty of a clinical training program operates on basic premises about the nature of therapy. These premises will be offered here in terms of polar extremes, one labeled Orientation A and the opposite extreme Z. It is recognized, of course, that many teachers of therapy try to be liberal and eclectic, and therefore waver between the extremes.

Spontaneous versus Planned Change.   Within Orientation A, the responsibility for therapeutic change resides with the patient. At this extreme, it is not the responsibility of the therapist to produce change but to help people change themselves. The therapist is a reflector, a consultant, or an advisor, but he is not an enforcer of change. Usually, in this approach, the therapist helps the person understand himself and his situation; what happens then is up to the client. Should therapy fail, that failure rests with the client and only partially, if at all, with the therapist.

At the other extreme, in Orientation Z, the responsibility for change belongs to the therapist. He is expected to plan a strategy of change to bring about what the patient is paying money to achieve. If change does not occur, he is a failure. Blaming the client for not changing is not allowed.

Although these opposite premises are general orientations to therapy, they become evident as the basis of operations in a single interview. In Orientation A, what is to happen between therapist and patient in the next interview is unpredictable; it is a happening and cannot be planned since the therapist must wait to see what the patient offers. He is a responder and must wait to comment on, or interpret, what the client initiates.

In Orientation Z, the therapist is expected to make a strategic plan that takes into account what is to happen in the next interview. He initiates the action. For example, it is his job to provide a reinforcement program or a directive for the client to follow.

In the clinical training programs of Orientation A, the teacher or supervisor is an advisor or consultant to the therapist. The teacher is not responsible for the success or failure of the case. If a case is going disastrously, the supervisor may intervene, but generally the supervisor does not consider a failure to be his fault. What happens between student and supervisor is spontaneous and unplanned. The supervisor must wait to see what the student brings him, and failure is on the head of the student. If the supervisor has helped the student understand himself and the dynamics of the case, he has done his job.

In Orientation Z, the supervisor is responsible for what happens with a case and is expected to plan with the ther-

apist what is to happen. In facilities where there is "live"
supervision, the teacher is placed behind a one-way mirror
watching the student work. He is expected to telephone the
student during the interview and guide him, if necessary,
or bring the therapist out and discuss what is happening.
In this arrangement, if change is not taking place, the supervisor is a failure. Not only is it his job to protect a client from
a beginning therapist, but also he must help a student in difficulty. If a client is provoking a student and so preventing
change, the supervisor's job is to find a way to help the student solve that problem. Just as the therapist is expected to
find a way to change the client if the client's life is going
badly, so is it the supervisor's job to find a way to change
the student if the student's therapy is going badly.

   A Growth versus a Problem Orientation.   One can think
of the goal of therapy either as the expansion of the life
of a human being or as the solution of specific problems.
Orientation A is based on the premise that the goal is to help
people develop themselves and so the therapist's task is essentially an educational one. He wishes to focus on enriching
people's lives. If a family presents a child as a problem because he sets fires, the therapist has as his goal the development of the child or family. The fire setting is thus "only
a symptom."

   At the opposite extreme, in Orientation Z, the therapist
is a problem solver. It is his job to clarify and get people over
the specific problems they bring to him. If a child is presented as a problem because he sets fires, the goal of the
therapist is to arrange that the child no longer sets fires. In
the process of solving the fire setting, organizational changes
may be made that allow the child and parents to grow and
develop, but the focus is on the symptom.

   These two orientations produce different therapeutic
action. Orientation A tends to leave the details of symptoms
unexamined and to focus instead on the general background
of the client. Directives are not used to bring about a change.
Instead, the approach is interpretive or experiential. Often
the therapist attempts to persuade the clients that what they

really want is something other than the complaint they offer. For example, parents who present a child as the problem may be influenced to see the marriage as the "real" problem. Or a therapist may describe a child as "scapegoated" and the therapist may feel his task is to point out other children who are problems, to get the problem child out of the scapegoat role. In contrast, Orientation Z accepts what the client offers as the problem and focuses on that. If a symptom is offered, the therapist engineers change through the symptom. If a child is offered as the problem, the therapist accepts the description and only later may he shift to other children or marital issues.

Training a student therapist can be conceived of as providing him with a rich philosophical life and helping him grow as an individual. Or it can be conceived of as teaching specific skills. In Orientation A, there is a trend toward helping the young therapist grow and develop himself. Instead of being taught interview skills, he is encouraged to enter therapy himself so that he can discover from his own experience what the human mind is about. It is assumed that the clinical program and his personal therapy will help him become a mature and developed individual and also an expert therapist. At the other extreme, in Orientation Z, it is assumed that a therapist grows with success in his work and the first task is to train him to do his work well. The focus is on helping him solve the problems he meets in therapy, not helping him enrich his personal life. For example, if a therapist has difficulty dealing with an authority figure, such as a grandfather, in therapy, the two training programs would have different emphases. In Orientation A, the therapist would be encouraged to understand how he feels about authority figures and to resolve that personal problem. In Orientation Z, the training program would be expected to train the therapist in specific ways to deal with grandfathers.

To put the matter another way, according to Orientation A the client should welcome therapy because it is good for people and will make them part of a special elite who have had a unique experience. In Orientation Z, therapy is for handicapped people who wish to get back to normal.

Understanding versus Action as a Cause of Change.   Orientation A includes therapists who assume that people should be more self-aware. They think that if a client understands what he is doing, and why, he will not do it anymore. Thus the therapist's job is to help the person understand himself both cognitively and experientially. The approach may be to lift repression by making conscious the unconscious, within the transference framework, or it may be to make interpretations about communication to help people understand how they are dealing with one another. This approach sometimes includes the idea that if a person expresses his emotions he will change, and so it emphasizes the honest and open expression of "real" feelings. Within this orientation, a case conference tends to focus on individual dynamics including the past history that led up to the problem. Or, if the conference expresses a family orientation, it tends to focus on interaction process and dynamics. The conference will involve discussion of the ways family members interact in both verbal and nonverbal ways. Such discussions do not usually emphasize what to do to bring about change.

In Orientation Z, it is assumed that neither understanding nor the expression of emotion causes change. Therefore the therapy will not involve interpretation or uncovering. Instead, the therapist must plan a strategy and devise directives requiring new behavior. These directives may be types of behavior programs for an individual, or directives for a family. The conference will involve little discussion of dynamics and a great deal of discussion of what to do in the therapy and how to do it.

Within Orientation Z, it is expected that a symptom cannot be resolved or a problem solved by merely talking about it. Therefore both therapy and training will emphasize bringing the problem into the therapy room. If a child has temper tantrums and bangs his head, only having a discussion about this behavior is not likely to lead to change. What is required is action—the head banging should happen in the therapy room. If a couple has a problem of fighting, they should fight in the room. Of course, some problems cannot be brought into the room, but those that can be should be put into action.

Because of the emphasis on self-awareness and individual experience, therapists in Orientation A are willing to bring clients together in group therapy. Since the emphasis is on changing the individuals, it does not matter if they are interacting with strangers or with a "pretend" family. Therapists with this view will also bring several families together in a large group, usually assuming that the members will learn from each other and, by thus understanding their own families differently, will change.

In Orientation Z, it is the behavior within a natural group that must change, because the therapist is trying to change repeating sequences involving several people habitually together. A man may understand how he relates to women in a group therapy setting, but that does not mean he will change his relationship with his wife. To change in relation to his wife he must be interviewed with the wife and not with other women.

Finally, the emphasis on understanding often leads therapists within Orientation A to help clients notice how they are treating the therapist. "Have you noticed that you are resisting me as if I were an authority figure?" says the authority-figure therapist. Or, "The way you are behaving is making me angry." It is assumed that if the client knows how he or she is treating the therapist they will not do that anymore. Orientation Z assumes that how the therapist feels is his or her own problem and need not be pointed out to clients in the hope they will stop doing what they are doing. It also assumes the therapist must behave differently if clients are resisting and must not comment on that resistance.

Training within these two approaches tends to reflect the basic orientations. One approach assumes that a therapist learns by understanding himself and supervision therefore consists of conversation about his conduct with a case. The other approach assumes that the problems of the student therapist must appear in action before the supervisor.

Within Orientation A, it is sometimes assumed that if a therapist understands his own personal involvement with his patients he will be a competent therapist. The teacher's talk is intended to make him aware of his biases and to change his way of thinking. If the student is cleared of his own neurosis and fully understands his involvement with his own family, he will be a good therapist. Given this assumption, therapists are persuaded to enter personal therapy or to have encounter experiences in groups. One premise carried over into the training is the idea that since the patient is expected to confess everything about himself, the therapist is also expected to confess all. In family therapy training programs within Orientation A, the therapist may be expected to go through simulated family exercises revealing his ideas and feelings about his personal family. He may also be assigned the task of contacting all his relatives to activate his extended kin network and to help him understand his involvement in his wider family.

Orientation Z does not assume that the therapist will be more effective if he understands himself or freely expresses his emotions. Instead, it assumes that he will only improve as a therapist by doing therapy under supervision and improving his skills. Instead of helping him understand his feelings or his transference involvement in a case, the teacher will offer him active ways to resolve the difficulties in the case. The teacher must teach the student ways to use himself, or herself, to bring about change. It will be assumed that the student will change with action, not reflection about himself. Just as the families treated by this approach are not expected to confess all, neither are the student therapists. In this approach, group exercises involving students having experiences together or sculpting their own family problems would not be done, since that would distract the student from the real issue, which is how to change a family.*

*A bill of rights being drafted by clinical students is now in the planning stage. The list includes an item that says that no teacher may

Self-Report versus Observation. The therapist within Orientation A tends to consider the ideas and fantasies of a person more relevant to therapy than the person's real life situation. Therefore he often does not feel it necessary to bring in the patient's intimates for observation but accepts the patient's self-report about them as adequate data. If the therapist interviews the whole family, action among the family members is not encouraged. Instead, each family member is asked about what happens in the family and reports about it to the therapist.

In Orientation Z there is grave doubt about the reliability of self-report. The primary concern is what is actually happening rather than the person's ideas about what is happening. The difference between observation and self-report was discovered a number of years ago, when therapists began to bring in whole families because they discovered that what a person said about his marriage or family and what could be observed were markedly different. When the whole family is brought in, the members are asked to deal with each other so that the therapist can see how they do that rather than listen to them describe how they do that.

As training is reflected within these two opposite orientations, the difference centers on the supervisor's data. Within Orientation A, the supervisor tends to accept the self-report of the therapist. The therapist makes notes and takes them to the supervisor who tries to guess what might have happened from that self-report. Lacking any other observable data, the supervisor naturally tends to discuss the therapist's ideas and fantasies about the case.

In Orientation Z, the supervisor observes the therapist in action with the family either live, through a one-way mirror, or on videotape or audiotape. He does not believe the therapist can accurately report what happened, just as a family member cannot accurately report what happens in

---

inquire into the personal life of a therapy student, no matter how benevolently, unless: (1) he can justify how this information is relevant to the immediate therapy task in a case, and (2) he can state specifically how this inquiry will change the therapist's behavior in the way desired.

his family. He wants the action in front of him so he can observe it. When supervisors learned that what a student therapist said about a session and what could be observed in the session were quite different, teaching began to focus on what really happens in the interview and therefore on interview skills. The training program is concerned with hierarchy and organization, not with the content of students' fantasies, just as in the therapy.*

Procedures Lead to Theory

Although some people think that a theory is created and then procedures are designed to carry it out, quite the opposite can occur. Procedures develop and then theories are created to rationalize them. It is also possible for a new procedure to develop that leads to a new theory, but the training of practitioners then suffers a time lag. The training operates on an old theory while the procedures suggest a new one. There are clearly parallels in the clinical field between a theory of change and a theory of training. But new theories of change may develop while traditional training methods continue.

There does not appear to be a single research study showing that a therapist who has had therapy himself, or understands his involvement with his personal family, has

---

*Although it may appear modern to have a supervisor watch the actual therapy of a student, this is an old-fashioned procedure. In the nineteenth century, when therapists were commonly using hypnosis, they were trained by someone who watched them work. It would have been thought absurd to think a hypnotist could learn his art by reading about it and—never having watched anyone be hypnotized—go off alone into a room and hypnotize someone and return to tell his teacher how he felt about the experience. As hypnosis was abandoned, therapy was taught by people who apparently thought therapy did not require as much skill as being a hypnotist. Therefore a student could learn to do therapy without watching anyone do it or being guided by an observer. When Freud discarded hypnosis, he also discarded the training in interpersonal skill that went with it and offered as a poor substitute a didactic analysis in which the student could make biased observations of one analyst at work on one case.

a better outcome in his therapy. Yet that assumption remains the center of some clinical training. Even teachers of family therapy continue to emphasize the personality and personal problems of a therapist when they would not emphasize the personality and personal problems of a family member in therapy. Some family therapists have only shifted from a one-to-one focus on the personal problems of the therapist to a group focus on the personal problems of the therapist. The students are brought together and asked to simulate families not only as a way of learning about family relationships but as a way of understanding themselves better. Encounter techniques and family sculpting techniques are used. In some cases these groups constitute the entire training process—a supervisor *never* watches a student do actual therapy. Perhaps the cause of this emphasis is a cultural lag. Many teachers of family therapy underwent individual therapy as a training procedure and so carry those ideas into their own training of family therapists. Others give brief workshops, in which supervision of real therapy is not possible.

Some of the conditioning therapists seem to train therapists on the basis of conditioning theory, but others do not. Supervisors will use systematic positive reinforcements with a student if that is their theory of change, but therapists who use aversive therapy with patients do not seem to train their students by aversive reinforcements. The student therapist who shocks a client incorrectly is not himself shocked to improve his skill.

Attempting Consistency

It should be possible to train a therapist in a theoretical framework consistent with the approach to therapy. What will be outlined here is a training program based on a theory most like Orientation Z in the premise system previously described. The task is to teach therapy as a skill.*

*Credit has already been given to others for many of the ideas in this book but should be especially emphasized here. The training ap-

Selecting Students. If one is doing a therapy that stresses problems in the real world, it is best to choose students with experience in that world. Therefore, mature students who have been married and have children will be easier to train than young people just starting out on courtship.

Besides a modicum of intelligence, the student should have a wide range of behavior so that he or she can adapt to a wide range of therapeutic approaches. At times a therapist must be authoritarian, at times playful, at times flirtatious, at times grim and serious, at times helpless, and so on. A student lacking skills in different kinds of social behavior will be more difficult to train than one who has had a range of experience.

One of the most necessary factors in training, and the one most difficult to achieve, is cutting the student therapist off from other teachers of therapy at the time he is in training. If he is in a training program part-time, while also receiving input from teachers at other settings, he will be receiving conflicting ideas about how to do therapy and he will be less likely to learn easily and successfully. When other teachers are influencing him, he screens what he knows in terms of what other teachers say, and can end up being so eclectic that he believes everything is so or nothing is so. At times he is a pawn in an ideological struggle between

---

proach described developed in the Institute of Family Counseling of the Philadelphia Child Guidance Clinic. Within that institute many ideas about training were generated by the faculty and by the students. When training a group for forty hours a week over two years, one learns a great deal from them. The faculty included the late Jerome Ford and the late Rae Weiner, who served as administrative directors at different times. Later Marianne Walters took over that task. Included as teachers were Braulio Montalvo, Cloé Madanes, Lydia Linan–Gervacio, and Mariano Barragan. The clinic director, Salvador Minuchin, not only helped work out the training ideas but also made a controversial program administratively possible.

schools of therapy and so his training time is wasted with irrelevant distractions.*

Learning by Doing.   The kind of therapy emphasized here cannot be learned by reading about it, by hearing lectures about it, or by having discussions. It cannot even be learned by watching others do it, although watching is valuable at certain points in the training. Therapy is a personal encounter and a therapist can only learn how to do it by doing it. All other training activity is peripheral if not irrelevant. Ideally he learns to do therapy by doing it while guided by a supervisor at the moment the therapy is happening.

With this approach, training starts when the therapist enters the room with a client, preferably a client and his family. Up to that point all that can help the therapist is some practice interviewing with simulated families so that he can learn how to do a first interview. He can practice saying hello to people, asking them about their problems, getting them to talk with each other if it is a family interview, and clarifying exactly what the problem is and what the goals of the therapy are to be. He should also practice any special techniques before they are used. Practice not only helps the beginner know what to do and how to do it, but it protects the client from a total novice.

Sharing.   The most economical way to train is in a group. In the traditional one-to-one supervision, the wisdom of a supervisor was available only to that one student. If a group of eight students are taught together, a variety of benefits accrue. First of all, the group observation from behind a one-way mirror multiplies the number of clients seen. If each student has seen four cases, they have seen thirty-two cases altogether. In this way they are exposed rapidly to a wide range of problems.

*The therapy and training issues are similar. Rather than have several therapists involved with a family either as cotherapists or as individual therapists with different members, it is better to have one therapist. This approach avoids trapping the client in a struggle between therapists, just as one avoids trapping the student therapist in a struggle between teachers of different schools.

What a supervisor offers a student dealing with a case is observed by all the students and becomes available to all. It is also possible for a supervisor to watch a student doing therapy from behind the one-way mirror with the remainder of the group and to lecture as he watches so that the group is guided through the interview.

When the group is studying a case together, many more ideas about what to do are available to everyone. Each student can make his contribution to the strategic planning so that each student not only has input from a supervisor but also from his peers.

The group provides a base of helpful support when a particular student is dealing with a difficult case. However, this support is only helpful if the supervisor deals with the group in a way consistent with the therapy. The group will have high morale if no psychiatric interpretations or group-therapy-style interpretations of each other are allowed, and so no innuendos about a student's personal problems. It is best if the rule is laid down that no one may criticize the work of anyone else unless he can offer a positive alternative. This rule prevents destructive comments as a way of attempting to impress a teacher.

Show and Tell.   With this approach, the goal is not to produce theoreticians but practitioners. A student will hopefully have developed a clear ideology after training, but the goal is to have him able to offer effective therapy. Examinations, if there are any, should be therapy sessions, not discussions of therapy.

However, even with this emphasis on action, it is necessary for the therapist to think through what he is doing and also be able to explain to others what he is doing. As a means to this end, it is helpful to have the students present videotapes of their work to each other and, later, to outsiders. By having to guide a group through an interview and to explain why he did what he did, the student learns to think tactically and learns to be articulate about his work.

Later in training, after he has learned skills as a therapist, reading seminars may be appropriate so the student can fit what he is doing into a broader model of the field. In this orientation, theory grows out of action, not action out of theory, and therefore reading of theories should come *after* the student has done therapy and has an idea of what he needs to know.

Motivating Students. Just as therapy works best when clients are involved and interested, so does clinical training. If students are given a client within two weeks of beginning their training, they are eager to learn because they feel so uncertain what to do. Similarly, if they are taught about a problem only when it comes up in therapy, they are interested because they are dealing with that problem. For example, if lectures are given first and readings offered in seminars about different types of abnormalities, the students learn about them as part of a duty. Later, if they meet a particular abnormality when doing therapy, they must recall the time they heard or read about that abnormality in their training. However, if a student is first faced with a problem, such as a withdrawn child, in therapy, then at that moment he is most receptive to learning about withdrawn children. When he is part of a group in which each student is meeting new problems that the whole group observes, then the whole group is motivated to learn about those problems because they are face-to-face with them. The motivation of the student is maximized. Teaching this way is the reverse of traditional training. Having a problem arise in therapy and generalizing from it is quite different from first generalizing and later having the student meet such a problem. Similarly, in therapy it is best to deal with an issue when it arises and then generalize from that issue rather than generalize first and hope that later the client will recall the ideas when an issue arises.

How to Tell Someone What to Do. Action therapy involves telling clients what to do whether inside the therapy room or outside. The clinician trained only in the traditional nondirective style is given no instructions in giving directives. After training he can only reflect, interpret, or offer advice as skillfully as the average layman. Skills in offering directives are not part of the curriculum and are even objected to so that a therapist trained in that way gives directives badly as well as reluctantly. He may say to a client, "I wonder if you have considered the possibility of perhaps under certain conditions thinking about talking to your wife in a different manner." Only with a premise that a therapist must take responsibility for change can a therapist tell someone "I want you to do this." He gives a vague and confused directive only for a tactical purpose.

A training program in directive therapy must include teaching students how to motivate someone to do what he is told, how to give the directives, how to clarify whether they have been understood, how to anticipate reluctance to follow them, and how to check to see if they have been followed. The training must include practice in giving directives. Simulated situations are used to develop skills in offering instructions to people. The student should learn to give straightforward directives as well as subtle, indirect, and metaphoric ones. One of the best ways to train a student therapist in the skillful use of directives is to give training in hypnosis.

An essential aspect of giving directives is learning what directives to give. A student must be taught to think strategically; he must develop skills in diagnosing a sequence and structure; and he must be able to design a directive that will produce the change he wants.

Fitting Therapeutic Problems to Students. Therapy should have a problem rather than a method orientation—a therapist should vary what he does depending on the problem. Similarly, the training of a student therapist should vary depending on the needs of a particular student. As a supervisor watches a student, he can observe deficits in his range of skills and can select future clients to fill out the operational skills of the student. For example, a student who seems to improve markedly with success should be presented with a series of cases where a successful outcome is most probable and only later have more difficult cases. Other students thrive on difficulty and should begin with

cases of that kind. A student therapist should meet, planned
in his training, the range of problems he will meet on the
job. He should deal with children, with young people, with
couples, with older people, with the poor, with the upper
class, and so on. Since most clinicians are expected to deal
with whatever comes in the door, their training should
touch upon issues they will be forced to solve. Learning to
cure a psychotic is as essential as learning to cure a bed-
wetter. Later in training students may specialize in types
of patients or particular social classes but they first need the
exposure to a range of problems. This range is needed not
only for the particular skills in dealing with those issues but
also for maximizing the flexibility of the student. Just as the
therapist should design a therapy for a particular client,
supervisors should design a training program for a particular student.

An essential part of the flexibility learned by the student is an ability to work in different contexts. A student
should have experience working in the home, in the school,
at work and in the neighborhood as well as in the office. As
therapy becomes more and more defined as working with
people at the interfaces of conflicting groups, such as between home and school, a therapist must learn to work
where the problem is when he cannot bring the problem
into the office.

Checking Outcome.   After a few months in a training
program, every therapy student should be required to bring
back the clients he has worked with and terminated to see
if he has produced a change. When students work in a
group, they can be taught to do follow-up interviews with
each other's cases. They should learn how to inquire of a
family whether they were satisfied with the therapy, how to
determine whether the changes sought have taken place,
and how to think about the biases of both therapist and
family in reporting on changes. The purpose is not to produce therapists who can do outcome research but to produce
therapists who think about the outcome they want as it will
appear months or years from now. Focusing on outcome

forces the therapist to orient toward change, to formulate problems that can be changed, and to think about how the people he is assisting now will manage without him in the future. It also helps a therapist think experimentally. If his outcome is not good, he can change his procedures to do better.

Choosing a Place for Training

Many apprentice therapists face the problem of selecting somewhere to train. Often they have minimal information about such places, and yet their whole career can be affected by the choice. A few points can be made specifically about training settings.

Where one trains should be determined by the nature of the future work planned as well as by the training opportunities available. If the apprentice plans to enter a peaceful private practice, he should train where he can find Orientation A as described here. The idea that change takes a long time and the initiative should be on the patient is best for private work. Private practice is most easy and lucrative when clients come several hours a week for many years. An active therapy approach requires three times as many referrals and many inconveniences. The place chosen to train for private practice should offer the advantage of meeting respectable people who will ultimately make referrals of well-to-do patients. Since most long-term therapy in private practice is now didactic, the apprentice therapist who has that goal should fit himself into an academic situation where future therapists can, if not must, come to him for personal therapy to improve their chances for future referrals.

If one is inclined toward Orientation Z and so wishes to train to be a therapist who takes the initiative for change and brings it about, the training opportunities are fewer and more difficult to find. Some students choose a place that is not especially good and use it as a base of operations while traveling to sample different approaches and experts over a wide geographic area. Often the situation is deceptive because many places appear to offer the right kind of training but in fact do not. Certain indicators can be suggested here. First one can list negative characteristics of training establishments as indicators for avoiding them.

1. One should avoid institutions where the emphasis is placed on the personality and personal problems of the therapist rather than on skills to bring about change. Similarly, if an emphasis is placed on using a group of students either as a form of group therapy or as an experiential focus "to loosen the student up," the setting should be avoided. When the focus is placed on the student's personal life, usually the teachers do not know how to teach how to do therapy. (This warning does not mean that students should not have a pleasant and stable personal life. The quality of one's work is always partly a product of one's intimate sources of support. A person's personal life is too important to be tampered with by teachers.)

2. One should avoid training in a place where only one class of people or ethnic group is available. For example, a university setting out in the wilds with only middle-class students as clients is a limited way to learn unless work placement opportunities offer variety.

3. One should avoid training in a clinic where the rules of the place are too rigid to allow experimentation in therapeutic approaches.

4. Generally, if the institution puts great emphasis on diagnostic skills, one can expect to learn little about how to do therapy.

5. One should avoid inpatient settings. These environments exist for purposes of social control. Therapy tends to make for trouble and instability because it encourages diversity and new alternatives. Social control, on the other hand, has the task of reducing diversity and forcing conformity on people who are out of control. It is difficult to learn to bring about change in places that seek to reduce instability.

Since inpatient settings are so common in the training of clinicians, the issue should be elaborated further. It was once thought that people could be changed by plucking them from their natural situations, reforming them, and then sending them back transformed. Therefore, people were plucked out of their communities and put in hospitals or juvenile halls. This system has failed and has adverse effects when compared with crisis work, which contains the person in his situation and changes that situation. Whether a person is mad, delinquent, or retarded, the first goal is to arrange that the family and the community solve the problem. Therapists should be trained to achieve that goal.

Certain handicaps are difficult to overcome when doing training within an inpatient institution. First, there are the impermeable walls. Most inpatient settings are of such a nature that the therapist does not control going in or going out. Also, they are often placed outside the community and are not easily accessible to families. I once taught a seminar on therapy for a group of psychologists in a Veterans Administration Hospital. After awhile I stopped, because there was no way to teach how to do therapy in that situation. The psychology interns did not control discharge and so had no power to influence the hospital career of the patient. They could not control medication and so had little influence over what was put into a patient. The hospital site had been chosen for political purposes and not for convenience and so was far from the families and communities of most patients. Therefore, families could not easily visit, nor could the patient easily visit home, and the therapist could do few home visits. Besides this handicap, the government paid the patients disability pay for being incapacitated so that they lost money if they improved. The psychologist could not change that system. All an intern could do was pass the time of day on a ward with a group, or sit alone with a patient listening to him ramble on. In the old days, when it was thought that sitting and having a conversation with a patient inside a hospital would transform him, this arrangement was considered therapy.

Another example can illustrate how the thinking and affect of therapists become disordered when therapists find themselves in the bureaucracy of a mental hospital. I recall two social workers in a state mental hospital who were deal-ing with a family in which the mother had become upset and was hospitalized when her mother-in-law moved into her home. The mother-in-law moved out two weeks later, and the woman was ready to go back to her husband and chil-dren. The therapists were not focusing on her going home but were bringing her husband and children into the hos-pital to help the family "clarify communication," whatever that means. When I asked if they had the power to discharge the woman so her communication could be improved at home, they replied that they did not and had not thought about it. They listed at least four members of the administra-tion who would have to approve discharge. They themselves had no say in the matter at all. Meanwhile the woman was being integrated into a variety of hospital programs, and her family was learning to function without her. When a ther-apist cannot easily move a patient in and out of an institu-tion, he may forget about the goals of therapy and think about working on communication or about therapeutic com-munities instead of changing people.

Secondly, inpatient settings emphasize diagnosis. Psy-chiatric residents often have the misfortune of training on psychiatric wards, even though few of them will become hospital psychiatrists. Usually, such a setting fixes their views and ways of working so that it is difficult for them to change later, particularly if they later meet anyone who has gone mad. Within the hospital, residents learn to spend their time in conferences on diagnosis and on the effects of dif-ferent kinds of medication. They learn little or nothing about therapy. When a psychiatrist trained in this way meets someone defined as psychotic, he is incapacitated as a ther-apist. He cannot think of what to do with the family and the social situation to change it. He can only think about whether the presenting problem is schizophrenia or an affect dis-order or the manic phase of a manic depressive cycle, and so on. Such questions are irrelevant to therapy and handicap the therapist in his thinking about what to do. All he has learned to do is diagnose, medicate, offer some insight, and pray. If the psychiatric resident begins his training in out-patient settings and *later* works on a psychiatric ward, he learns to see people less as medical entities and more as people with real human dilemmas.

A student therapist should avoid inpatient institutions unless the following conditions exist.

1. The therapist has control over discharge, whether from a mental institution or a juvenile hall. He must time the move back into the community to the needs of the therapy and not to the needs of the institution.

2. The therapist has control over medication if psychosis is involved. He must either be a physician and take that responsibility or he must have an agreement with the doctor in charge that medication will not be adjusted without the permission of the therapist on the case.

3. The therapist should have control over visits home or visits of family and friends from the community to the institution.

4. The therapist should control other forms of therapy given the patient in the institution so that he is not in conflict with other staff members over the approach to the problem.

Clinicians have had many years of experience failing when individual therapy is carried on with people defined as schizophrenic in institutions and almost as many years failing with family therapy when families are brought to the institution to pass the time of day with a member. Only if the therapy focuses on prompt discharge and its consequences is there a chance of forcing the family issues enough to bring about change. To achieve this focus, the therapist must control the exits and entrances. Since it is unlikely that a student therapist will be given sufficient power within an institution, a student should avoid custody settings and should rather work in community clinics.

Some of the positive characteristics to look for in a training setting are the following.

1. It is possible to observe therapists at work because there are one-way mirrors and they are used.

2. The student can be observed at work and given "live" supervision so that he can be guided while in the act of doing therapy.

3. Videotaping of sessions is easily and routinely done so that a student can go over the videotape with a supervisor at leisure.

4. It is assumed that the student needs to learn a variety of therapy techniques so that he can choose the one for a particular problem. The place should be one where whole families are interviewed as well as individuals.

5. The presenting problem is emphasized and taken seriously.

6. Outcome is emphasized so that case discussions are guided by the destination of therapy and not merely by the process of the journey.

Live Supervision

When estimating a place to work, as well as to train, the therapist should look into whether supervision is taken seriously enough to be taught. The fact that a person is a competent therapist does not make him a competent supervisor or teacher. Such skills must be taught just as one must be taught how to do therapy. A clinic program should include supervisory training.

The most effective form of supervision, and the most expensive for a training institution or clinic, is live supervision, in which the therapist is observed from behind a one-way mirror and so coached during the interview. Several criteria can be used to judge the procedure.

The supervisor's unit is the family *and* the therapist, not merely one or the other. If therapist and family get into a repetitive cycle, the supervisor must intervene to make a change. To do so properly, therapist and supervisor must agree on how this intervention is to be done. First of all, situations will differ, depending on whether the supervisor is supervising only this one case or the therapist's whole case load. The situations also vary depending on whether they are part of training students, of staff development, or merely assisting a colleague. Before the interview, the supervisor and therapist need to clarify just what their relationship is and what the purpose of the supervision is. The supervisor must be able to adapt to a relationship with an experienced colleague, to a student who is experienced but not in a particular approach being taught, or to a student who has never done any therapy at all.

A contract should be made between supervisor and therapist before the interview takes place. There should be agreement on at least the following points.

1. The supervisor will call reluctantly and will not interfere with the interview unless he considers it essential. (It is better to use a telephone rather than a "bug-in-the-ear." As the therapist listens to the bug, his eyes glaze and he is trying to attend to two different conversations at once and is not sufficiently involved in the therapy. Such a device also tends to make it too easy for the supervisor to interrupt and so he tends to talk to the student too often and too much. To sit in the room and guide the student is less effective as a training device since it involves the supervisor in the therapy and prevents private collaboration and strategy planning between therapist and supervisor.)

2. In a call, the supervisor should usually present only one idea. When a therapist is involved with a family, remembering a series of things can be difficult.

3. The supervisor should present the idea concisely so that telephone conversation is brief and to the point.

4. If the suggestion is more involved, or if the student wishes more clarification than can be offered on the telephone, the student should leave the room to discuss the issue. The student should be taught ways to leave the room gracefully, and outside the room the conversation should be as brief as possible.

5. The general strategy of a case can be discussed before the interview, and larger issues can be dealt with when student and supervisor go over the videotape of the interview later. What is crucial during live supervision is brief

interventions by the supervisor that make the interview go well and also teach the student some aspect of therapeutic skill.

6. A student should not deny that the family is being observed when it is or that he is being given suggestions when he is. Students will find that if they become comfortable with this arrangement the family usually does not mind at all. In fact, many families welcome the idea that more than one person is involved in their problem.

7. Perhaps the most important rule is that supervisor and therapist should agree that any suggestion is *only* a suggestion, since the therapist in the room has more information than the supervisor behind a one-way mirror. Behind the mirror one misses many empathic aspects of the interview. However, if the supervisor is responsible for the outcome of the therapy, when the supervisor says the therapist "has to do" something, that is not merely a suggestion and must be done. Such a directive should only be used when the therapy will otherwise be ruined or when people must be protected.

It should be clear that the supervisor's task is not only to make the therapy go well in this case and to teach a student therapist, but also to protect the family from a beginner's incompetence. Equally important, the family needs protection from intrusion into private areas that are not the therapist's business. For example, a therapist should only ask about how husband and wife get along with each other if the therapist can indicate how this information is related to the problem he is to solve. At times he may be exploring and therefore inquire without a clear contract about the relevance of his inquiry, but the supervisor should judge when the invasion of privacy is greater than is proper. Two examples may illustrate different aspects of this problem.

Once a student therapist was talking to a mother about a problem child. The mother mentioned something about her sex life with her husband. The student encouraged her to say more about that topic, and the supervisor behind the mirror allowed the discussion to go on. The woman did not

return for the next interview, apparently she was ashamed
of how much she had revealed to the student when it was not
clear to her how this information was necessary or relevant.
The supervisor should have intervened.

In another case a school counselor was brought in for
a session with the family, and the therapist began by asking
the family about their week. The mother began to talk about
the family problems. The supervisor called and asked the
student to deal with the school issues and then send the
school counselor out before dealing with the personal problems of the family that need not be revealed before the
counselor.

When a teacher observes therapists at work he realizes
the inadequacy of the former supervision model, in which
all that was revealed about a session was what the therapist
chose to tell someone about. We have progressed, over the
last twenty years, from a supervisory model in which a student made notes and took them to a supervisor who tried
to guess what happened from those comments. After that
we had audiotapes so that a supervisor could at least know
what was said. Then came videotapes, so that both the words
and the movement could be observed and commented on.
Yet in none of those procedures could there be any help and
guidance at the time the student most needed it—when he
was in the act of interviewing. With live supervision we
finally are able to protect the clients from incompetence
and overintrusion and also to teach how to do therapy at
the moment when the therapist is doing just that.

8

Ethical Issues
in Therapy

The main ethical issues in the field of therapy tend to fall either within the area of fair exchange, which involves issues common to any business or profession, or within the area of the control of information, which is especially important in the therapy enterprise. Fair exchange is a balance between what one receives and what one gives. In therapy the ethical issue arises because the therapist is a humanitarian helping people who need him, while he is also making money on that help. The therapist is paid by a sufferer, or by some advocate of the sufferer, to be helpful. The question of fair exchange inevitably arises, because to accept money and not give proper service in return is unethical, just as it is unethical to gain some personal advantage and not return sufficient compensation to the client. When we acknowledge that a therapist can make more or less money for himself or for his agency, depending on how he does his therapy, the ethical issue becomes tied to questions about therapy technique.

It can be argued that *good* in human relations is an equal balance of rewards, and that *evil* is unfair exchange. After therapy, if either client or therapist has given more than he has received, this imbalance indicates an ethical problem. What complicates the issue for many therapists is the obscurity of the therapeutic goal and therefore an uncertainty whether fair exchange has occurred. If a therapist has the goal of removing symptoms or solving problems, and he does so, he has done his job and earned his pay. Therapists who have the goal of helping people "grow," or providing a "human" experience, or of giving self-understanding to the client, have a more difficult ethical problem. They are uncertain as to whether or not they have succeeded. And they may feel they have offered fair exchange for their pay even if at termination the client still has the problems which he sought therapy to have cured. Clinical ideology, as well as technique, is inextricably mixed with the ethical issue.

One further aspect of fair exchange has become an issue in recent years. Despite its humanitarian nature, the clinical field is also an important arm of social control in society. Governments pay therapists to quiet segments of the population and keep them from making trouble. When the poor riot, mental health clinics proliferate in the slums. The ethical dilemma for many therapists is that they wish to help the poor and so welcome the government funds, but they do not wish to be used by the establishment to keep the peace and prevent basic social change. Each therapist must decide whether the impoverished client receiving his therapy truly gets a fair exchange for the money his government is providing.

A similar problem exists when therapists function as agents of social control in relation to people who are defined as psychotic and who make trouble, but not enough trouble to be legally put in jail. Does the person put in custody for bizarre behavior receive a fair exchange for what the therapist receives for custodizing and quieting him in an institution? The difference between therapy and social control hinges on who benefits from the procedures.

Controlling Information

The observation that a therapist functions at the boundary of conflicting groups makes it possible to define the ethical issue in terms of how the flow of information between those groups is controlled. When a therapist keeps something confidential, he is controlling information. It is possible to describe the groups involved from the smallest to the largest in the network.

The smallest unit could be considered to be the individual (although it is impossible for an "individual" to exist since even the act of observing an individual creates a dyadic group). If we arbitrarily suppose that an individual could be an independent entity, the issue of information control involves flow from outside awareness, or the "unconscious," to the "conscious." When the theory of repression was rampant, the obligation of the therapist was to bring ideas from the patient's unconsciousness into consciousness. An ethical issue thus centered on how quickly to reveal unconscious ideas so that the patient was not overwhelmed with anxiety. To help a patient permanently conceal ideas from himself would have been considered antitherapeutic, if not unethical.

In recent years it has become more accepted to help a person conceal ideas from himself not only for temporary periods but also permanently. We appreciate the value of natural amnesia more now, as we begin to realize that we forget things and overlook matters for sound reasons. In fact, a person with total awareness, if such awareness were possible, would be a strange and deviant individual. We seem to function best if many aspects of our lives continue outside awareness. (I recall Gregory Bateson once saying that it did not puzzle him that people had an unconscious mind but it did that they had a conscious.)

If it may do harm to make a person aware, then the therapist is involved in an ethical problem. For example, should a therapist help a person conceal from himself an idea which might upset him? Suppose that a person became anxious at being successful. Would it be wise to help him avoid realizing that he was successful? These issues arise when one accepts the idea that total awareness is not an ideal state. Some therapists may consider it patronizing, if not harmful, to help a person conceal an idea from himself. From another view, helping a person avoid facing more, whether shame or power or success, than he wishes to face, is an act of respect by a responsible person. Respecting the boundary within individuals can be considered as important as respecting the boundaries between people. From that view, the skillful control of amnesia becomes an essential part of therapy.*

Of course, the individual only exists in relation to someone else, and so the unit of the dyad is actually the smallest unit. The ethical issue of helping a person conceal from himself is inseparable from the issue of allowing the patient to conceal information from the therapist. How much will the therapist require that the patient reveal of himself? And how much of the therapist's ideas and operations will he reveal to the client? Some therapists argue that there must be no concealment between therapist and client because concealment prevents intimacy and sharing. Yet the same therapists often emphasize the importance of helping the client toward "individuation." It can be argued that individuation and total sharing of information are incompatible. The act of concealment between therapist and client defines a boundary between them and so individuates them.

Another dyadic unit the therapist deals with is the boundary between a married couple. Should the therapist reveal to a husband what the wife has told the therapist in private? If he withholds information, the therapist is drawing a boundary between the couple and saying that their interests may conflict. If he is for entirely "open" information between husband and wife, he is saying they are "one." The act of concealing or revealing information is not only an ethical one but a definition of marriage.

*J. Haley, *Uncommon Therapy: The Psychiatric Techniques of Milton Erickson, M.D.* (New York: Norton, 1973).

The next larger unit is the nuclear family, with the therapist functioning at the boundary between parents and children—the generation line. Should he conceal, or reveal to the parents information that has been given him by a child? If he reveals what the child has said, he may be betraying a confidence and so behaving "unethically." Yet what if the child is three years old and the therapist feels the parents should know what is on the child's mind?

A larger unit is the nuclear family and the extended kin, with the therapist functioning at the boundary between them. Should he conceal from the nuclear family what the grandparents have said, or vice versa? As a gatekeeper of information, the therapist may consider it unethical to pass information about a family's troubles to the wider kin network.

The largest unit is the family in relation to the community. It is generally accepted that the therapist is behaving unethically if he reveals to the agents of the community what has been told him in confidence in the family. By concealing information, he defines family and society as separate entities with conflicts of interest (while a therapist in a socialist state might not). Most therapists consider it ethical to conceal information from the community, but ethical issues arise when the therapist learns that a family member has murdered and plans to murder again. Less dramatically, a therapist sometimes knows something he learned in confidence about a family would help a teacher in school deal with a child. But should he reveal that information?

Although there are many ethical issues at the boundary between these various subsystems, the emphasis here will be largely placed on the boundary between therapist and client. Is it unethical for a therapist to conceal his operations from his clients?

Manipulation and the Therapist

Whether a therapist is "honest" with his client or is "manipulating" him has been a source of controversy. It is now accepted that one cannot do therapy without manipulating people in the sense of influencing them to change, since change is the purpose of therapy. The pretense that sitting with a deadpan expression and responding in monosyllables would not influence a patient's life decisions has been recognized as only a pretense. The question remains of how much of the therapist's maneuvering he should do outside the patient's awareness either by concealing information about his strategy or by using distraction techniques.

As actual therapy has been examined on videotapes and film in recent years, it has become increasingly clear how complex the interchange is between a therapist and one or more persons. Every minute hundreds of thousands of bits of information are exchanged in words and with body movement and vocal intonation. Both client and therapist may be conscious only of small amounts of so complex an interchange. A therapist may, for example, indicate displeasure with a topic by slightly averting his head. If he averts his head deliberately to block off the continuation of that topic, he is said to be a manipulator. If he makes this indication without realizing it, he is said not to be manipulative. One might say that the ignorant therapist is not a manipulator because he does not know what he is doing. But the issue is more complex than that.

If we deal with the concealment and revealing of information across the therapist–client boundary, and if we include the dimension of awareness or consciousness, we fall into an almost unresearchable bog. When a therapist does X with a patient and we wish to know whether he was aware that he did it, we must inquire. Not only may the therapist have a variety of reasons for not telling us the truth, or for offering biased information, but he may not have been aware of the act until the inquiry. Then he becomes aware that he was aware, even though he might not have been without that inquiry. If we wish to find out whether the patient was aware that the therapist did X, we have the same problem. The issue is one familiar to researchers in hypnosis, in which testing an amnesia may lift the amnesia. Not only are there many ways both subtle and obvious to communicate with someone, but there are also multiple levels of awareness.

An example arose with Braulio Montalvo and Salvador Minuchin. Working on a film of a therapy session, Montalvo noted that Minuchin in a variety of ways joined an inadequate father throughout the session. At the beginning of the interview Minuchin walked into the room with the family, not knowing what they were like. He stumbled and fumbled and knocked over an ash tray. Montalvo argued (in a private exchange) that Minuchin sized up that situation immediately and "joined" the father by this behavior. He cited as evidence that in other interviews Minuchin did not behave in that way. Minuchin could have "deliberately" fumbled as he entered the room with a fumbling father as a way of sharing something with the man. If so, he was consciously manipulating. He could also have been, as Montalvo suggested, deliberately unconscious of his act so that he would not be consciously manipulating. If he "accidentally" and "unconsciously" fumbled when such behavior was appropriate, was he manipulating? Questions of this kind are probably unanswerable.

Conscious Manipulation

When we leave the issue of the therapist manipulating outside his own awareness, we can focus on whether it is ethical for a therapist to manipulate outside the patient's awareness. This issue involves revealing and concealing information across the boundary line between therapist and client. When the therapist plans a strategy or a set of tactics, is it ethical for him to deceive a patient by giving false information? What about deceiving a patient by concealing information?

As a general rule it is unwise for a therapist to tell a falsehood to a patient, not only because it is improper to lie but also because it is naive to lie and believe that one will not be found out. In a temporary relationship, lying may be successfully carried out. But in any long-term relationship people learn to read each other so well that false information is recognized even though that fact may not be conceded.

It is said that one should not lie in therapy because it teaches the patient that the therapist is untrustworthy. An equally important issue is the fact that lying is usually patronizing toward the patient. It is treating him as if he were too dumb to recognize a lie. Most therapists do not lie to a client to take advantage of him but to "help" him. The deceit has a benevolent motive. Yet even the small white lie risks being patronizing when offered by a therapist.

There are several areas when lying or not lying is not so simple an issue. For example, it is unethical for a therapist to reassure a patient by telling a lie about himself, such as saying, "I too have that kind of problem with my children," when in fact the therapist does not. Yet there are times when the therapist says that something happened between him and his child when it may or may not have actually happened but is so "in character" with this therapist that it does not really matter whether it actually did happen or not.

When it is obvious to both participants that a statement is a lie, it is not necessarily unethical to lie. For example, a psychiatrist was treating a woman and her family for a period of time. One day, when angry at him, the woman asked, "Are you a doctor?" The psychiatrist replied, "No, I'm not." This statement was made for tactical reasons and was not a lie in the sense of a falsehood insofar as the context defined it explicitly as not true.

The lie as a joke is not quite a lie. For example, a mother was impatient with her child. The therapist said, "I get angry with my child, and I feel like throwing him out the window, except I don't want to put a dent in the top of my car. He's eighteen months old and should behave better." The mother responded by saying he should have more patience with a child. What the therapist said was a lie, and yet the "joke" indicators clarified that it was not true.

When a complex situation is discussed and the therapist emphasizes or even exaggerates one aspect of it, he is not simply lying. For example, if a therapist says he felt like doing such and such when he had a multitude of feelings in that situation and is only emphasizing a minor one, that is not clearly a lie.

Therapeutic maneuvers involved in encouraging symptomatic behavior are not simple lies. For example, if a person is afraid in a certain situation and the therapist tells the person he wants him to be afraid in that situation, the therapist is not telling the truth. In the larger context of the goal of therapy he does not want the person to be afraid, since he is curing him of fear. At that particular moment in that situation the therapist might actually want the person to be afraid so that the fear can be extinguished. However, often in using this approach the therapist does not want the person to be afraid but is only saying so to cure the fear. This statement is a benevolent lie and so must be approached with caution on both ethical and tactical grounds.

This type of situation arises by the nature of therapy where the goal of the therapist is to persuade a person to change "spontaneously." The therapist does not want the person to change because he says so. He must *arrange* a situation so the patient *initiates* the change. One of the many ways to do this is to encourage the client to rebel against the therapist. When encouraging a symptom, the therapist is provoking the client to respond by not having the symptom. In this sense the "lie" of encouraging the symptom forces the person to take more responsibility for his behavior. The therapist is tricking the patient out of his problem, a method traditionally used by shamans.

The question in this situation is not so much a question of whether the therapist is telling a lie but whether he is behaving unethically. Even if he is deceiving the patient for his own good, is it ethical to deceive a patient? If it is essential for the cure that deceit be used, it might be justified on that basis. However, one must also be concerned about the long-term effect of a person experiencing an expert as an untrustworthy person, which may be more harmful than the continuation of the symptom.

A more basic issue is raised by this approach. Is encouraging the symptom deceiving the client? It is a lie, but is it not a lie like a joke? If so, there is no deceit involved. This issue can be clarified for a doubtful therapist by having him explain to a client what he is doing when he encourages a symptom. Usually this procedure still produces a change—as long as the therapist insists the patient go through with the symptomatic behavior. In fact, some patients will point out that "reverse psychology" is being used, or they will say "you don't really want me to have the problem." The therapist simply agrees, since such "awareness" is irrelevant as long as the directive is given and followed. In that sense, the "deceit" is not necessary to the cure since the client is not being deceived, although less overt resistance is met if the "awareness" discussion is not held. Later one usually receives indications that the client knew all along what was happening.

The problem may be complicated if the therapist does not notice that he is encouraging a symptom. For example, a therapist may say to a complaining patient "It is important that you feel depressed right now so that you can learn to understand the lifelong pattern behind it." Some therapists say this sort of thing as a way of ending the depression—they are encouraging the symptom as a way of changing it. Other therapists may say the same thing but without intentionally being paradoxical or deceiving the client. They say it because they really do want the person to experience the depression and learn more about it. Similarly, one therapist may encourage anxiety as a way of getting rid of it while another may do the same as a way of providing less pressure for the patient, or of allowing him to notice what he really feels, or for some other reason. In one case, an expert is deceiving a patient as a way of tricking him into being cured, while in the other case, the therapist is not deceiving a patient, at least not deliberately. Once again, we have the problem that "deceit" may be a matter of the therapist's awareness or ignorance of what he is doing. It may be compared with a young person's coquetry in a courtship situation. Whether the coquetry is deliberate or is part of a natural response to the situation is difficult to determine. In either case, is it deceit? Equally important, is the therapeutic relationship comparable to normal relationships? Is "deceit" applicable in the therapeutic context?

Encouraging a symptom, or being "tricky" with a client, is sometimes said to be all right with adults, but not with children, because it could "distort their perception" and so do harm. The idea seems to be that a child has more fragile perception than an adult. Some therapists will make interpretations to a small child about quite adult matters and consider that less harmful than encouraging a symptom.

Concealing Information

One can deceive by concealing information as well as by giving false information. Some therapists are concerned about the flow of information between therapist and client and feel that any restriction on information by the therapist is unethical. The therapist should reveal whatever he thinks to the client. Other therapists are less expansive and feel that the therapist should not simply free-associate but should "time" his interpretations to the client, so that ultimately all information is revealed, but at different stages. The issue is not merely a tactical one but also an ethical one, if a therapist who conceals information from a client is said to be behaving unethically.

Whether a therapist should reveal what he observes to his clientele is one of the most important controversies in the field of therapy. Upon this question hinges one's view of a human being as a rational as well as an ethical animal. If a therapist believes it is proper and possible to change a person outside that person's awareness, he is conceptualizing men and women differently from the therapist who believes that whatever he observes must be shared with the people he is observing and that change comes about with their understanding of themselves.

In the past the therapist was said to be not responsible for what happened to a patient—he was only an advisor and a consultant. He was not influencing the life decisions of a patient, and he was not a judge of him or his family but merely a responder who would reflect back the patient's own views. The therapist was not really involved and therefore not responsible for what happened. He was largely helping the patient understand himself and his situation so the patient would be free to make his own decisions. In this mythological view of therapy, ethical issues were minimized. Any therapist who actively intervened in a patient's life, or changed the patients outside awareness, was considered unethical not only in his acts but in the very fact that he was so intrusive into the territory of another human being. Whether therapy cured people of their problems was considered less important than whether the therapist was behaving in a proper manner.

A major difference between the psychodynamic school of therapy on the one hand and the hypnotic approach, the conditioning methods, and other directive approaches on the other hand hinges on whether a therapist should help a client understand himself by the use of interpretations. It is a question of not only whether insight is a cause of change but also of whether the therapist is obligated to explain to the client what he observes.

Awareness and Ethics

It is now out of fashion to be an insight therapist, and therefore many therapists deny they operate with that theory. Yet often they continue with an insight approach while denying it. There are three basic types of interpretations used by an awareness therapist. One type involves insight interpretations that reveal to the patient some connection of the past with the present in a transference context. An example is to help a patient understand his response to authority figures by helping him connect his response to his boss and his father and the analyst. Another type involves past interpersonal interpretations in which the client is made aware that a relationship in the past is connected with one in the present. An example would be, "Have you noticed your fear about your heart came the same year your brother dropped dead of a heart attack?" The third type is the educational interpretation that brings about enlightenment on an issue in the person's present life. This type involves educational comments such as "You're overprotective of your child," or "You seem afraid of your wife," or "Have you thought you might be provoking people to criticize you?" and so on.

All of these types of interpretations assume the client will change if he understands himself and his situation better. Such interpretations are to be distinguished from strategic comments that the therapist uses to block off certain behavior and not to bring about self-understanding. For example, a therapist may point out to a wife that when she attacks her husband she is actually helping him. He may say this as a way of preventing her from attacking her husband, but the comment may appear to be an awareness interpretation.

If we define the use of insight broadly, to include all education of patients, we can focus on the issue whether it is ethical to change a person outside his awareness or whether one is obligated to help the person understand what is happening in the therapy as well as in his life.

At one extreme are the therapists who admit that they only explain to patients what is going on when they themselves do not know what to do and hope the patient will. At the other extreme are the therapists who believe that a human being is a rational animal and that changing him outside of his awareness denies his nature. Many therapists feel that sharing with a patient what they observe is treating the patient with respect and encouraging his autonomy. Should the therapist conceal from the patient what he sees, or make an intervention outside the patient's awareness, the therapist would be deceiving and manipulative. Some therapists with this view would even argue that whether the patient achieves the change he wants is less important than whether he has an honest, human experience with a therapist who is sharing understanding with him.

Disagreeing with such a view is rather like attacking home and mother. Yet several questions can be raised. First, we must accept the fact that the therapeutic situation is not an honest, human experience; it is a *paid* relationship. The therapist is receiving money to be human with a patient, which is rather inhuman. Second, it can be argued that no therapist of any school can share with a patient all of his observations and understanding. Third, it is doubtful that a patient can actually achieve autonomy when exposed to the understanding therapeutic approach. Finally, and most important, it is unlikely that an honest sharing of understanding within a paid relationship solves the problems the patient is paying his money to recover from.

When discussing such issues, a major problem is the fact that what actually happens in therapy and what is supposed to happen are not necessarily the same. If one observes therapists who claim to reveal all and share understanding with a patient, it is evident that they are doing neither. The therapist is carrying out many unmentioned maneuvers that he conceals from the patient, often for benevolent reasons, and even, hypocritically, from himself. (One has only to observe how such a therapist talks with a colleague about a patient and how he talks to the patient to note the discrepancies between his theory of honesty and his practice of concealment.)

In no therapy is all the machinery of therapy revealed to the patient. There would be no problem of "timing" or deciding what "depth" of interpretation to make, if the therapist immediately revealed all he sees. While ostensibly proposing full disclosure, the therapist actually conceals his observations from the patient until the patient "is ready" to receive them. One way therapists attempt to solve the ethical problem of being straightforward and honest while concealing is to develop a theory of resistance. By splitting the patient into a resistant side and a cooperative side, the therapist can conceal from the resistant side those interpretations that would not be effective at a particular time.

Therapists of the various conditioning schools face the concealment issue in different ways. Sometimes a learning therapist will "shape" a client's behavior by responding to the client with positive reinforcements whenever the "correct" behavior appears. The client might not be told this reinforcement is being given. If working with a marriage, such therapists may have a wife positively reinforce certain behavior of the husband outside the husband's knowledge. In such cases the therapist is forming a coalition with the wife to reform the husband; which is another way of saying that information is shared between therapist and wife but not between therapist and husband. Moreover, although controversies have arisen over the use of aversive stimuli to condition patients out of their symptoms, the concealment involved in some of the conditioning approaches has received less attention. The issue has been obscured by the enthusiasm with which some conditioning therapists educate their clientele about learning theory as a way of selling them on following the directives. Such therapists may appear to be revealing all by discussing theory, but in actuality they use many reinforcements, sometimes deliberately and sometimes not, that are not revealed to the clients.

One of the concerns about change outside patient awareness has been the idea that such an approach is incompatible with a major goal of therapy—helping a person achieve autonomy. Therapists often say they seek to have their patients achieve individuality and independence and make their own choices in life. Ostensibly, if a therapist shares his observations with a client, he is helping him to understand his problem and its causes, and is thus giving him freedom of choice about changing. Yet patients who have experienced such therapy may have their free choice limited by the indirect imposition of the therapist's ideology.

Any therapist trained in a school of therapy is going to learn an ideology of explanation about why people do what they do. Insofar as any ideology is narrow and limited compared with all the ways of thinking about human life, an "understanding" therapist is going to impose a narrow view on his patients. The result will be a person who is limited in his ways of thinking and behaving. His choices will be made within the framework of ideas that has been systematically inculcated in him over time.

If a therapist believes in his ideology, he is going to impose it on the patient (even if he tries not to) by words, body movement, vocal intonation, and instruction. The more hours therapist and patient spend together, and the more months and years the contract continues, the more the patient will be persuaded to accept the ideology of the therapist. The more interpretations are made and accepted, the less autonomous the patient will become, in the sense that he has less freedom to think differently from the therapist.

Furthermore, a therapist with a comprehensive ideology always has an ideal person against which he will judge his patient. For example, he may have an ideal model of a person cleared of all internal conflicts and repressed emotions. This model was not drawn from observation of normal people, since that observation never occurred in training. Such standards are not maps of actual human beings but of schematized ideal ones and the patient will always fall short of the ideal portrait. We also have the "ideal" family as a goal for many therapists. Both the "confronting" therapist who tries to bring out all emotions and the psychoanalyst who tries to lift repression with interpretations tend to have an ideal as a model. Another variation is the theory developed by Eric Berne, in which all behavior is to be explained according to a stereotyped schema of a "parent–adult–child" inside the client.

One aspect of the issue is whether the goal of therapy is to produce an ordinary person who is over his problem or a member of an elite who has been given a special knowledge or experience that ordinary people do not have. All elite therapies have ideologies that the clients accept as part of the therapy. The clients try to fit themselves into the models of how human beings should be. While emphasizing freedom and autonomy (which is an ideal in itself) a therapist may shape a client to a narrow ideology, thus preventing the diversity that human beings naturally display. To put the matter simply, if therapy is the introduction of more complexity, then imposing on clients a psychological explanation of their own and other people's behavior is antitherapeutic.

An example may clarify the issue of autonomy and illustrate how sharing understanding can prevent a good therapeutic outcome. A woman visits a therapist, brought by her husband, and says her problem is that she is afraid to go out of the house alone. If she attempts to go out without an adult with her, she panics and has an anxiety spell.

A therapist trained in the theory of repression may attempt to relieve the woman's fears by bringing out her ideas and emotions. The technique used might be an experiential group in which she expresses her emotions through various group experiences with strangers. Or she might be seen alone by an interpretive therapist who empathizes with her and explores the causes of her fears. He may help her understand how her past experiences have led to this state of being afraid to be autonomous. If she becomes a habitué of groups, or if she is seen in individual therapy over a period of years, the woman may be induced to think about herself in terms of inner guilts, anxiety, and so on. She may be taught a narrow explanation of why she cannot go out alone.

A more socially oriented therapist would relate the problem to her marriage and her husband's response when she goes out alone. Should the therapist be interpretive, he would share with the couple his view of the husband's involvement. Since the partners would not have the problem if they could concede the marital problem, they do not accept the therapist's interpretations. Exposed to unacceptable ideas, the partners may either terminate or set out to demonstrate that the therapist is wrong by an increase in the wife's anxiety, intended to show that the problem is really all her own. The therapist has been ethical in that he has honestly shared his views. Yet he has done nothing to help the couple solve the problem because he has only talked about understanding it.

A directive therapist who views the problem as a marital one will ask the husband to help him cure the wife of her problem, without suggesting that the husband has a part in the problem. He might, for example, ask the husband to help the wife leave the house step by step under the husband's supervision. He may tell the husband to stand on the front porch while the wife walks alone to the sidewalk, then stand on the sidewalk while the wife walks alone to the corner, and so on. The therapist will assume the wife will go as far as the husband can tolerate, and he will be working with the husband to extend that limit. In the process, the therapist will be revising the marital contract and dealing with the conflicts the couple could not previously concede— such as where will the wife go when she goes out alone and who will she be with. By dealing with the marriage without saying so, the therapist can effectively relieve this problem. Is his approach ethical? Obviously he has concealed his views, and he has "manipulated" the couple to change without making them aware of his therapeutic plan.

Whether one sees this latter approach as unethical is partly determined by one's philosophical views. From the "sharing understanding" view, the approach shows a lack of respect for people since the therapy is carried out outside their awareness. From the strategic view, such therapy is courtesy therapy. It is assumed that husband and wife know perfectly well that the wife's inability to leave the house is related to the husband and the marriage. They do not lack understanding but a way to resolve the problem. To force them to concede that the problem is a marital one is discourteous. Accepting their way of presenting the problem and offering a change within that framework shows respect for them. The crucial difference in point of view centers on whether the therapist thinks that patients need education and understanding. If the patient already understands, what he needs is a graceful way out of the problem.

In the same way, one can view either the presentation of a symptom or the presentation of a child as the problem.

Just because the parents of a problem child have an evident marital problem does not mean the therapist needs to "make them aware" they have such a problem. Similarly, if a wife is "depressed" and one notes that her depression occurs whenever her husband avoids her sexually, it is naive to assume that she and her husband do not know the depression is related to the marriage.

Along with the interpersonal explanation of symptoms has come the idea that people do not have problems because of ignorance but because of their social situations. If a therapist conceals information from a client, he is usually concealing what the client already knows. The therapist is showing both courtesy and respect by that concealment. Granting that some clients, and some therapists, are dumb, it is a more respectful view of people to assume that they are aware of their difficulties and that they need a therapist who will make change as easy as possible.

When clinicians are unwilling to draw a boundary between themselves and their clients and insist on sharing all, they not only risk failure but even risk doing harm. Priests and medicine men have traditionally drawn a firm boundary between themselves and their clientele by keeping their views and techniques secret. They did not expose the machinery of their work to the public they were helping. A new initiate had to take vows of secrecy before he was exposed to the esoteric teachings. If the knowledge could not otherwise be kept secret, it was put in an obscure language so that it was a code only understood by initiates. In the contemporary world that type of secrecy has been opposed. It is said that priests were concealing the fact that they had no special knowledge or skills but were exploiting the "faith" of the clients. It is also argued today that such secrecy is elitist and should be condemned as undemocratic. When clinicians adopt the total disclosure view, the person doing research in the field is put in an awkward position. For example, a researcher might suggest that a child's problem only changes if there is a change in the marriage of the parents. When this research is published, "awareness" clinicians who read it immediately rush off and tell parents their marriage must change if they want the child to change. Parents who do not like that way of being confronted, and who would have gone to marriage therapy if they wanted their marriage treated, will reject the therapy. The clinician is then likely to condemn them as uncooperative and resistant to the "truth." The idea that the researcher hoped would help the clinician is used in such a way that people in need of assistance are antagonized and avoid therapy.

The researcher is thus tempted to avoid publishing what he learns about therapy. He may seek instead to return to the idea that knowledge should be kept secret and not shared with everyone. Yet such a return to past ways prevents scientific validation and prevents the advancement of knowledge. Since therapy is also a business, secrecy encourages rascals who benefit when people are ignorant of their operations. Not only may the researcher's knowledge be misused, but it may be trivialized and stereotyped and watered down until it is meaningless. The dilemma is a severe one for serious clinicians, for researchers, and for writers of books like this one.

An obvious solution is to encourage clinicians to be sensible and not share all with their clientele. When the clinician concedes that he keeps private views to himself and offers his ideas to clients only with care and circumspection, then free presentation of ideas among clinicians will do less harm. It helps if clinicians admit, although few like to, that whatever they would tell the client is probably known already. Parents who have a problem child know their problem marriage is intertwined with that child. It is courtesy not to impose that awareness upon them and so help them "discover" what they already know and would rather not admit.

To emphasize the difference between an "awareness" and a "courtesy" approach, we can give an example showing how "awareness" can prevent change. A family enters therapy after the adolescent daughter took a dozen pills in an abortive suicide attempt. Parents and daughter are seen together the next day. The family shows the typical pattern of a child growing up to the age of leaving home. Often at such a time the parents' marriage is in difficulty. Not only is it a major change when children leave home, but often the parents have stabilized their marriage by communicating through a child, and now that child is leaving. The interview reveals that the parents have marital problems and that the father drinks to the point of being called alcoholic. The therapist views the girl's suicide attempt as a way of calling attention to the parental difficulty and the father's drinking so that the family can get help. Given that view, the therapist thought it reasonable, at the end of the first interview, to say to the girl in the parents' presence, "You seemed to be trying to get your parents some help by what you did, and attempting suicide was the hard way to do that." The therapist probably views this comment as a way of helping the girl get out of the scapegoat role by making the parents and the girl "aware" what the "real" purpose of the act had been.

From the research point of view, this kind of explanation of why the girl has attempted suicide might be of interest. But to confuse research ideas and clinical operations can be disastrous. It is naive, if not idiotic, to impose this explanation of the suicide attempt on the family. Should this in fact be the reason why the girl attempted suicide, the therapist is even more wrong to announce it to the family. The daughter would only arrange help in this indirect way if it was necessary because the parents would not accept help when offered. (The parents conceded during the interview that they had avoided therapy despite long-standing problems.) By announcing that the daughter is getting the family help by this act, the therapist has undermined and defeated the girl's attempt to take the blame for the problem on herself as a way of getting her parents to accept help. Shifting the blame off of her when she has put it on herself is demeaning to her and defeating the purpose of her act.

Let us suppose that the parents want to change in therapy after the situation is defined in this way by the therapist. Should the father now decide to quit drinking, this decision cannot be *his* contribution, because it has already been defined as caused by his daughter's attempt at suicide. Also, the mother has tried for years to get her husband to quit drinking. If he stops now after his daughter's act is defined in this way, he is letting his daughter help him when he would not let his wife do so. Rather than put his wife down in this way, he may go on drinking. Should the parents improve their marriage, they would be conceding that this improvement was arranged by their daughter. If they are angry at the daughter and would rather not give her credit for their better life, they will avoid improving their marriage. The act of making the family "aware" of why the girl did what she did is an act that prevents change. The odds are against any change in the marriage once this "insight" has been shared with the family. Instead of therapy increasing complexity, it has decreased alternatives and rigidified the social situation. The "awareness" therapist will not conclude that *his* act caused this unfortunate situation. Instead, he will say the parents have deep-seated character problems and long-standing marriage difficulties and are unreachable.

Information and Larger Units. Although we have been emphasizing the boundary between therapist and client, a similar issue arises at each of the other boundaries where a therapist functions. Should he reveal to a husband what he sees the wife doing and to the wife what he sees the husband doing? Just as some therapists argue that a therapist should share all his own operations with a client, so do they argue that if a wife is having an affair and secretly tells the therapist, he should reveal this information to the husband as part of an "honest" approach. Again, a therapist who assumes that if a wife is having a continuing affair her husband knows will view the problem as how to resolve it rather than whether to reveal the affair to the spouse.

At the boundary of the larger unit, the line between parents and children in the nuclear family, a therapist may feel required to reveal all he knows about the children's behavior to the parents and vice versa. In family sessions he may focus on total revelation and point out to parents and children how they are dealing with one another. Alternatively, he may assume that the problem is not sharing information but establishing rules for behavior. For example, a therapist might persuade parents to tell their adolescent children about their unhappy sex life. A more interpersonal therapist would assume the adolescent knows that a problem exists. For such a therapist, the therapeutic issue is the maintenance of a hierarchical line between the parents and the children rather than the sharing of information.

Information Theory and Communication Theory

When one views a therapist as gate-keeper of information between segments of society, a more general issue than therapy is involved. Implicit in this view is the idea that revealing or concealing information at a boundary between groups creates a boundary between groups. To not reveal to parents what their child has said is to draw a boundary between parents and child and define them as two separate groups. Information and boundary are synonymous.*

From this view, certain propositions follow: First, information and coalition are synonymous. The act of giving and

---

*An analogy is in order. Clerk Maxwell once proposed a model for describing negative entropy. If one places a gas in a container, the molecules move at a rate determined by the temperature of the gas. The molecules *average* the same speed, even though some move faster and some slower. Maxwell proposed that temperature could change on the basis of selectivity or ordering. He suggested that if one could conceive of the container as divided in half with a gate at which a "demon" is making selections of molecules, the temperature in the two halves could be changed. If the demon opened the gate when the fast molecule came along and let it through, and he closed the gate against any slow molecules, he would take randomness away from the activity. Soon he would have fast molecules on one side and slow ones on the other, changing temperature by selection. It is evident that he created the boundary between the two halves of the container by the very act of being gate-keeper who selected what could pass through the boundary.

In a way, the therapist is a "Maxwell's Demon" when he functions at the boundary between two segments of society. By selecting what information will be allowed to pass from one group to another, he is defining those groups as having a boundary between them (and he might also be changing the temperature of the groups). He is exhibiting preference and so "ordering" the two groups.

witholding information across a boundary is an act of forming and dissolving coalitions. To conceal from parents what their child has said is to form a coalition with the child on that issue. Second, information and power are synonymous. To be in a position to reveal or conceal information between groups is to be in a *meta-*, or power, position in relation to those groups. And third, a therapist's position in a hierarchy is largely determined by his control of information—the ability to reveal or withhold information.

One problem posed by many theoreticians is the distinction between information theory and communication theory. While information theory has a more solid base, perhaps because it has practical uses, communication theory has remained undeveloped. How information is coded between a sender and a receiver has appeared to be a different question from how a learning animal forms a hierarchy by communicative acts. One may deal with what information a creature has received in terms of bits, but not be able to connect that with a description of how the creature has formed a coalition against a rival. Observing a therapist, a change agent, functioning at the boundary between groups clarifies the relationship between information and hierarchy.

Given this view, it follows that a therapist who seeks power and influence over an individual or a group should establish himself as a gate-keeper of information between that group and a larger one. By actuality or illusion, he should be defined as the one who allows or prevents information to pass. Therefore, his power is enhanced if he is provided with secrets to be protected. The more an individual or group gives a therapist information it wishes concealed, the more power and status the therapist is given. Thus the ethical issues involved in the control of information are an essential aspect of therapy and so cannot be avoided or minimized.

It also follows that a therapist should not only see a whole family together but should also see members and factions alone. He must have, or appear to have, information that he controls at a boundary. If he only sees the whole family together, he can exchange covert information by innuendo and nonverbal communication, but the task of concealment is more difficult because everyone may receive the information.

There is a contradiction, or a tension, between the need of the therapist to have power and influence and his need to provide fair exchange. For example, if a therapist on the staff of a mental hospital sides with a patient against the remainder of the staff by not revealing something the patient has told him, he is disloyal to his fellow staff members. Yet if he does not persuade the patient to give him confidential information and then keep it concealed, he is not establishing a unique relationship or a sufficient coalition with the patient to make change possible. Although this dilemma is obvious in such a case, it is present in more subtle ways throughout therapeutic endeavors.

Let us suppose a therapist is treating a child and wishes to "reach" the child. He therefore encourages the child to reveal to him information he has not told others. As the child does so, the therapist conceals from the parents this information as a necessary factor in encouraging the child to trust him and reveal more information. Yet the therapist is also an adult, and is in natural coalition with the parents by that fact. He is an agent of the parents insofar as he is paid by them to cure their child. In that sense, he is in the position of the staff member of a mental hospital siding with a patient against the staff, because he is siding with the child against the parents. Yet if he does not side with the child by being gate-keeper at the boundary between child and parents, he will not be able to form a coalition with the child sufficient to bring about change.

One of the major points of organization theory is that consistently breaching power lines is pathological. If a staff member sides with a patient against other staff members and so crosses that hierarchical power line, the organization is in trouble. If a therapist sides with the child against the parents, he is like the grandmother siding with the child against the parents and is thus causing the difficulties he is trying to cure. At this point the paradoxical problem is evident. To gain power and influence in social systems, it is necessary for a therapist to conceal information between groups. Yet the act of concealing information from someone low in the hierarchy may force the therapist into a coalition across generation lines, which produces a disturbed system.

Let us take another example. It is often assumed that one should not side with a husband against a wife, or with a wife against a husband, when dealing with a marital couple. Insofar as the therapist is an expert he is higher in the hierarchy than husband or wife, and so siding with one against another is violating a hierarchical line. Yet if the therapist is gate-keeper of information between them, he can only be so if he conceals (even temporarily) from one the information he has received from the other. In fact, that act not only makes him an "expert" higher in the hierarchy but also places him in coalition with one partner against another.

One requirement for the resolution of these apparent paradoxes seems self-evident. The therapist must follow the fundamental rule of not consistently siding with anyone against anyone else. He must provide fair exchange not only between himself and his clientele but also between the subsystems of clientele. If he uses concealment of information to side with child against parents, he must do the same to join parents against child. In this sense, the therapist must be *meta* to all the groups with whom he works. The problems posed by his membership in a group with interests that differ from those of his client must be resolved at a higher level. The staff member who sides with a patient against his staff must do so in a way that allows him ultimately also to side with the staff against the patient. He must distribute himself equally, even within the group of which he is a member.* In this sense he must represent both his client and the

---

*Quite possibly there is an unresolvable paradox here that is central to therapy. One cannot be a member of a group and also be *meta* to the group. The same problem exists when an item is in a class and is also the class, as in the class of classes paradox of Russell and Whitehead. See A. N. Whitehead and B. Russell *Principia Mathematica* (Cambridge, England: Cambridge University Press, 1910).

community, using whatever devices allow him to place his weight equally with both systems in the long run. Of course in the short run he might at any time be siding with one against the other as he tips the coalition balance in ways that can bring about change.

Many therapists feel that too much is expected of them if they must judge what is best in the variety of social situations and make decisions for their clientele. They also feel that accepting the responsibility for changing people and keeping their knowledge of what is happening to themselves takes the wisdom of Solomon. Many therapists therefore choose to share their views with the client and push the responsibility for change onto him. Yet if the therapist is trained to be an expert, he should be willing to take responsibility and he should know what should be done in many different situations. Often he will not know, but that does not mean he should not. When therapy is seen from a social network point of view, the teachers of therapists clearly have more responsibility to do an effective job than they had when training therapists in the past.

In this brief review, many ethical issues have not been touched on. One crucial issue is whether it is ethical to take an experimental approach to therapy, tampering with people's lives with untried methods. Is it not more proper to use tested methods even if they have failed? The many social situations that appear in therapy force sudden ethical dilemmas on the clinician. With experience in the field, a therapist develops an ethical posture and learns to consider each situation on its merit. Practitioners who have done therapy for many years know what is ethical behavior and what is not. They may rationalize and attempt to deceive themselves and others about their own conduct, but they know.

Case Report

A Modern "Little Hans"

This complete case report illustrates the approach to therapy described in this book. The specificity of the problem and the obvious nature of the family situation make the case useful for illustration, even though the reader may find so clear a situation unusual. It is a child problem that is clearly defined, the stages of therapy occur as they should, the marital issue is a focused one, different types of directives are given, including paradoxical ones, and the outcome is good. The form of this case presentation is the script of a video training film. One of the earliest efforts at this type of training material, this film script represents a new form of case presentation.

Not so long ago, it was expected that a therapist would be closeted alone with one person who would talk at length about himself and his fantasies. Today, a therapy session may involve a whole family gathered together talking in a one-way mirror room with video cameras going and a supervisor watching and telephoning from behind the mirror. The room is full of action and emotion as the therapist shifts people from chair to chair and guides the action among the participants. When therapy takes this form, it becomes a human drama of action rather than a conversation about matters happening elsewhere. Husbands and wives negotiate and fight with each other, adolescents rebel against parents, children may be beaten on camera, and affection and tenderness appear in many forms and guises. The therapist is participant, guide, director, activator, and reflector as the important actions of life are recorded by video cameras.

Videotaped interviews can be shown to students so they can observe in detail how to conduct a therapy interview. After a complete case has been videotaped, parts from different interviews can be selected and copied on one tape so that several hours of therapy are compressed into a one-hour presentation. Narration and diagrams can be added so the tape can be used without the teacher being present. The videotape can thus become a therapy training film. When these training films take a "how to do it" form, the filmmaker has the problem of presenting a coherent way of doing therapy that students can understand and use with their cases. The filmmaker also has the responsibility for making a selection of the therapeutic moments that does not offer a distorted view of what actually happened.

It is possible that we have seen the last generation of expert therapists who present their work in written case history form. In the future, therapists can be expected to show what they do rather than offer a written summary of what they might or might not have done.* Although films

---

*At one time therapists objected to videotaping or filming interviews because clients would object to the invasion of privacy. It has become evident that if the therapist does not mind being videotaped, the family does not. Granting there are special situations, such as criminal confessions or professional colleagues, which can be legitimate reasons for not videotaping, in most cases there is no issue. This approach assumes that the client is properly informed about the videotaping and grants permission. As with all such technical matters, if it interferes with the therapy, observation and filming should not be done despite the enormous advantages gained for training and the overcoming of mythologies about what a therapist does in an interview.

of therapists doing an interview have been made in the past, only recently have clinicians filmed their actual therapy sessions, rather than demonstration interviews, and faced the special problems involved in editing a complete case down to a one-hour film. The case report here is in the form of an edited training videotape and so presents the highlights, or crucial aspects, of the case.

The therapist, Mariano Barragan, was in training as a Child Psychiatric Fellow when this work was done. Although he had experience previously as a therapist, he did not have experience with this therapeutic approach. The supervision was "live," with the supervisor behind a one-way mirror. Also present at each planning session and behind the one-way mirror were colleagues who were involved in a strategic therapy seminar, and therefore many ideas about what to do came from the group.

The film is called "A Modern Little Hans" because of the parallels between Freud's case in which a boy named Hans was afraid to go out on the street because of a fear of horses. This boy is afraid to go out because of a fear of dogs. In both cases, the therapist made use of the father–son relationship to produce a change.

The script of the training film is presented here verbatim except for changes made to protect the identity of the family.

Title: A Modern "Little Hans"
Therapist: Mariano Barragan, M.D.
Supervisor and Film Editor: Jay Haley

(In an interview room equipped with a one-way mirror a family is talking with the therapist.)

Narration: This is a family with a father, a mother, an eight-year-old boy and a six-year-old girl. The presenting problem is the boy, who has never in his life been able to associate with dogs. He cannot approach near a dog, cannot enter a house where a dog is present and he is largely

confined to his home because he avoids dogs on the street.
He will even run from them into traffic, and so his parents
are afraid to allow him out on the street alone and must
accompany him wherever he goes. Because of the severity
of the problem, the parents placed the boy in therapy. After
one year of individual child therapy, for what was called a
dog phobia, there was no improvement. The therapist left
the city, referring the boy to the Philadelphia Child Guidance Clinic for treatment. The whole family was interviewed, and in the first session the family discussed the
problem and their history. A treatment strategy was planned
and in the second interview with the family it has begun.
The first step is to obtain a clear statement of the problem,
particularly from the boy, since he had said little in the first
interview. The boy discusses his fear and then he begins
to minimize it, making it necessary for the parents to correct him.

Boy:	And I thought this was the end of me being afraid of them but it wasn't.
Therapist:	When you got one?
Boy:	A dog.
Therapist:	Yeah.
Boy:	It was a puppy.
Therapist:	So what happened?
Boy:	We gave it back.
Therapist:	Because?
Boy:	Because I was too afraid of it.
Therapist:	But you thought you wouldn't be.
Boy:	Yeah.
Therapist:	It was a puppy?
Boy:	Yes.

Therapist: And you were still afraid of a puppy?

Boy: Umhuh.

Therapist: A little tiny puppy?

Boy: No, it was about this big and . . .

Mother: It was tiny.

Boy: It was about this wide, wasn't it?

(Later in the interview, the conversation continues.)

Boy: I don't really want to stay away like that, and
                 as for German Shepherds, because I'm afraid
                 of those. Those are the dogs that I am most
                 afraid of.

Mother: Stuart, now, be very honest, be very honest
                 about it all. Princess or Bruce, Bruce is not a
                 German Shepherd.

Boy: I'm not talking about . . .

Mother: I know, I know you're not talking about, you're
                 talking about the German Shepherds and
                 you're saying that's the dog that you are really
                 afraid of.

Boy: Yes.

Mother: Tell him about, also about Princess when you
                 come home in the car, I mean Bruce, and if
                 Bruce is outside, which is all the time now, and
                 we all get out of the car, what happens? And
                 he's not a German Shepherd.

Narration: Now let us look at a family interview three
weeks later. The boy has a puppy in the room and is petting
it. What must have happened in three weeks that had not
happened previously in the boy's life despite a year of ther-

apy? How can we explain that he is now touching a dog when he could not do so before? Various explanations are possible: there might have been spontaneous remission. There could have been insight that resolved the problem. There might also have been a deconditioning process where the boy was brought closer and closer to a dog until his anxiety was allayed and he could touch it. In actuality, a quite different approach was used. It was assumed that the avoidance of dogs by the boy has a function in the family. If family relationships are changed, the boy will be over the problem. It is not assumed that insight or understanding is necessary, or a step-by-step conditioning process. Instead, it is assumed that a therapist must intervene actively and directively in a series of stages to bring about changes in family relationships. By this fourth family interview the change has begun but six more interviews were necessary to complete the therapy.

We will show, in oversimplified form, the strategy of treatment in this case, using excerpts from family interviews to illustrate the process. Arbitrarily choosing mother, father, and child as a unit, leaving out other family members, one can say that when a child has a problem that handicaps him, usually one parent is intensely involved with the child. This parent often speaks for the child, hovers over him, and is both overprotective and exasperated with him. The other parent is more peripheral, tending to be disengaged from both child and spouse. Sometimes it is not two parents but a parent and grandmother or sibling that have this arrangement. In this particular family the mother is overinvolved with the child and excessively concerned about his fears. The father is more peripheral. He holds down two jobs and so is rarely at home. His contacts with the boy are largely because he must take him places because of his fear of dogs. The goal of therapy can be put simply. It is to shift the relationships in the family so that mother and father are more intensely involved with each other and the boy is disengaged from them and more involved with his peers. Although the goal can be described simply, the tactics to achieve that goal will be complex and determined by the unique nature of each family. To change the family from the beginning arrangement to the end point cannot be done abruptly. There are several stages in the treatment process. The first step is to change the relationship between overinvolved parent and child. When a therapist enters the family, he can take this first step in many different ways. One particular way was used in this case. The parent who was more peripheral was directed to become more involved with the child, thus disengaging the intensely involved parent. In this case, the mother was the authority on the child, particularly on his fears. The therapist intervened to make father an authority, thus bringing about more action between father and boy and excluding the mother.

The intervention to achieve this first stage came about in family interview number two, when the mother left the room briefly. The use of the father as an authority on dogs was previously planned as part of the treatment strategy. To begin the intervention when the mother was absent was not planned.

(A return to the first scene when father is talking about the boy's fear of dogs. Mother leaves the room to take daughter to the bathroom)

Therapist: How much do you ask your father about dogs?

Boy: Very little.

Therapist: Very little?

Boy: Mhmm.

Therapist: Do you know what a—well, tell me, what is your father's job? What is his job?

Boy: A letter carrier.

Therapist: Right. Do you know that letter carriers, you know, are supposed to be pretty good with dogs?

Boy: Uh uh.

Therapist: Yeah.

Boy: But I know dogs don't like them. Most dogs don't.

Therapist: Alright, how many times has a dog bit your father?

Boy: None.

Therapist: None, so that must mean that he is pretty good, because dogs don't like letter carriers. Right?

Boy: Right.

Therapist: So he must be pretty good if no dogs bite him.

Boy: Well, dad, can I ask you a question?

Father: Yeah.

Boy: How do you get them away from you?

Therapist: That's what I wanted to hear.

(The therapist sits back while father and son talk.)

Boy: Like, I mean, like, you know, like at Gerald's house.

Father: Yeah.

Boy: Or Miss Jones's house.

Father: Uh uh.

Boy: Like if the dog was loose, like that big white dog over there.

Father: Uh huh.

Boy: If he got loose, how would you get the dog away from you, if he was a mean dog?

Father: Holler. Scream at him.

Boy: Yeah, but what if they didn't go then?

Father: Well, then you have to get ready to do something else, but whatever you do, you try not to run.

Boy: Now, that big white dog . . .

Father: If I had a coat on, I would try to take my coat off and put it in front of me.

Boy: Why that?

Father: Well, if the dog is gonna bite me, he's gonna bite the coat.

Boy: Yeah, but what if you didn't have the coat and it was summer time?

Father: Well, then the thing that I would be able to do to ward off a dog, to fight a dog, probably you wouldn't be able to think of it at the time, I know that . . .

Boy: Kick him.

Father: If you take your hat and you put it in front of a dog, and the dog grabs ahold of the hat, he's gonna grab the hat, he's not gonna pass the hat and grab your arm. He's gonna grab the cap. Right?

Boy: Uh huh.

Father: You kick him under the chin, while he's grabbing ahold of the hat.

Boy: You kick him under the chin?

Father: Uh yeah.

Boy: That be . . .

Father: It fits real nice, you see. (*Shows foot movement.*)

Boy: Yeah.

(*Mother entering the room with daughter.*)

Mother:	We got lost.
Boy:	*(Continuing with father.)* So isn't that cruel?
Father:	If the dog is trying to bite you, nothing is cruel.
Boy:	Uh huh.
Father:	Nothing is ever cruel if the dog is trying to bite you, defending yourself is not cruel.
Therapist:	You see, I think maybe you haven't thought that you have an expert on dogs right at home.
Boy:	I know.
Therapist:	Your father deals with dogs every day.

(Later in the conversation.)

Mother:	If he sees a dog one time, he never forgets it. When we left here the last time we went downtown to a store and he said as we were going in, "Have we been in this store before?" I said "We were never at this store," he said "Yes, we were, because they have a big dog in there." I said "Well, I don't know anything about it." Well, when we walked in the store there was a great big dog. And I really had forgotten that, that's how long it's been since we were there. And this great big brown, pretty dog was in there.
Father:	A Doberman Pinscher.
Mother:	A Doberman Pinscher.
Therapist:	Think Stu, have you ever seen your father handling a dog?
Boy:	Yeah.
Father:	What?
Mother:	Handling dogs.

Father: Handling dogs?

Boy: Yeah, I seen you do it. You kicked that dog the other day, didn't you?

Mother: Oh. *(Laughs.)* Did you kick a dog?

(Later in the conversation.)

Therapist: You said that you know that dogs don't like letter carriers.

Boy: Uh huh.

Therapist: Right? So you know, your father has been dealing with dogs, maybe you can learn from him.

Narration: The first step has been taken. Father and son are interacting over the issue of dogs in an area where father is the authority and mother is not. When mother mentions the boy's fears, the therapist neutralizes her words by emphasizing the father's knowledge of dogs.

The next step was to get a dog into the home. This step was necessary to continue the involvement of father and boy over a dog. It was also done to bring the boy into proximity with a dog so that changes in the family could be estimated. That is, the boy's association with dogs becomes a measuring stick for change. The closer his contact with a dog, the more family relationships are changing. To introduce a dog into the home was difficult, since the family had attempted to do so previously and the boy became frightened. When one gives a directive to do a task that has previously failed it is necessary to make the situation a new one. The therapist makes the addition of a dog a new kind of situation as interview number two continues.

Therapist: Alright, Stu, so it sounds as though you have to learn a few things.

Boy: Yes.

Therapist: You know what I want you to do?

Boy: No.

Therapist: If it's agreeable with your parents? Okay? I want you to go and adopt a dog.* But you pick one who is afraid.

Boy: Afraid of me?

Therapist: No, not one that is afraid of you.

Boy: Afraid of anybody?

Therapist: One that you think is afraid.

Boy: Why would I think?

Therapist: No, no, no, I want you to pick a dog who you think might be afraid. I know there is no way of knowing that and you can't ask the dog.

Boy: I know, but I'd know how to do that.

Therapist: Would you?

Boy: Yeah, it would probably be a dog that was running, not running around and come back to me and stuff, that would be a dog that I wouldn't think would be afraid of me, it would like me. I would say a dog that would—like go away.

Therapist: Okay, then I want you to adopt a dog that you think is afraid, and I want you to *cure* this dog. With the help of your parents. You are all to get together and cure this little puppy who is going to be a fearful puppy. *(To parents.)* Is that alright with you?

---

*This is an example of good collaboration between supervisor and therapist. The supervisor said a dog must be brought into the home and it must be done in a new way since they had tried it before and failed. The therapist thought of this new way which was acceptable to the family.

Mother: Yeah, it's alright.

Therapist: How about you?

Father: It will be alright. It will be alright if he goes to get it.

Therapist: That's what I had in mind.

Boy: What you mean, Dad?

Father: Just what I said.

Boy: Oh, you mean if you take me but I pick it out.

Father: Just like I told you all along, all along, I'll take you and get a dog. Haven't I said that?

Boy: Yes.

Father: I'll take you to get a dog as long as you get the dog, you pick the dog up and bring it home.

Boy: Uh huh.

Father: Okay, I'm not gonna.

Therapist: Is that okay with you?

Father: I'm not gonna bring it home.

Therapist: Now wait a minute, you know that's . . .

Father: No, I mean I'm not gonna . . .

Therapist: Yeah, I know what you mean but I want you to get together and—today is Friday, I want you to get together and talk about the dog. Alright?

Boy: Yes.

Therapist: And then I want you to decide exactly what you have to do and then I want you to go and do it. But first I want you to talk about it with your parents.

Narration: That ended the second interview with the family. The following week the family had not obtained a dog and the session was a general one on their family life. At the fourth family interview, the family arrived with a puppy.

(The boy is opening a box and letting a puppy out. It was a frightened puppy, the only survivor of a litter discarded on a highway.)

Therapist: You take him out, Stuart.

Boy: He can jump out like that.

Mother: I hope he doesn't go to the bathroom.

Therapist: Don't worry about that.

Mother: Oh, okay. But it looks like he's smelling, doesn't it.

Father: Yeah, it looks like it.

Therapist: You know, you can put your box over there if you want to.

(The dog puddles on the rug.)

Mother: Oh, that's a shame. But he didn't do it in his box, did he?

Therapist: Don't worry, we'll get some paper later on. *(To boy.)* What I want to see you do is, you know that he is afraid, don't you? Right.

Boy: Right.

Therapist: Now, how are you going to do something about that?

Boy: You want me to do something?

Therapist: Uh huh.

Boy: But how am I gonna do it?

Therapist: We know that you have to get this little puppy over his fears. Right?

Boy: Right.

Therapist: Well, Stuart?

Boy: Huh?

Therapist: I want to see some action.

Boy: What?

Therapist: I don't know, you got a problem.

Father: Pick the dog up.

Boy: I can't pick him up.

Father: You held him.

Therapist: There are a lot of people here helping you. You can ask your parents, you can ask Sharon *(the sister)*.

Boy: I held him *(as his sister pets the dog)*. No, Sharon, no, Sharon, no.

(Later in the interview.)

Mother: I think he's come a long way, he has.

Therapist: You think what? I didn't hear you.

Mother: He's come a long way. He's doing good, the only thing is that he just won't pick him up and carry him, he won't carry him anywhere or pick him up.

Father: I've seen him hold him.

Mother: Tom says he's held him, I don't ever remember seeing him hold him.

Boy: At Aunt Sarah's.

Father: He'll hold . . .

Mother: Oh right, at Aunt Sarah's house, Sunday.

Father: He'll hold him.

Mother: Yeah, right, Sunday at Aunt Sarah's you picked him up and brought back, oh, Aunt Sarah had him, right?

Boy: Yeah.

Mother: She handed him to you and you brought him to the car.

Boy: Yeah.

Mother: That's right.

Therapist: What do you think, Mr. Crosby?

Father: I think he's doing alright, maybe it may not seem like that, but I think he's doing a whole lot better.

Mother: I feel as though he's doing good, too, because I am sure we can both remember when he didn't even want me to touch a dog, a puppy, like one was in the yard and they were on the back porch, and I went down in the yard to pet the puppy and he screamed, "Don't touch him," and I thought he was going to pass out.

Therapist: So you agree with Mr. Crosby.

Mother: Yes.

Narration: At this point the boy has improved sufficiently so that the therapist can begin to shift to the next stage of therapy, where the focus is on the marriage. To deal with the marriage before there is a change in the boy would be a mistake. Just because the child's problem is part of a triangular marital problem does not mean that the child's problem can be solved by immediately dealing with the marriage. There must be a step-by-step process and the

first step is producing a change in the child. The way the
therapist begins the shift to the next stage is by giving credit
to the parents for improvement in the child. They deserve
this credit for the ways they have cooperated and have gone
to the trouble of finding the right puppy. Giving credit to
the parents does two things: it makes it possible to focus on
the marriage. It also prepares for the ultimate disengagement of the therapist later in the therapy, when he must
leave the family system. It is easier to leave if the responsibility for the change has been placed within the family.

Therapist: What I want to say is that whatever progress
Stuart has made has been basically because
of you.

Father: I don't know.

Therapist: I think so, and I think that it's not time to be
modest now.

Father: I'm not trying to be modest.

Therapist: You see, what I am trying to point out to you,
both of you, but basically to you, is that there is
a lot of things that are—there are a lot of things
that you have done about Stuart's fears.

Father: Well, answer this, why couldn't we do it, why
couldn't I or my wife do it by ourselves?

Therapist: Well first of all, you didn't think about the
business of you being an expert on dogs. Which
you are. I mean, let's face it, whether you admit
it or not, it seems very easy for you now-a-days
and as a matter of fact it was such a part of
everyday life that you never knew about it.

Father: Uh huh.

Therapist: But your being a letter carrier has helped
Stuart.

Mother:　　I agree. I agree, but you put it in words, that mailmen are experts on dogs.

Narration:　Giving credit to the parents for producing a change in the child serves another purpose. Parents have usually tried every way they could to help their child and have failed. If an expert comes in and quickly produces a change in the child, the expert becomes too powerful. The parents are pleased but they have also developed a natural resentment for someone who has succeeded where they have failed. This resentment can only be expressed and pride salvaged by arranging that the therapist also fail. If the parents are given credit for the change, this failure does not happen.

Therapist:　What I'm trying to say is that you have done a lot in here to produce whatever change has happened.

Father:　That makes you feel good anyway.

Therapist:　Huh?

Father:　I said that makes you feel good.

Narration:　The therapist moved the family to the next stage by asking them, as a reward for having done so well with their child, to go away together for the weekend. This request forces a focus upon the marriage. The task is also a natural process that helps the family move to the marital stage. When mother is excluded from the relationship with the boy, she does not like to be excluded and wishes to return. If she is blocked off from engaging with the child, she will engage with the father. The form this engagement will take is complaints about his neglect of her and demands for more from him. Such a response allows the therapist to shift to the relationship between the spouses, and at this point he can leave the child out of that struggle.

Therapist:　And this is why I was pointing out what you have done. So I suggest something more ob-

240   **Problem-Solving Therapy**

vious. Go along with me, because this is important for what we are seeing here. A couple who is relaxed, you know, usually takes things easy.

Mother: Uh huh.

Therapist: Do you agree with that?

Mother: Uh huh.

Therapist: I don't know how you feel about it, but I think that what is important is that you get a reward for what you have done.

Mother: Uh huh.

Therapist: Because I think what you've done is great. Now for a reward for both of you, I can think of several. For instance, how about a weekend away by yourselves?

Mother: Yeah, that would be nice.

(Both parents laugh.)

Therapist: Would that be nice?

Mother: Yeah, that would really be nice. I don't know if Stuart heard that.*

Boy: What? What? *(Looking up from playing with the dog.)*

Therapist: Never mind, Stuart.

Father: What did you say, never mind?

Therapist: This is both of *you*.

Mother: Yeah.

Therapist: But it's for *him*.

*The triangular involvement of parent and child is illustrated by mother's response here. When it is suggested that she and her husband do something together, the son is immediately brought into the issue.

Father: Can you remember that far back?

Therapist: That would be ideal in terms of his realizing that you are not so concerned about him.

Mother: Yeah.

Therapist: Okay?

Father: Yes.

Therapist: Which is what I am trying to do, I don't have anything else in mind.

Father: Uh huh.

Therapist: What I have in mind is that this boy can come to realize that you and you are not so worried about him anymore.

Mother: Right.

Narration: In terms of the stages of therapy the family is now on the edge of entering Stage Two, where the marriage is the issue. However, in the sixth interview the parents had not gone out alone together and were not talking about their marriage. The boy was still partially afraid of dogs. The therapist dealt with this impasse by first focusing on the boy and then on the married couple, repeating the general pattern of the therapy in order to shift from the child to the parents.

Because of the danger of a relapse at this point, the therapist took action to prevent it. Instead of letting the family shift back and talk about the child's fears, the therapist did so. The way he focused on the boy was by encouraging him to have a relapse and by asking the parents to cooperate. Such a move stabilizes the improvement and prevents the family from going back to old patterns. The therapist encouraged this relapse in a playful way by asking the boy to help the puppy by pretending to be afraid of him. The boy's expression when this is said is a classical response to a paradoxical therapeutic maneuver.

Mother: The dog goes for Stuart so much. He whines when Stuart goes out the door. You know, but we can't bring ourselves to pick him up and fondle him.

Therapist: Stuart, do you think that we can play a trick on that dog so that he will be alright?

Boy: Like what?

Therapist: But you have to be pretty smart. And I'll show you the way, you know, in which you can measure how smart you are being. Alright?

Boy: How are you gonna do it?

Therapist: How am I gonna do it?

Boy: Uh huh.

Therapist: I will ask you to do something and I'll ask your parents to participate on that. Alright?

Boy: Like what?

Therapist: See actually we have to—we have to trick this little puppy into thinking that *you* are afraid of *him*.

Boy: Make him think *I'm* afraid? (*The boy looks stunned.*)

Therapist: Do you get the idea? See, I want the puppy to try to convince you not to be afraid of him. This is just a make-believe, I know that you are not afraid of the puppy. Are you?

Boy: No.

Therapist: Alright. This is just tricking the little puppy into thinking that *you* are afraid of *him*. Do you get the idea?

Boy: But how are you gonna do that after I've already been touching him and holding him and everything?

Therapist:	Well, somehow you have to give him the message that you are afraid of him. Like, you know you have to kind of . . .
Boy:	Run from him?
Therapist:	And show him that you are afraid of him.
Boy:	Like what? Chasing him away and everything?
Therapist:	Yeah.
Boy:	I think that would be mean to him.
Therapist:	You don't have to chase him away. You know, do you think that if you are afraid of me you are gonna chase me away? No, you're just gonna run from me. Right?
Boy:	Uh huh.
Therapist:	*(To parents.)* Do you think that you can help Stuart to get afraid of the puppy?
Mother:	I'll try.
Therapist:	Huh?
Mother:	I'll try.
Therapist:	No, no, no, that's not, that's not very enthusiastic.
Mother:	Help him to be afraid of the puppy?

(Father and Mother look at each other, puzzled.)

Therapist:	Yes. See I'm very serious about this and I'm sure you get the idea. The idea is to get the puppy to think that Stuart is afraid of *him*. So that the little puppy will understand that it is his job to convince Stuart not to be afraid of him. Now we all know that he is not afraid of the puppy, but it's just tricking the puppy for the puppy's benefit.

Boy: Well, what I think is, I think, he knows that I'm *not* afraid of him.

Therapist: I know that, that's why it is a *trick*. And you only have to do it for a couple of days. I'll tell you what. I want you to ask your parents about what they think about it and how do they think you can do it. Look, you don't seem too happy about the idea. Do you?

Boy: No.

Therapist: Why not?

Boy: Because.

Therapist: Look, you are an expert on that. Weren't you afraid of dogs for a long time?

Boy: Yeah.

Therapist: Well, . . .

Mother: How did you like it?

Boy: I think I acted crazy.

Therapist: You think you acted crazy? When you were afraid of dogs?

Boy: Uh huh.

Therapist: All you have to do is the same things that you were doing before.

Boy: It's gonna be hard.

Therapist: Oh, I know it's gonna be hard.

Boy: After all this time, seven or eight years, almost eight years I been afraid of them, but now it's slipping off of me.

Narration: The parents had not succeeded in getting away for the weekend. But they had a pleasant evening alone at home, which was unusual for them. The therapist continued to insist that they get away together without the children. This was a way of forcing attention more on the marital dyad. A marital difficulty was finally conceded.

Therapist: There is a dog in this room. And Stuart isn't afraid.

Father: Uh huh.

Therapist: Because of the kind of parents that you've been. He's been able to do all these things.

Father: Uh huh.

Therapist: Unquestionably that speaks very highly about the quality of parenting that he's getting. Yet, you haven't taken care of each other.

Mother: Well, we don't see very much of each other.

Therapist: (*After a pause.*) You don't like that do you?

Mother: No.

Therapist: When was the last time that you even talked about it?

Mother: We don't.

Therapist: You don't?

Mother: Uh uh.

Therapist: You mean that you don't talk about things that you dislike?

Mother: No, we don't.

Therapist: How come?

Mother: Because, well, I guess that we can't talk about those kind of things, really.

Narration: This decision point is typical in family therapy. The contract of the therapist with the family is to work on the child's problem. The marriage is now an issue. He can work on the marriage indirectly or he can make a new contract explicitly saying that they should deal with the marriage. In this case, the therapist decides to make an explicit contract.

Mother:	And that would lead to arguments and what not and rather than argue, we don't talk, I guess, about some things. Right? Right.
Father:	I guess. I don't see why, but . . .
Mother:	I don't see why but . . .
Therapist:	*(After a pause.)* This, this is not my business, right, Mr. Crosby?
Mother:	Evidently it is part of the therapy.
Therapist:	Do you agree with that?
Father:	It must be.
Therapist:	Because I'm doing this for Stuart and for Sharon. There is nothing wrong with her, so far. Let me speak very frankly with you. I feel very optimistic about Stuart's fear of dogs.
Mother:	Uh huh.
Therapist:	That will be gone. I don't feel so optimistic about the overall picture for Stuart and Sharon because even though you are excellent parents, you seem to lack the knowledge that good parenting begins with each other.
Mother:	Uh huh.
Therapist:	And if you want to, uh—stop at the level of Stuart getting rid of the fear of dogs, we can do it. But what I really had intentions of asking you today is, do you want the whole thing? Or just get rid of this?

Father: *(After a long pause.)** Do the whole thing.

Therapist: The whole thing?

Father: Yeah.

Therapist: Then I have your permission?

Father: Yes.

Therapist: Uh huh.

(Later in the interview.)

Mother: He knows me and I know him but I don't know . . .

Therapist: I'm sure that . . .

Mother: I'm pretty uptight and I know it myself and I said it, all week in so many words I said that they've gotten on my nerves and I do need to get out of the house and what not, but it's like just saying it, but toward the end you just get tired of saying it . . .

Therapist: You know a lot of things.

Mother: I feel a lot of things.

Therapist: That are not being done.

Mother: I know that in order to, uh—make a happy home and what not, it's not just the children and what not, it's time together, going places together so that when you come back you can appreciate them, you can appreciate being away from them and being back with them, but

---

*There are what could be considered two technical errors at this point. One is the implied threat that something might go wrong with the sister later when the therapist says "There is nothing wrong with her, so far." That is unnecessary. The other error is when the therapist asks if father wants "the whole thing." That is so global that father is not clear what he is agreeing to. It would be better to ask if he wishes to deal with specific marital issues.

I never was, if I went away myself, the whole weekend, I'd be happy.

Therapist: Why do you think we're talking like this today?

Father: Because of the way she sounded on the telephone.

Therapist: Huh?

Father: On account of the way she sounded on the telephone.

Therapist: Not only that, on account of the way she looks now.

Father: Yeah, I know, I saw her, I saw her.

Therapist: Saw what?

Father: The tiredness, the look on her face, the droop. I know.

Mother: I *am* tired. And my nature, it's against my nature to prolong things.

Therapist: I think you're lonely.

Mother: I know that, I admit that, I admit that. *(To husband.)* I've admitted that to you, haven't I?

Father: Uh huh.

Mother: Haven't I said that?

Father: Yes.

Mother: Many times. You're not telling me anything. I am lonely, I am tired. I am, I've said, a lot of times, that you know, I can talk to them for a while but after a while you know you get the craving for the conversation of grownups, and, being a woman, not only just grownups but the male.

Narration: When a couple with a child problem have reached an impasse and cannot deal with the marriage there is always the possibility that they will begin to include the child and his problem again as a way of dealing with each other. Then they never solve the marriage issue. One way to prevent this regression is for the therapist to encourage them to do just that. Previously the therapist encouraged a relapse with the boy. Now he does the same with the parents, blocking them off from returning to the past triangular patterns.

Therapist: You seem to be a little bit more aware of what's going on here with this couple. Therefore, you know, that's the point to start. But there is a very good way to settle this situation.

Mother: Which is?

Therapist: Why don't you both try, I'll ask Stuart to help you, try making him afraid of dogs.

Mother: Making Stuart afraid of dogs?

Therapist: Yeah, just as afraid as he was when he walked in here and then we can get busy working on that and we won't get to talk about this anymore. As a matter of fact, I'll help Stuart to help you by pretending that he is afraid.

Father: That's a nice waste of time. Is that what you're saying?

Mother: He's saying that maybe that will be a mutual meeting ground; Stuart.

Therapist: And I'm saying that we would have something to talk about and we wouldn't talk about the important things. So in a way, not in a way, your husband is right. And as soon as he comes back, we can ask him to be afraid of the dog. This is a temporary measure until you decide, okay?

Father: Well, we'll talk it over.

Therapist: Will you?

Father: Yes.

Therapist: Okay, then we can get busy on the dog today.

Father: We don't need to talk about the dog.

Therapist: Why not?

Father: Stuart doesn't—he doesn't need the fear of the dog.

Therapist: Doesn't need it?

Father: No. And we don't need to keep on talking about it. I mean the way you say it, that's the only time that my wife and I get to talk is about Stu and if we don't talk about the dog, we won't have anything to talk about.

Therapist: We won't?

Father: Huh?

Therapist: We won't?

Father: No, I say that's what you're trying to say.

Therapist: Yeah. If you don't talk about the dog you won't have anything to talk about. So really, you know, you are making me feel like a villain. You are. Because if I come into the picture and I make you work on the problem and you get the problem solved and all of a sudden Stuart is not afraid of the dog, you know I get the feeling that you worked against yourself because then you are left kind of empty.

Narration: Despite a variety of efforts the therapist could not get the couple to talk about their marital problems. The father was particularly silent and although he would talk about his relationship with the boy he was very reluctant to talk about his relationship with his wife. There was obviously a marital problem and the children were left out of the session while an effort was made to get the couple to talk out marital issues in interview number eight.

Therapist: I wasn't really implying that your marriage was shaky, I was talking about things that can be improved and, uh—for godsake, you just said one.

Father: What did I say?

Therapist: Didn't you say you were walking arm and arm?

Father: Well, I said it like that because, uh—we haven't been out.

Therapist: Well, I know, and that I . . .

Mother: We haven't been out, we don't talk.

Father: Not even if it was, uh—not even to be shopping, we haven't been out.

Mother: Right.

Therapist: Yeah, but, you know, that is exactly what I meant, you know, things, small things like that.

Mother: I would say our marriage is blocked, in a way, you know, not shaky, it's just going along like—from day to day, so to speak because everything is child, everything is for them. You know, we have no time together and we have no time for conversation and what not.

Narration: The therapist tried in many ways to get the couple to deal with one another but without success.*

---

*It should be emphasized that when the child is presented as the problem, it is not necessarily the therapist's obligation to make a happier

At this point he asks them to describe their average day at home. They reveal that they spend almost no time together and in fact avoid each other both during the week and on weekends. The therapist takes a different approach and finally the couple brings up an issue that has kept them apart for a number of years.

Therapist: By being so worried about losing the love of these kids, you've lost sight of each other.

Mother: Uh huh.

Therapist: Like, does it worry you that you might lose the love of your wife?

Father: Yes.

Therapist: Yes?

Father: Yes.

Therapist: I think that you haven't thought about it because you take it very much for granted.

Mother: Right, right, I don't take his love for granted anymore. Tom will tell you, he'll tell you so, but I do feel as though *I'm* taken for granted. Stuart has his place, Tom has his place, you know, but I don't feel as though we are supposed to devote all our time to him, I don't because I really, truthfully I feel I, I, I guess I do, I hate to put this in words, I resent it. All the time, that you know I don't have any time, I guess I do resent it.

---

marriage for the parents unless he specifically makes that therapy contract. His task is done if the child is free of symptoms and the parents are involved with each other directly and not communicating with each other through the child. Many marriages are quite unhappy and the children in the family are not involved and do not have problems. In this case, the boy was not yet completely over the problem. It seemed there was an issue between the parents that was unresolved, since the boy was still triangulated.

Therapist: Does it worry you that you might lose his love?

Mother: Yeah, I . . .

Therapist: You don't take him for granted?

Mother: No.

Therapist: No?

Mother: I *have* taken him for granted, but I don't think I do now, I know I don't.

Therapist: What made you change?

Mother: Well, I, that's a different story, I guess. *(After a pause.)* Just something that happened between us and, which made me not take *him* for granted, but then I think that now he takes *me* for granted.

Therapist: Something that happened between both of you?

Mother: Right.

Therapist: Do you want to talk about it?

Mother: I don't know, not if Tom wouldn't want to talk about it, I wouldn't talk about it.

Therapist: Why don't you ask him?

Mother: Do you want to talk about it?

Father: I don't know.

Mother: Um.

Father: I don't know.

Narration: In effective therapy, it is not necessary to explore unsavory aspects of the past or family secrets. The problem is how to get past them and move on. In this case, there is obviously a problem from the past between this couple. The therapist handles it in such a way that they can go on from where they are.

Therapist: Would it produce some embarassment?

Mother: No, not, I don't know, it wouldn't on my part but I think maybe . . .

Therapist: I'll tell you something, why don't you *pretend* that you told me, and then go on.

Mother: Pretend that what?

Therapist: That you told me about it.

Mother: Uh huh, alright well, I'll say that we had Stuart and I was on cloud nine because this is what I really wanted. A month after that, then something happened, and I think that then I started realizing, you know, that maybe I was too wrapped up in Stuart. That you know, that maybe I wasn't giving enough attention to Tom, which caused what happened to happen. And I wanted to, you know, maybe give him more attention but I don't know if he wanted it. So that's the way it happened.

Therapist: Alright, well, you said it.

Mother: I think that, I don't know, I think that we changed, Tom changed.

Therapist: How much resentment was left?

Mother: How much what?

Therapist: Resentment.

Mother: A lot.

Therapist: A lot.

Mother: Yeah.

Therapist: It's still there? Is that 95 percent for this situation?

Mother: I think so.

Therapist: If not 100 percent?

Mother: Uh huh. Because I think, you put it in words and it's something that I just been thinking all along and you know that, maybe the kids were being used.* You know they were being used to, uh, like, bridge the gap. It's like what we had in common. I've said this to you, though, right? I've said these things to you, right?

Father: That's right.

Narration: The couple has now brought out into the open a major issue that has divided them for many years. It is an issue they were unable to resolve by themselves. The therapist begins to help them resolve it. First he changes the idea of who is the villain and who is the victim, making them mutual victims. He also persuades them to drop the issue by reducing it to absurdity, putting the problem far into the past.

Therapist: Now I know you've been punished for, how many years?

Mother: I wouldn't know, alright, six and a half years, now he's being punished for many years. And I admit it.

Therapist: Six and a half years.

Mother: Right, maybe that is so but I'd say that I too, I was being punished, too. I've been punished as much as you know. I've always said that he was a good man and a good person but he is also a person who will let you talk yourself blue in the face and argue yourself crazy and you will end up with no concession, no concession,

---

*The therapist had not suggested that the kids were being used since this is not interpretive therapy. This example shows that people already know their situation and understand it, and when there is a change they can concede what they know.

nothing, not even nothing, because he will never say that you are right or that you are wrong.

Therapist: Now wait a second, I never implied that he was the victim and you were the . . .

Mother: Villain.

Therapist: The villain.

Mother: No, I . . .

Therapist: No.

Mother: I can't just have blind faith in you, I have to be proven. I have to show things and know things and to feel a part of things before I can say that everything is alright. Maybe that's why I hold myself so tensely and what not. In other words, say, for instance, say, for the time that we might have to sneak a word in edgewise, there are some subjects that are taboo, that I can't talk about. Like, for instance, to bring it all out, he'll keep, which he didn't used to do, job and home is entirely separate. It's like my husband is living two lives. From the minute my husband walks out the door in the morning to go to the post office, and until he comes home, that's one life that I dare not even ask a question about. But he never was like that before. So there he is punishing me. I mean he holds back.

Therapist: Oh yeah, I don't believe for a second that you were doing it all.

Mother: Yeah, but he won't talk to me, which he used to, and I don't know why, and I'd like to know why, you know, uh, you . . .

Therapist: You'd like to know why?

Mother: Sure, you can forgive or you can understand anything if you can talk it out.

(Later in the interview.)

Therapist: If whatever happened six and a half years ago, hasn't changed, and continues in your mind even though it might be long ago dead . . .

Mother: Uh huh.

Therapist: You know, not happening anymore, but it continues to exist in your minds and in your hearts.

Narration: Besides talking about the issue and providing a different way of viewing it, the therapist requires different behavior from the couple. Talk alone will not solve a problem. At the end of the interview he gives a directive to the father that provides an opportunity for the couple to have a fresh start.

Therapist: You know, freely tell me whether you will be willing to do it or not. You know, uh—what I would like you to do is to do something that she wouldn't expect from you. You know her very well and you know what she wouldn't expect. Would you do something, anything?

Narration: The following week, in the ninth interview, the boy had partially changed and was beginning to make friends. The couple had partially changed and the father had brought the wife flowers unexpectedly. The therapist began to move to complete the change and then begin his disengagement from the family.

Therapist: And how's he coming along? The puppy, I mean?

Mother: Big.

Father: The puppy is getting bigger every day.

Therapist: Is the puppy getting over the fear?

Mother: Yes, and everybody else has to be afraid of him.

Father: Yeah.

Therapist: Oh.

Mother: He doesn't let anybody come in the house, any-body but the four of us. And he's only a puppy.

Therapist: That's good, isn't it?

Mother: Yeah, that's beautiful. That's good, so he's not afraid.

Father: He's not afraid anymore.

Mother: No, he's a very good watchdog.

Father: He oughta be.

Mother: He isn't afraid when I get the paper behind him.

Therapist: *(Turning toward the boy and smiling.)* Then it sounds as though you've done a pretty good job, you and your dad. *(To mother, referring to father.)* But he, he really did what I wanted him, what I asked him to do?

Father: I did some things.

Mother: He did some things.

Therapist: You did some things?

Mother: He did some things.

Therapist: Well, you tell me, I mean, after all, you were the one who did the job.

Father: Got some things that she didn't know anything about.

Therapist: Like what?

Father:	Uh, some extraordinary Christmas present, for one. I brought some flowers home a few times.
Therapist:	Uh huh.
Father:	Last time it was more or less a real surprise, wasn't it?
Mother:	What?
Father:	The flowers, the last time I brought you some flowers.
Mother:	Right, right, the last time, because the first time he brought the flowers home was the day before we were supposed to come down here. Right?
Father:	Yeah.
Mother:	That is, you just made the deadline.

(They all laugh.)

Therapist:	Is that right?
Father:	Yeah.
Mother:	I was teasing him about it.
Therapist:	When was the last time?
Mother:	He knows that I like flowers. When was the last time what?
Therapist:	That he brought the . . .
Mother:	Brought me flowers?
Therapist:	Yeah.
Mother:	For our anniversary, in August. Right?
Therapist:	No, no, no, the very last time.
Mother:	Oh, for New Year's Eve, he brought flowers.

Therapist: And you weren't expecting it?

Mother: Right, I wasn't expecting it, no.

Narration: To continue the improvement and to disengage himself, the therapist does two things. He recesses the family for three weeks, which suggests in action that they can improve without him. He also suggests that mother and father will have a major disagreement. He does so partly to prevent a fight that might develop because of the changes they are going through. More important, by suggesting that they will have a fight with each other when they would rather not, the therapist pulls the couple together against him. This approach allows them to free themselves from him. To avoid the major disagreement they will maintain an amiability with each other that will help them past this difficult time of change.

(Later in the interview.)

Therapist: For some reason I get the feeling that you are getting a little closer to each other than you were. Sometimes when this happens, people tend to have some kind of disagreement, like a big fight.

Mother: When they get closer, they have a fight?

Therapist: Right.

Mother: Oh.

Therapist: To go back to the same. So I'm afraid that you are in for a major disagreement.

Mother: Oh, oh. *(To husband.)* Are you ready for that?

Father: Uh huh.

Therapist: Well, and the reason I am telling you is so that when you have it, it won't catch you by surprise. But you doubt it. But let me tell you . . .

Mother: *(Interrupting.)* But I'll tell you, I doubt, let me tell you how I feel, I doubt that we'll have a major disagreement, what I would call a major disagreement.

Therapist: How about you, Mr. Crosby?

Father: I doubt it.

Therapist: Okay, then let's do this, you will still have it even though you don't believe it.

Mother: Well, if we have it even though we don't believe it . . .

Therapist: You see, the way it happens is you are not gonna have it because I say so.

Mother: Oh.

Therapist: It's gonna happen because of the way that things are coming along, which are very good. I like the way things are coming along.

Mother: Well, suppose we don't have it, just to say you're wrong? You know we'd do those kind of things. *(Laughing with husband.)*

Therapist: Oh.

Mother: We are very good at proving the other person wrong.

Therapist: I don't think you are that kind of person.

Mother: Oh, boy, we've proved a lot of them wrong.

Therapist: But you wouldn't do that, would you?

Narration: The tenth and final interview is a disengagement session. Let us review briefly what the family has been through. Beginning with an overinvolved mother and child and a peripheral father, the therapist decided to use the father to disengage mother and child. Therefore he began the stage of getting father and child to do something excluding mother. This process led to the next stage, where mother and father become more involved with each other and the child begins to become involved with peers. Finally, as this stage stabilizes, the problem of the therapist is to leave the family with this improvement continuing.

Therapist: The reason why we were getting together was because Stuart was afraid of dogs.

Mother: Right.

Therapist: Was the main reason.

Father: Uh huh.

Therapist: How is that situation?

Father: Good.

Mother: Can I say something?

Therapist: Sure.

Mother: The dog on the street that he was afraid of from the very beginning, you heard him talk about him, Bruce?

Therapist: Bruce.

Mother: Bruce, well him and Bruce are friends.

Therapist: Are friends?

Father: He wants to pet Bruce.

Mother: And now I don't want him to look at the dog—Bruce is the dirtiest dog in the whole block and Saturday—well, he is, and I told his master that he needs a bath.

Therapist: How about Princess?

Mother: Princess, Princess is Bruce's mother and Princess lives at the corner.

Therapist: Oh.

Boy: And Bruce lives next door.

Mother: And Bruce lives next door, Bruce is the frisky one, Bruce is the one that, all the kids he runs after. And that's what turned him off, you know he chases them and all. And Saturday, I was trying to keep him away from Bruce.

Therapist: He wanted to go to Bruce?

Mother: He missed Bruce.

Therapist: *(To Stuart.)* That sounds great, I'm proud of you. Let me tell you, the reason that I am proud of Stuart is that he is all over it . . .

Mother: I'm proud of him too.

Therapist: What he came originally for, right?

Mother: Right.

Therapist: Okay. Then I guess we don't have to worry about you anymore, Stuart, right?

(Later in the interview, parents alone.)

Mother: He's changing, in fact, he's even gotten a little more aggressive, you know. Whereas before he might not have started anything with you, but now he's, you know, I think all of that was in with the dog bit. You know he was afraid of dogs, so he was a little afraid of other things, you know what I mean? Like even certain kids and what not. One day I saw him and he just walked right up into a mob of kids.

(Later in the interview.)

Therapist: *(To boy.)* You know your dad and your mommy and I have agreed that you don't have a problem anymore, so from now on we're just gonna be friends. Okay?

Boy: I guess so. I never saw how anybody could be friends and never see them again.

Therapist: Oh, that doesn't mean that you can't come over and visit me. You can come over anytime.

Boy: I don't know.

Mother: He's telling you that you can.

Boy: *(Pleased.)* Oh!

Therapist: You can.

Narration: At the end of this session, the family discontinued. The follow-up interview, which was done two years later, shows the family still over the problem.* The daughter, Sharon, is doing well, and on that particular day the teacher sent a note to mother complimenting her. The son, Stuart, is not restricted in his behavior by *any* avoidance of dogs.

Father: He walks down the street with me now and . . .

Mother: Right.

Father: And he doesn't even pay them any attention.

Therapist: Uh huh.

Father: Like I mean, he used to come up in back of me, and coming up on this side, and all this kind of stuff.

Narration: At the end of therapy, there did not seem to be a major change in the marriage relationship except

---

* This follow-up was a clinical one and not for purposes of research. The intent was to make sure that the child continued to be over the presenting problem and was developing normally. There was also an interest in whether the parent's marriage was stable and whether they were more involved with each other and with friends rather than focused on the children.

that the son was out of it. In this two-year follow-up, there was an inquiry into the current marital situation.

Therapist: Your wife was looking very tired and she was, those were hard times for us.

Father: They were.

Therapist: What happened with them?

Father: They left us.

Therapist: Huh?

Mother: You didn't really remember, did you, Tom?

Father: I remember some of it. Yeah.

Mother: Yeah, okay, *I* remember.

Therapist: There is one thing I can tell you, you don't look the same as when that thing was happening. You used to be very silent. And now you are not.

Father: Who? Me?

Therapist: Yeah.

Mother: Yeah. I hope you're over it.

Therapist: Would you rather not talk about it?

Mother: It doesn't matter to me if we talk about it or we don't talk about it. Because I don't feel as though there is any problem, now, I don't.

Therapist: That's all I wanted to know, really, I don't want to go into any detail, I just wanted to know.

Mother: I think in my own mind, maybe any fault or anything that I may have been doing wrong, have been all solved, in my mind because I went back to church. So I just feel better on that score. And the kids, I had them baptized.

And, I don't get there that often, but I go to church. Just the fact that I started back has made me feel that much better, I think. You know. Because, we—then we started having company, we have company a lot. Which we weren't doing at the time.

Father: True, we have card parties.

Mother: Yeah, and now we go from house to house. It is mostly people who can't leave their kids at home or who don't leave them with sitters. So we play pinochle.

Father: You know, so we have this thing going and we play cards, you know, and we have a lot of people into dinner for the holidays. This is something that we used to do when we first got married, when we first got married our house was like Grand Central Station.

Therapist: Would you say you see more of each other than you were before?

Mother: Yes, because he doesn't work at night.

Therapist: Oh, you don't have two jobs now?

Father: No.

Therapist: Just one?

Father: Uh huh.

Mother: So he is home and I . . .

(Therapist shakes hands with father, congratulating him.)

Therapist: That's really a major change, right, Tom?

Mother: And he helps with the dishes.

Father: Yeah.

Mother:	And he usually puts the kids to bed. But they just about go to bed themselves, you know.
Therapist:	How do you feel about seeing your husband more?
Mother:	I, I, I know that he is in the house, I don't say that I see him that much more.
Therapist:	Uh huh.
Mother:	Because the competition is too great (with the children).

(Therapist laughs.)

Mother:	But I, I don't mind because this way I don't have them to really worry about in the evening, so I can sew or I can go upstairs and watch television.
Therapist:	You look about a hundred times more relaxed. You look very pleased about what you have done, you know, with the kids and with each other, and I really congratulate you both.
Mother:	Do you want me to tell you why?
Therapist:	Why?
Mother:	Because two years ago, two summers ago, we must have just finished here, right?
Therapist:	Uh huh.
Mother:	Tom got a bonus, and we took the bonus and we went down the shore. All of us went, you know, we have never gone away, even before the kids, for any length of time, right?
Father:	Right.
Mother:	And it was nice and we went again this summer and we sent Stuart to camp last summer. He

has so much to tell you. He's joined the Boy
Scouts. He has a lot to tell you about.

Narration: The parents viewed this film and gave
permission for it to be shown to professional audiences.

Index